ART AND SOCIETY IN THE VICTORIAN NOVEL

Art and Society in the Victorian Novel

Essays on Dickens and his Contemporaries

Edited by

COLIN GIBSON
Donald Collie Professor of English
University of Otago, New Zealand

St. Martin's Press New York

Scholarly and Reference Division,
St. Martin's Press, Inc., 175 Fifth Avenue, New York, NY 10010

First published in the United States of America in 1989

Printed in Hong Kong

ISBN 0–312–02064–3

Library of Congress Cataloging-in-Publication Data
Art and society in the Victorian novel: essays on Dickens and his contemporaries / edited by Colin Gibson.
p. cm.
Includes index.
ISBN 0–312–02064–3: $35.00 (est.)
1. English fiction—19th century—History and criticism
2. Social problems in literature. 3. Literature and society—Great Britain—History—19th century. 4. Dickens, Charles, 1812–1870—Political and social views. I. Gibson, Colin.
PR878.S62A78 1989
823'.8'09—dc19 88–10123
CIP

To Alan Horsman

Contents

Preface

The essays gathered in this volume have as their central theme the interface of personal vision and social address in the work of the greatest of the Victorian novelists. The art of writers such as Dickens, Eliot, Hardy and James had a Janus-like quality, displaying on the one side an idiosyncratic and sometimes highly unorthodox personal sensibility, and on the other exhibiting a shrewdly analytic and frequently reforming interest in the elaborate social structure and complex morality of Victorian society.

Craftsmanship, the struggle to bring into being a form that adequately expresses the writer's artistic conception and yet satisfies the requirements of the reading public, becomes an issue here, and several essays explore different facets of it, from Dickens's creation and development of Jo's prominent role in *Bleak House* to Hardy's attempts to match the expectations of his readers and critics in his depiction of rural life 'under the greenwood tree' and Henry James's working out of his theme of lost youth in the complexities of *The Ambassadors*.

Dickens offers a crucial example of a major novelist whose rich and complex art both reflected the writer's active engagement with his society and his own distinctive temperament; four essays are devoted to important works spanning his triumphant career, from *Oliver Twist* to the unfinished *Mystery of Edwin Drood*. Charlotte Brontë and (perhaps surprisingly) Trollope figure as novelists who express highly individual attitudes in their fictions dealing with female personality and sexual relationships, and there are studies of George Eliot's quest for a valid historical awareness and understanding, Kipling's assimilation of his many borrowings from earlier writers, and the portrait of the physician, that respected member of Victorian society, that emerges from a wide range of Victorian novels.

The essays collected here are the work of colleagues and friends of Professor Alan Horsman, former Donald Collie Professor of English in the Department of English, University of Otago, who is currently engaged in writing a volume of the Oxford History of English Literature dealing with the Victorian period and whose distinguished career as an editor, literary critic, teacher and university administrator is only partly recorded in the list of his publications printed at the end of this volume. It is the editor's agreeable duty to thank the authors both for their contributions and their patience during the process of publication. Thanks must also go to Lindsay Francis and Mary Sullivan, who typed successive drafts of the manuscript accurately and with unfailing cheerfulness, and to Valery Rose and Frances Arnold for their editorial work.

COLIN GIBSON

Acknowledgements

The editor and publishers wish to thank the following who have kindly granted permission for the use of copyright material:

The Bodley Head, for the extracts from *The Ambassadors*, in *The Bodley Head Henry James*, edited by Leon Edel, vol. 8 (1970);

The British Council, for John Holloway's 'Form and Fable in *Hard Times*';

Oxford University Press, for the extracts from the World Classics edition of *Jane Eyre*, edited by Margaret Smith (1980).

Notes on the Contributors

Miriam Allott has held chairs in English at the Universities of Liverpool and London. She is the editor of Keats and Arnold, and has published many articles and essays on the Brontës and other Victorian novelists and prose writers. She is currently completing (in collaboration with Nicholas Shrimpton) a critical edition of Arnold, and is preparing a critical biography of Clough as well as her book *Poets on Poetry*.

Philip Collins is Emeritus Professor of English at the University of Leicester. He has published studies of Boswell, Trollope, Thackeray and Tennyson. His work on Dickens as novelist and public performer includes *Dickens and Crime, Dickens and Education, A Dickens Bibliography, Dickens: The Critical Heritage* and *Dickens's Public Readings*.

D. W. Harding is Emeritus Professor of Psychology at the University of London. He has published a number of papers in the field of literary criticism, and his books include *Social Psychology and Individual Values, Experience into Words: Essays on Poetry* and *Words into Rhythm*.

Jocelyn Harris is Associate Professor of English at the University of Otago, the editor of Richardson's *Sir Charles Grandison* and Duncombe's *The Feminead*. Other books include *Samuel Richardson*, and a study of Jane Austen. She has published a number of articles and essays on eighteenth-century and Victorian writers, and is currently engaged on a new edition of Richardson's *Clarissa*.

John Holloway is Emeritus Professor of Modern English, University of Cambridge, and Fellow of Queens' College. His many books on English language and literature include *The Victorian Sage, The*

Charted Mirror, Narrative and Structure and (as co-editor) two collections of *Later English Broadside Ballads*. His most recent publications are *The Slumber of Apollo* and *The Oxford Book of Local Verses*.

Lawrence Jones is Associate Professor of English at the University of Otago, author of *Barbed Wire and Mirrors: Two Traditions in New Zealand Prose* and an edition of Dan Davin's *Roads from Home*. He has published on Hardy and other Victorian writers as well as on New Zealand poets and prose writers. He is currently preparing a history of the New Zealand novel.

Juliet McMaster is Professor of English at the University of Alberta. Her publications on Victorian and earlier writers include *Thackeray: The Major Novels, Trollope's Palliser Novels, Jane Austen on Love* and *Dickens the Designer*. She is also the editor of *Jane Austen's Achievement* and co-author of *The Novel from Sterne to James*.

Ian Milner is Emeritus Associate Professor of English at Charles University, Prague, and has been Visiting Professor in English at the University of Otago. Author of *The Structure of Values in George Eliot*, he has written a number of articles and essays on nineteenth-century English fiction, particularly George Eliot and Dickens. He is also a well-known translator of Czech poetry.

At the time of his death in September 1987, **Sydney Musgrove** was Emeritus Professor of English at the University of Auckland. His publications were chiefly concerned with Renaissance drama and poetry, including studies of Shakespeare, Jonson and Herrick, and editions of *Twelfth Night* and *The Alchemist*. He also wrote on T. S. Eliot and Whitman; Kipling was a favourite author.

W. W. Robson is Masson Professor of English at the University of Edinburgh. He has published several collections of critical essays dealing with nineteenth- and twentieth-century English authors and with the business of criticism itself. He is at present preparing a volume dealing with the twentieth century for the Oxford history of English literature.

Kathleen Tillotson is Emeritus Professor of English at the University of London and a Fellow of the British Academy. She has published widely on such Victorians as Arnold, Carlyle, Dickens,

Thackeray, Trollope and Wilkie Collins; her books include *Novels of the Eighteen-Forties*, *Dickens at Work* (with John Butt), *Mid-Victorian Studies* (with Geoffrey Tillotson) and editions of *Oliver Twist* and Dickens's letters. She is General Editor of the Clarendon Edition of Dickens's novels, and of his letters, being joint editor of the latest volume of the letters (vol. VI), covering the years 1850–2.

John Watson is a Senior Lecturer at the University of Otago. He has edited a collection of the literary criticism of the New Zealand writer Charles Brasch, *The Universal Dance*, and published work on Dickens. He has recently completed a book, *Dickens and the Cruelty of Life*.

1

Laughter, Imagination and the Cruelty of Life: a View of *Oliver Twist*

JOHN WATSON

That Dickens is not a 'realist'[1] has always been apparent to readers, though not to film directors, who have, for instance, flattened Mr Bounderby from an inflated windbag to a surly Lancashire businessman, whose sudden comic reference to Mrs Sparsit's 'seemingly swallowing marbles' pokes up incongruously from the pervasive greyness.[2] Madame Defarge on television is not a monster, but a luminously beautiful woman who even manages to produce a few tears.[3] Conversely, non-realist versions of the novels also manage to offend: the starving boys, in a scene that lingers unforgettably among memories of the outrages perpetrated upon Dickens, burst forth into a colourful song and dance routine in the musical *Oliver!*[4] A fair treatment of Dickens's characters must therefore take account of both comedy (Bounderby) and imaginative transformation (Mme Defarge); yet the mixing of these tonal elements, while customary in Dickens's own narration, is certainly not to be tampered with lightly in the presentation of human suffering, as *Oliver!* shows us.

The overall effect of the Dickensian mixture has always divided the critics. Writing of comic characters such as Mr Bumble, John Carey concludes: 'Because Dickens' main comic characters are magnificent performers, but have no emotions, they provided him with no way of bringing within the scope of his comedy real suffering or real cruelty. But it is clear that he wanted to make his comedy confront and embrace the cruelty of life.'[5] *Oliver Twist* is certainly full of the 'cruelty of life', to which the critics have responded, emphasising, for instance, the nightmare of fear and cruelty suffered by Oliver,[6] 'the squalor and misery' of the underworld,[7] the 'confrontation between good and evil',[8] and the contrast between the trials endured by the good child and the disruption of ordinary time endured by the guilty criminal adult.[9] Yet Carey's reference to Mr Bumble reminds us that comedy inhabits this same world and is often linked with imagination to produce effects more or less comic. I view *Oliver Twist* as an early attempt by Dickens to confront the 'cruelty of life' with the aid of comedy and imagination, by a careful manipulation of the point of view, which fluctuates continually between the narrator (external, formal, sometimes apparently unfeeling) and the characters (sometimes external and unfeeling, sometimes internal and childlike). Only at the end does the comedy fail, as imagination assumes feverish intensity and the nightmare shifts from the victims to the predators.

At the simplest level are the characters whose suffering is quite obscured, even derided, by comedy and imagination. Mr Bumble, who sells himself for Mrs Corney's cutlery and comes a cropper, need not be taken seriously, as the narrator's jocular image of the paper fly-cage makes clear: 'A paper fly-cage dangled from the ceiling, to which he occasionally raised his eyes in gloomy thought; . . . it might be that the insects brought to mind some painful passage in his own past life' (p. 239).[10] He tries his eye of mastery on his wife, suffers her manual assault in private (ch. 37) and a public confrontation with a bowl of soap-suds in front of the paupers, then retires defeated. Not that his spirit is defeated: his anarchic vitality provides the only life during the sullen account of Monk's life-history (ch. 51), and quite overwhelms the judgement of the righteous. 'You may leave the room', says Mr Brownlow (p. 354). 'The law is a ass – a idiot', says Mr Bumble (p. 354). Comedy here has only a surface relation to cruelty. Noah Claypole, whom we hate for his earlier bullying of Oliver, provides a nastier model of weakness and depravity. Noah's fear when he first encounters Fagin's power in the Three Cripples becomes the object of our contempt and laughter, spurred on by the Heep-like shuffling and writhing of his legs, which retreat until he gets them 'by gradual degrees abroad again' (p. 290). Fagin pokes and fingers him with 'grotesque politeness' (p. 292), finally drawing him down into the underworld into a state of 'wholesome fear' (p. 294). The contrast with Oliver's purity is obvious and the comic effects punitive, calling up the reader's antagonism in a way that Mr Bumble seldom does.

More difficult to evaluate is the fate of the Artful Dodger, whose criminal activities Dickens can hardly condone since the Artful Dodger embraces criminal philosophy whole-heartedly (ch. 18). Yet his vitality and resilience draw the author imaginatively towards him, so that the trial and sentencing of the Dodger becomes a joke, full of wit, malapropisms and a comic exit in which the young criminal condemns the bench: 'I wouldn't go free, now, if you was to fall down on your knees and ask me. . . . Take me away!' (p. 300). Yet whereas that other Cockney wit Sam Weller turns the jokes against the court, here the jokes tend to rebound harmlessly, giving the laughter an uncomfortably impotent effect: laughter maintains the boy's 'self-approval' but fails to disguise his helplessness, in spite of the narrator's apparent agreement with Noah about the Dodger's 'glorious reputation' (p. 301).

If comedy and imagination may obscure suffering, then conversely their absence may deprive it altogether of interest, as when Rose Maylie lies ill while Oliver nobly suppresses his own emotional anxieties and Harry Maylie sobs in the wings (ch. 33). Our interest drifts fitfully instead towards the butler Giles sitting distracted on the *chaise* with white nightcap and red eyes, comically concerned lest he be seen by the maids in this state and thus lose his authority over them forever (p. 222). Indeed, one of Monks's fits provides a welcome diversion in these troubled days (p. 217), though Oliver does not quite know how to respond and soon forgets the incident. But not even such touches as these are provided to give a lift to the pallid romantic *Angst* which follows in the love-scene between Rose and Harry.[11]

When cruelty is treated with jocose humour, either in the characters' inappropriately heartless responses or in the author's jovial pretence that he approves of the monstrosities he details, the effect is to arouse our intense anger, if not our pity. Underneath the jarring inappropriateness of response, we recognise the common humanity to which Dickens appeals, but, because the point of view is largely that of the unfeeling onlookers rather than the sufferers, we feel hatred and shame surging outwards, rather than sympathy focusing inwards. Gamfield's comic defence of boy chimney-sweepers is a case in point: 'Boys is wery obstinit, and wery lazy, gen'lmen, and there's nothink like a good hot blaze to make 'em come down vith a run. It's humane too, gen'lmen, acause, even if they've stuck in the chimbley, roastin' their feet makes 'em struggle to hextricate theirselves' (p. 14). Whereupon there is bargaining over a suitable price for Oliver to participate in this process, and the scene concludes with convivial laughter amongst the old gentlemen of the board. John Carey gives fuller details of the deformities and cancers suffered by chimney-sweepers, as recorded in Mayhew's *London Labour and the London Poor,* and concludes that laughter undercuts the seriousness: 'Gamfield the sweep seems suddenly less funny when we look back at him from these facts. We end up feeling ashamed of Dickens for making us laugh.'[12] But the shame is directed against the characters who laugh, not against the author, because the horror is retained ('good hot blaze', 'roastin' their feet') with the added obscenity of making a joke about it. Then, after Oliver personalises the attack by his terrified appeal against Gamfield, the author himself retreats into apparent acquiescence: 'The next morning, the public were once more informed that Oliver Twist was again To Let; and that five pounds would be paid to anybody who would take possession of him' (p. 19). This acquiescence further fuels our anger, as even the narrator now seems to have withdrawn his sympathy from the child-victim. So laughter intensifies the reader's angry humaneness by its apparent refusal to acknowledge humane considerations; of which Dickens is fully aware, as he trades on the point of view of the reader.

These elements of jocose insensitivity and inappropriateness are combined with other elements – such as aggression, conflict and the strongly felt presence of Oliver to focus the suffering – in the big scenes such as the 'asking for more', and the fight with Noah and the Sowerberrys. Here, a finer balance is achieved, between the child's desperation, into which we are drawn imaginatively and emotionally, and the authoritarian responses of the adult world. In the workhouse scene, the pantomime of adult astonishment, showing a misplaced sensitivity towards Oliver's rebellion against the official diet, is emphatic: 'The master . . . gazed in stupefied astonishment on the small rebel for some seconds; and then clung for support to the copper' (p. 11). But the engagement of the imagination first, on the boys' behalf, together with a certain macabre comedy, intensifies the feeling of dislocation. The empty bowls polished with spoons 'till they shone again', the staring eyes devouring the bricks, the sucked fingers (pp. 10–11) – these all intensify the children's point of view, which is given a comic cannibalistic twist in the aggressive threat from the tall boy that he 'might happen some night to eat the boy who slept next him'.

We are thus imaginatively ready for the act of aggression on Oliver's part, the asking for more. The suffering boys, paralysed 'with fear', weigh equally against the indignant adults, 'paralysed with wonder' (p. 11). Aggression is met by aggression, macabre comedy by pantomime comedy.

At the Sowerberrys', Oliver's reactions progress from his initial imaginative response of expecting 'to see some frightful form slowly rear its head' from the unfinished coffin where he must sleep (p. 25), to a culmination in violent anger which bursts out against the jeering Noah. Laughter is one-sided and painful: it is linked with Noah's jeering 'Tol de rol lol lol, right fol lairy, Work 'us' (p. 36); with his blubbering cowardice when Oliver at last comes to life and fells him; with Mrs Sowerberry's exaggerated relief that 'we have not all been murdered in our beds!' (p. 38); with Mr Bumble's comic explanation that 'It's not Madness, ma'am. . . . It's Meat' (p. 41); with the hen-pecking of Mr Sowerberry (p. 42); and with the jeering of his wife against the memory of Oliver's mother (p. 48). The injustice of the laughter catches us. Furthermore, Oliver's response of anger is ultimately quite exceeded by our knowledge of what Oliver cannot know or hear, such as Mr Sowerberry's uxorious motives for beating him and Mr Bumble's discourse on 'Meat', delivered while Oliver is locked out of earshot in the cellar. Our anger is more comprehensive, and laughter fuels it.

So far, the underworld has figured little in my argument. Philip Collins, indeed, claims that Dickens errs in 'over-emphasising the squalor and misery, and suppressing its feckless jollity'.[13] Yet the jollity, the vitality of evil and the Pinteresque laughter accompanying the menace are all given due emphasis. At its simplest, this jollity extends the range of comic contrasts, as when Oliver lies recovering in Mr Brownlow's house (ch. 12) after his first pickpocketing experience and consequent brush with Mr Fang the magistrate. The dream-like atmosphere, liable to be watered away by pathos (even Mr Brownlow cries), is touched incongruously with comic ignorance and incompetence, when the self-satisfied doctor pretends to know how Oliver feels, and then hurries away, 'his boots creaking in a very important and wealthy manner' (p. 69), to be succeeded by a fat old pious woman who spends the night tumbling towards the fire with 'divers moans and chokings' (p. 69). Oliver during this lies weakly counting the circles of light reflected on the ceiling (p. 69). His suffering is thus placed in a context of ignorance and laughter, as well as pathos, the narrative working towards a full range of human responses to it. But for completeness, we must wait until the contrast at the end of the chapter, when the narrative returns to the Dodger and Charley Bates, who have escaped by directing the hunt towards Oliver. Charley gives quite a different, vividly imagined account of Oliver's affairs: 'To see him a-splitting away at that pace; and cutting round the corners; and knocking up against the posts; and starting on again as if he was made of iron as well as them; and me with the wipe in my pocket, singing out arter him – oh, my eye!' (p. 74). The contrast, then, is between the comic and uncaring imagination of the underworld[14] and the dream-like imagination which follows Oliver's wandering consciousness; one reflects human sympathies, the other reflects human drives.

When the boys return without Oliver to the den (ch. 13), somewhat sobered by the thought 'What'll Fagin say?', Dickens explores the way in which laughter and play-acting come naturally to the thieves, covering an undercurrent of menacing fear and aggression, before finally giving way to a climax of coarse brutality. The episode begins with simple physical strife between toasting fork and pewter pot, rendered comic by the jocular references to letting 'a little more merriment out' of the 'merry old gentleman's waistcoat' with the fork 'than could have been easily replaced' (p. 76). With the entry of Bill Sikes to receive the pot head-on from Fagin, aggression brings both grim humour and comic imagination: Sikes concludes sarcastically as the beer splashes over him that 'nobody but an infernal, rich, plundering, thundering, old Jew, could afford to throw away any drink but water' (p. 76), and proceeds to imagine in precise detail keeping Fagin 'as a curiosity of ugliness in a glass bottle' (p. 77). As the fear gathers strength, Fagin acts vacant innocence with his shoulders 'shrugged up to his ears' while actually threatening to blab if they get caught (p. 78), Sikes mimes hanging, and Nancy gives a dress rehearsal preview as Oliver's distressed sister, 'to the immeasurable delight of her hearers' (p. 80), before going off to the police station for the official performance. Even the dog seems to be 'meditating an attack upon the legs' of the general public (p. 78). Fear stimulates the imagination to comic effect, which only intensifies our sense of the menace. This is followed by the scene in which Mr Brownlow and Mr Grimwig await Oliver's return from his errand of trust. The safely comic expression of aggression by Mr Grimwig shows the relative devitalising of the subterranean energies in the daylight world: 'If ever that boy returns to this house, sir, I'll eat my head' (p. 91). But the voltage is increased by the immediate return to the coarse brutality of the den (ch. 15), where Sikes fights his dog viciously with poker and clasp-knife and then transfers the quarrel to Fagin. When Sikes and Nancy leave to recapture Oliver, Fagin performs a malicious solo pantomime with 'clenched fist' and 'deep curse' (p. 95). The inexhaustible vitality, resourcefulness and sense of the comic shown by these demonic characters draw laughter and cruelty together in a vicious embrace. The sense of foreboding intensifies the reader's feeling that the child-adults (Brownlow and Grimwig) have far less power in Oliver's world than the evil adults (Fagin) and adult-like children (the Dodger and Charley Bates).

Soon, Oliver is returned to the nightmare world, its cruelty now intensified by his innocent presence. At first we are drawn into experiencing at the child's level the fearful dream-like irruption of the forces of aggression upon him. This makes the comic vitality of life in the den all the more disturbing. Narrative attempts at facetiousness, particularly in describing Nancy's suffering, pale before her passion and rhetoric. Hooking the imagination at the child's level is what gives the scene its power, even though Oliver's responses are not given in detail. Comedy here does not so much 'confront the cruelty of life',[15] as join sides with it, until there is another climax of physical brutality after which Oliver gives in and gives up, accepting again his old suit of clothes previously disposed of, he thought, forever.

The capture has the arbitrary qualities of a nightmare for Oliver: when he accidentally takes the wrong turning, a pair of arms suddenly grip his neck, his protestations of innocence are ignored and overturned by the unfeeling crowd as he belatedly recognises Nancy beneath her strange mask, a man bursts upon them violently, a white dog eyes his throat; finally he is absorbed, hands held, into 'a labyrinth of dark narrow courts' (p. 97) through 'the door of a low earthy-smelling room' (p. 100) to be met by shouts of laughter. What follows depends on this nightmare introduction for its full effect. Charley Bates circles Oliver joyfully, nearly setting him on fire as he examines his 'togs' (p. 100), while the Dodger steadily rifles his pockets. Fagin enacts a charade of mocking bowing politeness: 'Why didn't you write, my dear, and say you were coming? We'd have got you something warm for supper' (p. 100). Then Oliver himself provides the key to further power over him – his friends will think he stole the books, a realisation which brings desperation to the boy and chuckling satisfaction to Fagin. In the ensuing violence of Oliver's escape bid, the brutal assault by Fagin's club and Nancy's equally violent defence and vehement torrent of remorse and despair, some authorial attempts at facetiousness, as if to reduce this passion to a manageable level, merely echo feebly: 'Mr Sikes . . . possibly feeling his personal pride and influence interested in the immediate reduction of Miss Nancy to reason, gave utterance to about a couple of score of curses and threats, the rapid production of which reflected great credit on the fertility of his invention' (p. 103). But we have just witnessed Nancy fling the club into the fire so that sparks whirl out and even Fagin shrinks back in fear. Finally, 'sick and weary' (p. 105), Oliver falls asleep in the dark behind a locked door. Admittedly, the reader is likely to respond with greater imaginative intensity than Oliver (who makes no response, for instance, to the blow from Fagin's club). Oliver becomes an object around whom are gathered our feelings of outrage, anger, desperation, despair and pity.

Similarly, in the breaking-down of Oliver (ch. 18) preparatory to the Chertsey burglary attempt, the boy's response is much simpler than the total response evoked by the variation in point of view. The boy's point of view includes both the dreariness of his imprisonment, imaginatively spread around him (in the spiders and terrified mice, the confused mass of house-tops, the occasional grotesque glimpse of a distant 'grizzly head' – p. 115), and the drollness of the psychological effect on him of Fagin's stories of robberies in the old days, 'mixed up with so much that was droll and curious, that Oliver could not help laughing heartily, and showing that he was amused in spite of all his better feelings' (p. 120). But there is also the vitality of temptation as expressed from the point of view of the other boys, who explode in choking mirth, give pantomime explanations of 'scragging' (Charley, p. 118) and put the thieves' philosophy of picking pockets before 'some other cove' can (the Dodger, p. 118). Finally, the narrator's analytic comments provide full understanding of what is happening to Oliver: 'In short, the wily old Jew had the boy in his toils; and, having prepared his mind, by solitude and gloom, . . . was now slowly instilling into his soul the poison which he hoped would blacken it, and change its hue for ever' (p. 120).

Oliver himself is not a large enough character to contain all this complexity of laughter and imagination poured into the story in response to his experiences of suffering and cruelty; only with the discovery of Pip, and perhaps David Copperfield, does Dickens find such a character. But there is no doubt about our intense involvement in Oliver's fate.

This intense involvement survives even the recurrent dislocation, seen in the lead up to the burglary (ch. 20), between a sort of parental view of Oliver, as model child attending impeccably to his role as 'principle of Good' (Dickens's phrase in the 1841 Preface) for the benefit of Victorian parents, and the imaginative involvement in a real child's real responses. On the one hand Oliver's slow naïvety makes for a telling, believable contrast with the intelligent thieves – as when Nancy discerns Oliver's thoughts of calling for help in the street, prompted by his realistically selfish perception that he has 'some power over the girl's better feelings' (p. 131). But on the other hand he soon knuckles down to improbably altruistic thoughts: 'a cry for help hung upon his lips. But the girl's voice was in his ear: beseeching him in such tones of agony to remember her, that he had not the heart to utter it' (p. 132). When Oliver reads the book of criminals given him by Fagin, the writing starts up into the most intense imaginative life as the sallow pages seem to turn red and the words seem to be whispered by spirits in his ears (p. 130). Naturally, he undergoes a paroxysm of fear, but unnaturally averts the crisis with a paroxysm of prayer. As he journeys with Sikes, the boy's anxious mood is transferred to the setting, to the 'cheerless morning . . . blowing and raining hard' (p. 135) and to the gaunt trees they pass in the labourer's cart, trees 'whose branches waved grimly to and fro, as if in some fantastic joy at the desolation of the scene' (p. 139). At midnight, stupefied and half-awake, he goes forth into the half-frozen atmosphere with hair and eyebrows stiffened (p. 143). But the delayed discovery of the real nature of his expedition brings again a rush of piety, saved only by the swift transition to impressionistic writing as Oliver is wounded: 'a vision of two terrified half-dressed men at the top of the stairs swam before his eyes – a flash – a loud noise – a smoke – a crash somewhere . . . – and he staggered back' (p. 145). The moral distress is spooned into the child by the parental narrator, but the fears and sensory projections arise naturally.

That reference to the 'terrified half-dressed men' provides Dickens's link with the episode of Oliver's rescue (chs 28–31), which exploits what might be called the 'comedy of transition', the transition from the rough brutality of Sikes to the benevolent atmosphere of the Maylies' house by way of the comic cowardice of the servants. To begin with, the point of view alternates between Oliver and his comic rescuers, before finally fusing harmoniously as Oliver shows how grateful he is, happy to run up and down the whole day long to please Rose Maylie. Sikes, about to kill Oliver, flees before the servants, whose state is accurately expressed by the terrified Mr Giles: 'it's wonderful . . . what a man will do, when his blood is up' (p. 181). Oliver, into whose fevered consciousness we are then taken, relives the last moments with Sikes and Crackit, now talking to them, now alone with Sikes (p. 182), before sinking exhausted on the portico; behind which, in the kitchen, a comic version of the housebreaking is being given, replete with boasts and macabre details of possible throat-cuttings. This is interrupted by Oliver's knocking, which thus becomes part of the comic fear: ' "It was a knock," said Mr. Giles, assuming perfect serenity. "Open the door, somebody" ' (p. 185). Finally, all the servants manage to muster sufficient courage to creep up to the door, aided by the ingenious stroke of pinching the dogs' tails 'to make them bark savagely' (p. 185). Thus the narrative leads to the meeting between the two parties, looking up with Oliver's fearful, heavy eyes and down with the servants' newly valiant eyes. The double point of view incorporates suffering within a comic setting. So, Oliver is saved. The comedy of menace is succeeded by the comedy of eccentricity, cowardice and ineptitude; as also, unfortunately, the primitive imagination within Oliver is succeeded by an imagination of pastoral innocence touched with a lingering attraction to the local graveyard (p. 210).

But the plot grinds on, as Oliver's enemies magically hide their traces and Monks's plotting gains momentum, before the climax is reached when Dickens turns his main attention to the fate of the thieves, leaving the trapped Monks to give one of those sullen narratives of past machinations we all have come to dread in Dickens even as late as *Little Dorrit*. During this period, comedy and nightmare are fused, first in the encounter with the dwarf during the fruitless search for Mr Brownlow and then in the encounter between the Bumbles and Monks, when the vital evidence in the gold locket is thrown into the Thames. The dream-like attributes of the underworld persist in Oliver's experience as he comes again with Dr Losberne to the house where he was taken on the night before the housebreaking (ch. 32). It is clearly the same house; yet inside, everything that Oliver described has vanished. Only a Quilp-like hump-backed man appears, full of fantastic demonic vitality. He exhibits a quite unnecessary comic exuberance – unnecessary for the plot, but necessary for Dickens, to convey his sense of the comedy of menace, the exuberance of evil. Oliver is safe, yet not safe. The 'mis-shapen little demon' (p. 207) opens the door so suddenly that the doctor nearly kicks himself into the passage, then he twists away dexterously from the doctor's grasp, full of oaths, yells and wild dancing movements. They see him in the distance when they leave, 'beating his feet upon the ground, and tearing his hair' (p. 208); but not before that evil eye has set upon Oliver 'a glance so sharp and fierce, . . . that, waking or sleeping, he could not forget it' (p. 207). This eye links the demon with Fagin, whose eye keeps fastening upon Oliver even in sleep, as when Oliver first watches Fagin gloating over his treasure and meets his 'bright dark eyes' (p. 52), or later when Oliver is roused from sleep at his little study desk at the Maylies' and finds Fagin 'with his eyes peering into the room, and meeting his' (p. 222). Again, all traces magically vanish, even the footprints in the grass (p. 230). All that remains, as with the hump-backed man, is an image imprinted in Oliver's memory 'as if it had been deeply carved in stone' (p. 228).

When the Bumbles meet Monks (ch. 38), comedy and nightmare are again brought together, though with a different balance. This time the comedy is inept, powerless, poured into the quivering bulk of Mr Bumble, while the menace retains a melodramatic grimness spread about the characters in the atmosphere. Imagination arouses fear; comedy incorporates Bumble's ineptitude into it, intensifying the nervousness. Mr and Mrs Bumble come to meet Monks at night in an old building among the jumbled hovels, leaky boats and mud of the Thames-side, complete with lightning and thunder and a view of the turbid tide underneath them, 'foaming and chafing round the few rotten stakes' (p. 255), while the three conspirators hover together under the sickly rays of the lantern 'encircled by the deepest gloom and darkness' (p. 253). Mrs Bumble is resolute, intent on getting the twenty-five sovereigns for her knowledge. Monks is tense and jittery, liable to have another fit at the next rumble of thunder. But Mr Bumble is petrified, his teeth chattering as he assures his wife he only wants 'a little rousing' (p. 252), while the perspiration trickles down his nose. His one feeble attempt at facetiousness pales as they all look through the trap-door at the water; he leaves backwards, bowing himself towards the ladder so as to risk being 'pitched headlong into the room below' (p. 256); and finally he negotiates this lower room with a delicate regard for the possibility of hidden trap-doors. It is a comic *tour de force*, neatly delineating the distinction between Fagin's world of savagely comic menace and the Monks–Bumble world of melodrama suffused with nervous comedy.

Up to this point in the novel, comedy has overturned suffering; has aroused anger against the perpetrators of cruelty (sometimes turning attention away from the sufferers); has provided contrasts of various kinds, between the two worlds of light and darkness; has intensified the menace and cruelty of one while easing us into the benevolent atmosphere of the other; has underlined the predicament of the pitiably helpless victim surrounded by raucous laughter; has nervously jolted the melodrama into life and has given the nightmare visions a kind of grotesque enthusiasm. Imagination has provided us with images of Fagin preserved in a bottle, eyes carved in stone, a dancing imp, a cannibalistic boy, coffins expected to disgorge their lodgers, head-eating old eccentrics and grizzly heads appearing and disappearing above the roof-tops; all in the course of our progress through a world of friendly, gesticulating villains giving command performances of grief and cowardice, crime and death, righteous indignation and amazed disbelief.

In the last episodes of the novel, however, Dickens abandons comedy in the account of the fates of the three main thieves, whose anarchic vitality is now redirected into primitive fears and fantasies. The nightmare world which they took for granted, and from which only Oliver fled, now settles into their own consciousness with a new terror and consumes them. Pious Oliver and plot-bound Mr Brownlow make what amounts to a merely absurd intrusion at the end, their righteousness appearing quite irrelevant beside Fagin's terror. Morality is given only a token justification: the evil must destroy themselves in a just world, but the righteous characters join in the chase with a bloodlust not very different from Sikes's rage against Nancy. Dickens is caught up in the excitement of justified destruction, as his public readings of the murder of Nancy were to demonstrate later.

Nancy's fate stirs Dickens's imagination in several ways, none of them comic. When Fagin observes Nancy's baulked rage over the broken appointment with Rose, he tempts her to turn against Sikes, almost touching her ear with his mouth, his eyes looking into hers, his hand groping obscenely towards hers (p. 305). Nancy finally does manage to meet Rose and Mr Brownlow after dosing Sikes with laudanum, and stands shaking from the effect of her visions of 'shrouds with blood' (p. 312) and the coffin 'carried . . . close to [her], in the streets', a vision which she knows is not 'real'. She is witnessing her own approaching death. When Noah peaches on her, and Fagin goads Sikes to the highest pitch of animal fury, Nancy meets death in a manner reminiscent of Desdemona, protesting her innocence and holding up a white handkerchief towards heaven while she 'breathe[s] one prayer for mercy to her Maker' (p. 323).

Bill Sikes, as the critics recognise,[16] is newly humanised by the terrifying consequences of his act of murder. The animal references (teeth tightly compressed, strained jaw, p. 321) give way to a kind of parody of Othello, as Sikes draws back the curtain upon the sleeping Nancy, violently puts out the light (p. 322), looks at her with dilated nostrils and heaving breast, calls her a 'she devil' (p. 322) and beats down her upturned face (p. 322) with its beseeching eyes. Then he flees, pursued by her eyes and ghastly phantom, losing himself in a warm pub only to have a wandering mountebank centre all eyes upon his blood-spotted hat, wandering distracted in a state of terror emphasised all the more by Dickens's controlled rhetoric: 'Those widely staring eyes, so lustreless and so glassy, . . . appeared in the midst of the darkness: light in themselves, but giving light to nothing' (pp. 327–8). Finally, he circles back to London, to the hideout on Jacob's Island. The writing reaches a pitch of intense excitement, balancing the fevered point of view of the isolated, tormented robber with the equally fevered point of view of the gathering crowds, joined by Mr Brownlow, who adds £50 to the £100 reward as his 'blood boils to avenge' Nancy (p. 338), and a changed Charley Bates, who now sees Sikes as 'monster' (p. 343) and raises the alarm to bring the crowd: 'On pressed the people from the front – on, on, on, in a strong struggling current of angry faces' (p. 345). With the hunting down of Oliver, Dickens felt obliged to moralise ('One wretched breathless child', p. 59); here he joins in the excitement. But the balance is restored by the final horror of the eye motif, which brings us back to Sikes's point of view as it brings about his death: ' "The eyes again!", he crie[s] in an unearthly screech' (p. 347) and plunges to his death, joined by his familiar the dog, which dashes out its brains against a stone. Nancy's swift death, the hunting down of Oliver and Fagin's eyes are all intended to be feared and deplored; Sikes's protracted torments, particularly the vision of Nancy's eyes, are dwelt upon with an extraordinary fascination, felt along the narrator's blood.

Finally, Fagin meets his fate. There is the same balance in point of view between the wandering consciousness of the condemned man, looking up at the 'firmament' of 'gleaming eyes' in court (p. 358), and the external view of the public, giving a 'peal of joy' (p. 359) at the news of his impending death; they are joined by Oliver, who would like to pray for him, and Mr Brownlow, who wants the plot cleared up: 'You have some papers', he insists at their final interview (p. 363). Oliver begs, 'Let me say a prayer. Do!' (p. 364). Piety is not in itself offensive, but is certainly inappropriate here, coming from a child – useless, feeble, patronising and ill-timed, when responsible adults like Mr Brownlow have given up and are concentrating on the plot. Above all, the moral view pales into insignificance beside the power with which Fagin's struggle is rendered, as we share his sense of detachment in court ('Will the sketch turn out a good likeness?' he wonders – p. 359), followed by his struggle against the passing of time and his disintegration as fragments from his past flood into the present:[17] 'Take him away to bed! . . . He has been the – the – somehow the cause of all this. It's worth the money to bring him up to it – Bolter's throat, Bill; never mind the girl – Bolter's throat as deep as you can cut. Saw his head off!' (p. 363). Dickens the artist has soared far beyond Dickens the moralist, and Dickens the comic writer has withdrawn. Comedy in this novel seems to him finally to be inappropriate for depicting the last hours of characters whose terror quite freezes laughter, as he imagines them in their torment.

NOTES

1. Dickens defends the conduct and character of Nancy with the emphatic declaration that 'IT IS TRUE' (1891 Preface); which of course is not the same as the realism of George Eliot: 'It is for this rare, precious quality of truthfulness that I delight in many Dutch paintings, which lofty-minded people despise' (*Adam Bede*, ch. 17).

2. Timothy West played Bounderby thus in a television adaptation of *Hard Times*.
3. Judy Parfitt appeared thus in the Tribunal scene in a television adaptation, at the point where Dickens writes: ' "Much influence around him, has that Doctor?" murmured Madame Defarge smiling to the Vengeance' (*A Tale of Two Cities*, III, ch. 10).
4. They sing 'Food, Glorious Food'.
5. John Carey, *The Violent Effigy* (London, 1973) p. 68.
6. John Bayley, '*Oliver Twist*: "Things as They Really Are" ', in *Dickens and the Twentieth Century*, ed. John Gross and Gabriel Pearson (London, 1962) pp. 49–64.
7. Philip Collins, *Dickens and Crime*, 2nd edn (London, 1964) p. 262.
8. G. Thurley, *The Dickens Myth* (Queensland, 1976) p. 50.
9. B. Westburg, *The Confessional Fictions of Charles Dickens* (Illinois, 1977) pp. 1–28.
10. Quotations from *Oliver Twist* are taken from the Clarendon Edition, ed. Kathleen Tillotson (Oxford, 1966).
11. As George J. Worth points out, 'Dickens' valiant attempt to pump the colour of life into such ciphers by having them deliver melodramatic lines results in little more than mere inflation' (*Dickensian Melodrama: A Reading of the Novels* (Lawrence, Kansas, 1978) p. 43).
12. Carey, *The Violent Effigy*, p. 72; see also 'They started climbing chimneys when they were anything from four to seven years old, and frequently developed deformity of the spine, legs and arms as a result, but more frequent still was cancer of the scrotum' (ibid., p. 72).
13. Collins, *Dickens and Crime*, p. 262.
14. Kathleen Tillotson links this use of the thieves' point of view with that of the readers of 1837: 'Dickens, with some daring, lets us see Oliver from the Dodger's point of view: "He is so jolly green". Readers of 1837 were also tinged with green when it came to meeting the pickpockets of Saffron Hill' ('*Oliver Twist*', in *Essays and Studies* (1959) p. 95).
15. Carey, *The Violent Effigy*, p. 68.
16. 'Other murderers become conscienceless animals, but he acquires the form and conscience of a man' (Bayley, '*Oliver Twist*', p. 60).
17. Analysed by Westburg in his section 'Crime, Time, and Psychological Complexity' (*The Confessional Fictions of Charles Dickens*, pp. 24–8).

2

Bleak House: Another Look at Jo

KATHLEEN TILLOTSON

Bleak House, published in the usual monthly numbers from March 1852 to September 1853, had been growing in Dickens's mind at first intermittently, then steadily, throughout 1851, an exceptionally busy and distracting year. By October it was 'whirling through [his] mind' with a wild impatience to start writing, which house removal and dilatory workmen prevented. Writing began in the first foggy weeks of November; by January it seemed safe to advertise 'a new story', though without a title; early in February it was announced as *Bleak House*, two numbers (Chapters 1–7) were in proof, giving clear evidence that plot, theme and many of the main characters were designed and coming developments foreseen.

But with one important exception – Jo. In his account of *Bleak House* Forster makes one of his rare mistakes and has thereby misdirected many of his successors.

> The first intention was to have made Jo more prominent in the story, and its earliest title was taken from the tumbling tenements in Chancery, 'Tom-all-Alone's', where he finds his wretched habitation; but this was abandoned.[1]

On the contrary, Jo as we know him seems not to have been included in Dickens's 'first intention' at all. Forster has been misled by the name 'Tom-all-Alone's', which the sequence of trial titles shows was not originally applied to the 'tumbling tenements', but to the once ruined Jarndyce mansion, restored and renamed Bleak House.[2] It is not easy to prove a negative, and the absence of any hint of Jo in the memoranda for the numbers or chapters preceding his appearance in Chapter 11 (the first in the June number) need not be significant; such notes were made solely for Dickens's private use and it could be argued that he had long had Jo in mind while planning to delay his introduction. But the pictorial cover is another matter; this was devised to attract the first readers as a kind of prospectus of the serial and must remain (since it recurred each month) appropriate to the completed novel.

This cover would be discussed with the illustrator (Hablot K. Browne), designed and finally approved by mid-February at latest, for publication in the March number on 28 February. It is unusually explicit, as the following details will show, 'shadowing out'[3] the main themes and introducing several leading figures. The top section represents the follies, greed and confusion of Chancery, with a motley crowd harassed by blindfolded lawyers in fools' caps, tumbling over woolsack and mace; lawyers are seen again at the foot, playing battledore and chess with human shuttlecocks and pawns, flanking a picturesque gabled house with a fox as weather-vane pointing to the east. In front of the house stands a hunched and depressed figure clearly intended for Mr Jarndyce, surrounded by a number of futile, humbugging philanthropists signalised by an Exeter Hall porter and two negro children. Minor figures down the sides are: on the left, a lawyer with a spade (conceivably Mr Tulkinghorn), digging up documents;[4] a young woman, obviously Esther, being approached by an ingratiating fox (again suggesting the law, with its cunning and hypocrisy), while a dancer in the background on the edge of an expanse of water or marsh bears a terrestrial globe on his head and a lantern in one hand;[5] an obvious Miss Flite with her birds; on the right, perhaps balancing these, Krook with his cat drawing letters on the wall; an older, aristocratic lady with carriage and footman; two temporarily estranged lovers; a copying clerk at a desk with bottle, glass and guttering candle at hand. With all this included, it is surely inconceivable that Jo would not have been somewhere on the cover if he had been part of the original plan; his prominence is admitted at the conclusion of the novel when he is represented on the vignette title page, published with the final double number in September 1853 and facing the frontispiece of Chesney Wold. Purchasers of the novel in volume form were left in no doubt of his importance.

There may be other reasons for thinking that Jo did not take shape in Dickens's mind before March (or even April) when he was beginning to write the May number and therefore looking ahead to June.[6] The general idea of such a character as Jo would come naturally to the creator of those two terrifying figures, Ignorance and Want, in the *Carol* nine years before, of the brutalised boy in *The Haunted Man*; and especially to the journalist of the *Daily News*, *Examiner*, and *Household Words*,[7] the promoter of Ragged Schools and of the Metropolitan Sanitary Association. The notorious case of the crossing-sweeper George Ruby two years before, constantly adduced as a real-life 'original' for the rejection of Jo's evidence at the inquest – because he does not know what will be done to him after death if he lies, only that lying is wicked – was doubtless in the author's mind, though in fact this was only one of many such cases.[8] But the spark that ignited these materials is surely to be seen in a painfully impressive incident witnessed by Dickens at a crucial time. One day in the week of 23 February 1852 he visited the Ragged School in Farringdon Street with a view to an article for *Household Words*, because certain improvements in the school and the addition of a dormitory had recently occurred. 'A Sleep to Startle us' was published in the issue of 13 March, therefore appearing on the previous Wednesday, 10 March; it struck readers and reviewers of the periodical perhaps the more forcibly since it followed so closely on the blazing success of the first number of the novel.

After describing the present state of the school and then the exact layout of the dormitory, Dickens tells how he watched the men and boys, 167 of them, being admitted by the night officer – 'thieves, cadgers, trampers, vagrants, common outcasts of all sorts' – and given a wooden crib and a small loaf. All were accepted, except those who were near death – such as an aged, emaciated drunkard, and one other:

> Beside this wreck, but all unconnected with it and with the whole world, was an orphan boy with burning cheeks and great gaunt eager eyes, who was in pressing peril of death too, and who had no possession under the broad sky but a bottle of physic and a scrap of writing. He brought both from the house-surgeon of a Hospital that was too full to admit him, and stood, giddily staggering . . . while the Chief Samaritan read, in hasty characters underlined, how momentous his necessities were. He held the bottle of physic in his claw of a hand, and stood, apparently unconscious of it, staggering, and staring with his bright glazed eyes; a creature surely as forlorn and desolate as Mother Earth can have supported on her breast that night.

> He was gently taken away, along with the dying man, to the workhouse; and he passed into darkness with his physic bottle as if he were going to his grave.

This harrowing figure with the burning eyes of high fever, being 'moved on' by authority – albeit gently – would obviously anticipate Jo, especially as we see him in Chapter 31; even without what follows in the article, with its criticism of the government's neglect and the rhetorical final apostrophes to 'my Lords and Gentlemen' and 'Dearly beloved brethren'. The latter, to the clergy, was especially topical in 1852:

> Do you know that between Gorham controversies, and Pusey controversies, and Newman controversies and twenty other edifying controversies, a certain large class of minds in the community is gradually being driven out of all religion?

The implication that the crying needs, spiritual as well as material, of the outcast poor, are being neglected by a Church preoccupied with other matters, takes in the novel a different but related form, initially indicated in the witty title of Chapter 4, 'Telescopic Philanthropy', introducing Mrs Jellyby. The contrast between true and false philanthropy is developed in various ways, ultimately becoming more important than the attack on Chancery abuses.[9] Much of this intention is carried by Jo, who yet remains touchingly individual and convincing, though arguably in some of his longer speeches too much the author's mouthpiece. As with many of Dickens's suffering characters he is most moving when silent (like his prototype in the Ragged School dormitory) or barely articulate. In Chapter 16, where Jo is making his morning way from Tom-all-alone's to his crossing, along with 'the other lower animals', and 'munches his dirty bit of bread as he comes along' –

> His way lying through many streets, and the houses not yet being open, he sits down to breakfast on the door-step of the Society for the Propagation of the Gospel in Foreign Parts, and gives it a brush when he has finished, as an acknowledgment of the accommodation. He admires the size of the edifice, and wonders what it's all about. He has no idea, poor wretch, of the spiritual destitution of a coral reef in the Pacific, or what it

> costs to look up the precious souls among the cocoa-nuts and bread-fruit.

The point is sharply made, and with more precision than the modern reader might guess. Jo's route, like so much of the novel's action, topographical and symbolical, is concentrated in the small area adjacent to Lincoln's Inn Fields, and that was the location of the Society's headquarters[10] from 1824 to 1835, which of course includes the relevant period. But as we shall presently see, Dickens also has in mind the status of the Society at the time of writing;[11] this gave an extra edge to his stroke and added to the offence given to its supporters.

Within a few days of reading the passage in Number 5 one of them, as is well known, wrote to Dickens to protest. His letter is quoted in the first collection of Dickens's *Letters* as that of 'an anonymous correspondent', though as we now know it was not in fact anonymous – and had it been, Dickens would not have replied.

> Do the supporters of Christian missions to the heathen really deserve the attack that is conveyed in the sentence about Jo seated in his anguish on the door-step of the Society for the Propagation of the Gospel in Foreign Parts? The allusion is severe, but is it just? Are such boys as Jo neglected? What are ragged schools, town missions, and many of those societies. . . ?[12]

Dickens replied immediately, politely but strongly, with a decisive affirmative to all three questions.

> There was a long time during which benevolent societies were spending immense sums on missions abroad, when there was no such thing as a Ragged School in England, or any kind of associated endeavour to penetrate to those horrible domestic depths in which such schools are now to be found; and where they were, to my most certain knowledge, neither placed nor discovered by the Society for the propagation of the gospel in foreign parts.

Dickens's 'certain knowledge' of the conditions in which Ragged Schools were started in London dated from 1843, as may be seen from his letters to Miss Coutts. But what most strongly vindicated his severity was the disproportion of expenditure and endeavour.

> If you think the balance between the home mission and the foreign mission justly held in the present time – I do not. I abstain from drawing the strange comparison that might be drawn, between the sums even now expended on foreign missions, and the sums expended in endeavours to remove the darkest ignorance and degradation from our very doors, because I have some respect for mistakes that may be founded in a sincere wish to do good. But, I present a general suggestion of the still-existing anomaly (in such a paragraph as that which offends you) in the hope of inducing some people to reflect on this matter, and to adjust the balance more correctly. I am decidedly of opinion that the two worlds, the home and the foreign, are *not* conducted with an equal hand; and that the home claim is by far the stronger and the more pressing of the two.

Far from being 'Anti-christian' or 'irreligious' – accusations evidently made in the letter and referred to by Dickens 'in all good humour' – he proposes that the 'making of good Christians at home' might take precedence of missions to the 'benighted portions of the world'.[13]

The offending passage had a fiercely topical reference in 1852. Fresh in the reader's mind were the Society's lavish public celebrations in the previous year, its 'Third Jubilee' or 150th anniversary. These occupied an entire week at the height of the season, and included a public meeting with Prince Albert presiding, services in Westminster Abbey and St Paul's and a dinner at the Mansion House. A special fund was raised which increased the Society's annual income to nearly £90,000. Dickens's point about disproportion was not in doubt.

That this is not incidental but an essential part of his purpose is evident at the climax of Jo's history in Chapter 47 (Number 15, May 1853) where Dickens may well be recalling the earlier protest and making a further indirect reply to his correspondent of ten months before:

> Jo is brought in. He is not one of Mrs Pardiggle's Tockahoopo Indians; he is not one of Mrs Jellyby's lambs, being wholly

> unconnected with Borrioboola-Gha; he is not softened by distance and unfamiliarity; he is not a genuine foreign-grown savage; he is the ordinary home-made article. Dirty, ugly, disagreeable to all the senses, in body a common creature of the common streets, only in soul a heathen.

The paragraph ends with the Carlylian outburst:

> Stand forth, Jo, in uncompromising colors! From the sole of thy foot to the crown of thy head, there is nothing interesting about thee.

Dickens is manifestly addressing his readers (one thinks of them as hearers) without reference to anyone present at this scene; Jo has been 'brought in' to his last and sole refuge, George's shooting gallery, after being traced with difficulty by the physician Allan Woodcourt, and, though he cannot yet believe it, is among friends. He will not be moved on again. As the end approaches, Allan asks if he ever knew a prayer: 'No, sir. Nothink at all'; of Mr Chadband's praying he could make nothing, and the others who came to Tom-all-alone's 'mostly sed as the t'other wuns prayed wrong'. But trusting in Allan and sinking into the ultimate darkness and hoped-for light, he repeats after him the opening words of the Lord's Prayer, reaching as far as 'Hallowed be – thy –', after which the last words of the chapter are the author's apostrophe:

> The light is come upon the dark benighted way. Dead!
>
> Dead, Your Majesty. Dead, my lords and gentlemen. Dead, Right Reverends and Wrong Reverends of every order. Dead, men and women, born with Heavenly compassion in your hearts. And dying thus around us, every day.

If the citation of this famous and (for most readers) very moving passage requires excuse here, it is the need to emphasise an aspect sometimes overlooked: Dickens's forcible challenge to the *Churches* ('Right Reverends and Wrong Reverends of every order') and the Chadbands, as also to philanthropic movements and societies that were partisan and exclusive,[14] or 'telescopic' and blind to what was 'around them, every day'. Its implications extend over the whole novel, including the ten chapters before Jo appears and the twenty that follow his death – we easily forget that at this point the novel has almost a quarter of its length still to run. Their relation to Chapter 4 in the opening number (Mrs Jellyby) is obvious enough; and to Chapter 8, though it will develop more subtly, with Mr Jarndyce's two classes of charitable people – one, who 'did a little and made a great deal of noise', and the other, 'who did a great deal and made no noise at all', and the introduction of Mrs Pardiggle as a type of the former. Later, examples of the two classes will multiply – for instance, Mr Chadband and Allan Woodcourt in their treatment of Jo. But before that, in Chapter 11, crucial distinctions are being firmly and delicately drawn in a way that will further the plot by means as yet unforeseen. Jo's account of the dead law-writer's compassion ('He wos wery good to me, he wos!') is given by him, the rejected witness, to Mr Tulkinghorn, who, the reader already suspects, is using it for his own dark ends, treating Jo as a mere means, a thing; in further contrast to the humble and disinterested Mr Snagsby who from inarticulate pity for the ragged waif ('no noise at all') lies in wait and secretly 'puts a half-crown in his hand'.

Narrative suspense is tautened and a vital question asked in Chapter 16, entitled 'Tom-all-alone's' but beginning with Lady Dedlock's restless move from Chesney Wold to London: 'What connexion can there be, between the place in Lincolnshire, the house in town, the Mercury in powder, and the whereabout of Jo the outlaw with the broom. . . ?' Vital, not only for the plot, but because it carries, not obtrusively, Dickens's social and moral theme. The world of fashion, of Chesney Wold, cannot cut itself off from Tom-all-alone's whose 'tumbling tenements contain, by night, a swarm of misery . . . in maggot numbers' however alien and repulsive that place appears, and however strongly on the level of individual characters the 'connexion' is resisted.[15] To Lady Dedlock, Jo is a 'horrible creature', 'loathsome to her'; she will not touch him even to give him the promised payment, 'shuddering as their hands approach'; he is endured only because he can show her where her former lover died, and the rat-ridden graveyard where, says Jo, 'they was obliged to stamp upon it to git it in'. Neither she nor Jo ever learns that they are connected not only by their knowledge of the dead law-writer but by their love and devotion to his memory. On the same 'dreadful spot' Lady Dedlock will be found dead; unknown to her it is Jo's grave too, for dying, he asked to be 'put along with him', giving directions

– 'there's a step there, as I used fur to clean with my broom'; the only return he could make.

There indeed lies Dickens's deeper answer to the question 'What connexion can there be'; its basis, the 'distant ray of light' in the gloom, must be the bond of common humanity expressed in simple acts of kindness, and of reverence for the individual. When the book is seen as a whole, of all its characters the nearest to its heart is Esther; not so much by positive actions, which are constrained by the limits of the young girl heroine, as by the whole tone of her own narrative, so evidently designed as a running contrast and relief to the rest, and the truth and tenderness of her responses to persons and situations. This is noticeable with the neglected Jellyby children, and then more significantly in Chapter 8 when she is being dragooned by Mrs Pardiggle. Esther tries to explain her hesitance about joining that lady's 'visiting rounds', for good reasons, including this: 'That I had not that delicate knowledge of the heart which must be essential to such a work.' She and Ada are made 'uncomfortable' at the brickmaker's cottage by Mrs Pardiggle's bullying of the family and 'her mechanical way of taking possession of people', rightly resented by the husband:

> We both felt intrusive and out of place . . . painfully sensible that between us and these people there was an iron barrier, which could not be removed by our new friend. By whom, or how, it could be removed, we did not know; but we knew that.

As time goes on, Esther, aided by Mr Jarndyce, does learn to cross that barrier, if not to remove it, showing 'that delicate knowledge of the heart' in her relations with Charley, with Jenny and the brickmaker's wife, and with Jo; shown by his words of surprise that he is not blamed for giving her the fever: 'The lady come herself and see me yesday, and she ses, "Ah Jo!" she ses, "we thought we'd lost you, Jo!" she ses. And she sits down a smilin so quiet.'

But within the world of the book the few who have this capacity are felt to be exceptional. The suffering poor are helped by those on the same side of the barrier, those hardly less poor: the orphaned Charley and her babies first by old Mrs Blinder ('it's not much, Sir, to forgive them the rent'). And so also with Jo; Guster the slavey offers him bread and a gentle touch; to care for him on his death-bed, George deputes Phil Squod, 'who was found, when a baby, in the gutter' and so will 'take a natural interest in this poor creature'. They echo the keynote: ' "I am as poor as you, today, Jo", he ses to me.'

No one in his time did more towards the removal of that barrier than Dickens, opening the eyes and hearts of his immense public so that they could at least see and feel what lay on the other side. This is the cumulative effect of all his writings[16] – novels, journalism, speeches – but strongest of all, and at the same time most controlled and inspired, in *Bleak House*. Let one contemporary, perhaps unexpected witness testify: exactly in July 1852[17] when the novel has reached Tom-all-alone's, Dickens's old friend Walter Savage Landor, the 'Boythorn' of the novel, a man of seventy-seven, dedicated a volume to him

> to register my judgment that, in breaking up and cultivating the unreclaimed wastes of Humanity, no labours have been so strenuous, so continuous, or half so successful as yours.

NOTES

1. John Forster, *The Life of Charles Dickens* (1874) III, ch. 1, p. 29 (VII, ch. 1, in modern editions).
2. MS (Forster collection, Victoria and Albert Museum). The title is extended by such additions as 'The Solitary House', 'The Ruined House' (or 'Building', or 'Mill'); then more elaborately, 'Where the Grass Grew', later 'Where the Wind howled', and with added references to Chancery; finally, these are superseded by 'Bleak House and the East Wind', which was retained as the heading of the memoranda of numbers 1 and 2. Comparison with Mr Jarndyce's retrospective description of his great-uncle Tom Jarndyce's house in Chapter 8 is decisive as to Dickens's change of intention.
3. 'Shadowing out its drift and bearing', referring to the cover of *Dombey and Son* (*The Letters of Charles Dickens*, ed. Madeline House, Graham Storey and Kathleen Tillotson (Oxford, 1965–) IV, p. 648; letter of 26–9 October 1846).
4. The comparison in Chapter 8 of a Master in Chancery to 'a sort of ridiculous Sexton, digging graves for the merits of causes' may have been already in Dickens's mind; but the other details on the cover seem mostly related to Chapter 5.
5. Not explained; perhaps Esther is metaphorically facing the world, and the figure symbolises Skimpole's light-hearted attitude towards it, combined with the suspicions of Inspector Bucket. His bull's-eye lantern is emphasised not only in Chapter 22 but in the earlier

'Inspector Field' sketches, and here directed at the 'waters' of Chesney Wold. (One such sketch compares the detective's discoveries with Columbus's of a new continent.) But proximity to the fox might suggest a possible reference to the sly tricks in *Reynard the Fox* (then very well known, with various translations, one of 1845 being in Dickens's library). Reynard's pretended gifts to the king and queen included a magic mirror or crystal globe, revealing things distant in time and place. Browne, if not Dickens, may have unconsciously recalled the dancing figure of Till Eulenspiegel holding the mirror, on the striking engraved titlepage of the 1846 (London) edition of Goethe's *Reineke Fuchs*, illustrated by Wilhelm Kaulbach.

6. In spite (or partly because?) of the great success of the first number, Dickens's letters to Forster in March show him restless and anxious about his writing. The proofs of number 2 gave trouble because of the necessary Skimpole revisions, and ahead of him in April and May lay certain weeks occupied by the amateurs' theatrical tour. Little is known of the writing of number 3; but by 8 May, before leaving, he had finished number 4 (chs 11–13) and sounded satisfied with it – with good reason.
7. Especially 'Crime and Education' (*Daily News*, 4 February 1846) and 'Ignorance and Crime' (*Examiner*, 22 April 1848); more recently, 'On Duty with Inspector Field', *Household Words*, 14 June 1851.
8. On Ruby, and the probability that the *Examiner*'s comment is by Dickens, see K. J. Fielding and A. W. Brice in *The Dickensian*, September 1968. An extract from the report is in the Norton edition of *Bleak House*, ed. George Ford and Sylvère Monod (New York, 1977). But that such cases were familiar is evident from the reference in *David Copperfield*, ch. 1 (May, 1849), to Ham as a 'credible witness', being a National (i.e. Church) School pupil and 'a very dragon at his catechism'.
9. For the former, see his *Examiner* article on 'The Niger Expedition', 19 August 1848, especially 'To your tents, O Israel! but see they are your own tents! set *them* in order.' It is carried on in later novels, to the end (Mr Honeythunder in *Edwin Drood*).
10. At the north-west corner, 77 Great Queen Street, a building erected by the Society. Dickens originally wrote 'His way lying through Lincolns-Inn-fields' and named the site of Jo's crossing as Holborn, revising in proof probably to obscure the exact location of Tom-all-alone's. For some years before 1852 the Society had been at 79 Pall Mall, and some commentators have wrongly supposed that Dickens took Jo far out of his way in order to make the satiric point.
11. This is one of several examples of his deliberate combining of material from the period of the novel's action with that of its publication, not through any confusion but to emphasise the continuance of abuses.
12. *The Letters of Charles Dickens Edited by his Sister-in-Law and his Eldest Daughter* (London, 1880) p. 272; the text of Dickens's letter appears (not quite accurately) on pp. 277–9 and again in the National Edition and Nonesuch Edition.

13. Extracts here quoted from the MS in the Morgan library, printed in *The Letters of Charles Dickens*, VI (1988), which has the correspondent's name, 'The Reverend Henry Christopherson', in the subscription. Earlier texts omitted the words 'on foreign missions, and the sums expended', an easy error of transcription, to the detriment of the sense. Christopherson is an interesting man and by no means the bigoted partisan one might imagine. Born in 1822, apparently a cousin of the Blackheath family (people of substance, several of whom, and their descendants, attained eminence in the Church and public life), he was at this time a Congregational minister; was prominent in the early history of New College, London, but after the 1865 Act was ordained in the Church of England, held curacies in London and finally at the famous Trinity Church (formerly the Revd F. W. Robertson's) in Brighton. He died there in 1874, greatly loved and esteemed, with several columns of tributes in the local press. Published writings (all sermons, the British Museum catalogue wrongly attributing hymns by an 'H. Christophers') show no special advocacy of foreign missions; he was an earnest, eloquent and cultured preacher, and not in the least like Chadband. One sermon, for example, 'Actions speak louder than Words' (on James 2: 15–16), collected in his *The Fight of Faith* (1861), urges the kind of practical and compassionate charity towards the suffering poor that Dickens most approved; and 'Strangers and Angels' (ibid.) is fierce on the unfairness of society to the seduced woman. His reference in 'The Many Crowns' (ibid.) to 'some novelist who . . . is willing to be slanderous, if only he may be amusing' may be aimed at Dickens. But much more significant is his quotation of part of the letter, 'a kind, a conciliatory, and in some respects admirable note' from 'one of our greatest and most popular of the light literature writers of the day', in his address to the annual meeting of the London City Mission of 7 May 1857. To Christianise the 'benighted' at home, the 'untaught childhood' of the streets, as Dickens wished, was indeed the concern of the City Mission; by that date it had 339 workers in London, and was certainly not 'exclusive' in its philanthropy. Clearly, Christopherson treasured the letter, and his widow (daughter of John Fenwick, FSA) must have sent it on condition of anonymity, with a copy of his letter of complaint, when Georgina Hogarth appealed for such loans in 1878.
14. Dickens had attacked them effectively in two *Household Words* articles written and published just when the novel was shaping itself in his mind: 'Whole Hogs', 23 August 1851 (Peace Societies, Bands of Hope, Vegetarians) and 'Sucking Pigs', 8 November 1851 (women-with-a-mission and specifically 'Bloomerism'; the latter too obviously a passing craze – it reached its peak in midwinter – to figure in the novel).
15. The 'connexion' supplied by fever and cholera was often recognised, then and since; vigorously by Carlyle in *Past and Present* (1843) III, ch. 2, and frequently throughout the 1840s. Hence the double sense of Dickens's last trial-title, *Bleak House and the East Wind*; compare

his speech to the Metropolitan Sanitary Association in May 1851: 'the air of Gin Lane is carried, when the wind is Easterly, into May Fair' (*The Speeches of Charles Dickens*, ed. K. J. Fielding (Oxford, 1960) p. 128).

16. As was recognised in the famous words of Dean Stanley's sermon on the Sunday after his death: 'By him that veil was rent asunder that parts the different classes of society.'
17. *Imaginary Conversations of Greeks and Romans*, not published until 1853, but printed, and copies inscribed, by 19 July 1852.

3

Form and Fable in *Hard Times*

JOHN HOLLOWAY

A recent re-reading of *Hard Times* brought me to an unexpected and indeed somewhat unwelcome conclusion. I found myself thinking that, in the end, the most interesting character in the book is Bounderby. More than that, in a certain extremely limited but nevertheless quite real sense, he is also the most impressive.

Many readers, I believe, are likely to find that such a thought verges upon the nauseating; and I must admit to having been disquieted. Am I, as the years pass (I even wondered), growing into something of a Bounderby myself, and now simply finding interest in my own image? The thought was an unwelcome one. Bounderby, intensely narrow, self-righteous and overbearing, is a most unattractive man. There is no need to catalogue the many occasions when that is only too obvious in his behaviour; though there is perhaps need to notice how often Dickens is at pains to underline the point by an aside of his own. In fact, one must go a little further than that. Dickens sometimes tells us that Bounderby has lost face, or is ridiculous, when really that is not quite what we see for ourselves.

It is not quite what we see because, as the novel proceeds, Bounderby moves in one direction while all the other characters to a greater or lesser extent move in another. One must say, of course, that that is simply because Bounderby is an unteachable bonehead and bully – the latter something that his creator is rather fond of pointing out to us. Yet, once the real difficulties begin for him, it transpires that he is rather more than those things. Despite his extreme unlikeableness, and defectiveness, of character, it remains the case that Bounderby can resist difficulty and crisis when these things confront him. How little is that true of any of the other major characters! Gradgrind, once he sees how he has miscared for his children, becomes an abject figure. His head is always in his hands, and he can sink to the unutterable feebleness of 'Bitzer . . . have you a heart?' (III, ch. 8). Young Tom, when the 'net' closes in on him, becomes feebler and feebler, and ends up looking like a surly monkey. Louisa, after her flight in the storm, falls ill, becomes a Victorian invalid, has her life taken out of her hands (by Sissy, in Book III, ch. 2) and never – we are assured in the closing chapter – makes a life for herself again. Stephen falls down the mine-shaft and has to ask others to clear his name. Rachael succeeds in nothing for the man she loves, save sterilely to devote her life to his drunken and vicious widow. Mrs Sparsit, when her own crisis arrives, wrecks her position twice over by uncharacteristic acts of impetuosity. Harthouse sits idle in his hotel, absurdly waiting for Louisa to come to him through the storm, and is then discomfited by a teenager. None of them has much of what, about thirty years before the novel was written, the Victorians had begun to call 'grit' ('firmness or solidity of character; indomitable pluck or spirit', *OED*).

Save, I am afraid, Bounderby. It is true that, in refusing to allow Louisa 'a period of repose and reflection' at her father's house (III, ch. 3), Bounderby acts, as Dickens tells us, with 'determined obstinacy'. But it is also true that he does not look like a poltroon. He is the first to give the reason why Gradgrind proposes the temporary separation ('what people call some incompatibility'), and of course he acts brutally, but all the same, what he does has the merit that he claims for it himself – it is 'consistent'; and moreover it is in his own interest. Bounderby lost nothing when he 'resumed a bachelor life'. Two chapters later, it is Gradgrind whom the author uses as a pawn to reveal (much to Gradgrind's own discomfiture and embarrassment) that Mrs Pegler is Bounderby's mother. Dickens, once again, tells us of Bounderby's 'blustering sheepishness', and of how he looked 'superlatively absurd'. But I cannot find that this is a true description of what the reader is actually shown in the book. Bounderby quickly and, one must add, astutely fixes on, and exploits, the weak position of those present, which is that they have all come into his room uninvited; and with his curt 'In reference to the bank robbery, there has been a mistake made. . . . Good evening!', circumstances (or the author) have indeed shown Bounderby up for a humbug, but he has also shown himself for a man with a certain measure of 'grit' and even a certain minimal dignity. When hard pressed, the loquacious humbug can be tellingly laconic.

What are we to make of facts like these? The view, I think, begins to form in our minds that Bounderby is, from the author's point of view, getting a little out of hand. The role is beginning to take on an independent life, and to guide the author's mind, or his pen, willy-nilly, as he portrays the character. Later, however, I shall suggest that that may well be part of the truth but not the whole of it.

In the final incident of the book (III, ch. 9), Bounderby dismisses Mrs Sparsit. Dickens has the lady tell him (and us) that he is and looks like a 'Noodle', a simpleton. Again, however, the reader is likely to sense that there is a gap between what he is told to see and what shows itself to him in fact. As Bounderby finds means to insist on opening the door for his departing housekeeper, to drop the cheque, already drawn, into the work-basket that she is imprudently carrying, open, on her arm, and to give her what time she likes to go, while sarcastically laying down that henceforth she is to eat alone, Bounderby – one accords him this with reluctance and a little surprise, but the facts remain – Bounderby looks not only clear-headed and strong-minded, not only of a certain dignity, but even something of a gentleman. Finally, where all the other characters fail, more or less abjectly, in what they set out to be in life, Bounderby – judged of course by his own standards, which make the appropriate standard for the point at issue – succeeds. Dickens even confirms this in the brilliant notion he has for Bounderby's will. I shall return to this point later. At the present stage of the discussion we may wonder what this character stood for that made him into something his originator, labour as he might to disparage him, could not bear to, or did not know how to, or – I shall suggest later – had anyhow one good reason not to, deflate.

A good deal in more recent Dickens criticism can come to our aid, generally, in suggesting how to understand these difficulties and discrepancies better. We can even see Bounderby as more of a fabulous than a real character. His 'ate venison off a gold spoon' and 'Josiah Bounderby of Coketown' are like the giant's 'wife, bring me my gold', or the 'small little black thing with a long tail' that sang 'Nimmy nimmy not,/ My name's Tom Tit Tot'.[1] Bounderby is something of a fable-giant in his castle. In likening him also, as happens several times, to a bear, Dickens may be recalling Grimm's 'Man in the Bear's Skin': not simply because of his repellent bearish appearance, which so intimidated the old man's daughter, and not simply because of the shock of hair (like Bounderby's, 'standing up in disorder' and constantly being shaken by its owner) that the unshorn folk-tale hero had; but also because the Bear-skin Man in Grimm's tale was a much more self-assured and powerful personality than at first he seemed.

Some of Grimm's other tales, or other related tales, may have been in Dickens's mind as *Hard Times* began to take shape. Sissy Jupe is not only something of a Cinderella figure, her story is also much like that of the poor girl adopted into the rich family. 'Give me your daughter', says the queen to the girl's mother in Grimm's 'Three Spinning Women': and this very tale may have supplied another motif for the novel, because we read in it of the Lachesis Spinner-Woman whose foot was greatly enlarged through continual use of the spinning-wheel treadle, and we cannot but see in her the Parcae-like figure of Mrs Sparsit, constantly 'netting at the fire-side, in a side-saddle attitude, *with one foot in a cotton stirrup*' (my italics). Besides this, the girl's fate in the Grimm tale is not really unlike that of the 'hands' in Coketown. 'The girl was terrified, because she could not spin all that, not if she had sat down to it from morning till night until she was three hundred years old.' In *Hard Times* we read, 'People as has been broughten into bein' heer, fur to weave, an' to card, 'as to piece out a livin', aw the same way, somehows, 'twixt their cradles and their graves.' Stephen Blackpool, here (II, ch. 5) is almost beginning to paraphrase Grimm. Moreover, next to 'The Three Spinning Women' in Grimm's collection comes 'Hansel and Gretel': the story of an ill-reared brother and sister who became parentless, and who suffered from the hook-nosed, the *Sparsit*-nosed witch.

There are other and similar things in the book, things that help to extend its legendary dimension, or as it were to throw that into relief. The legend – Dickens is at least likely to have known that Rabelais attributed it to Heraclitus – that Truth lies at the bottom of a well is re-enacted in Stephen's last moments. 'He was gazing at a star. "It ha' shined upon me . . . in my pain and trouble down below. It ha' shined into my mind . . . till the muddle in my mind have cleared away" '. The staircase down which Mrs Sparsit imagines Louisa to descend looks a good deal like another version of the same symbol. Louisa is likened, at one point, to a descending 'weight in deep water' (II, ch. 11). In the end she 'falls from the lowermost stair, and is swallowed up in the gulf'. This dark sea merged into the flood of night-time rain as the two women arrive in Coketown in the storm. The moment of truth is, once again, at the bottom of a well.

Remarkably, the very same fable-image comes again in III, ch. 7, when Sissy and Louisa journey all night, so as to make contact with Tom at Sleary's circus: 'The two travelled all night, except when they were left . . . at branch-places, *up illimitable flights of steps, or down wells* – which was the only variety of such branches – and, early in the morning, were turned out on a swamp' (my italics). Finally, the idea is made quite explicit, just before the death of Mrs Gradgrind: 'She might have been lying *at the bottom of a well*. The poor lady was *nearer Truth* than she had ever been: which had much to do with it' (II, ch. 9; my italics).

'Sowing', 'Reaping', 'Garnering', the subtitles of the three parts of the novel, are also full of traditional associations, in this case biblical ones, that give them a legendary dimension. Sowing and reaping adages like Job 4:8, 'Even as I have seen, they that . . . sow wickedness, reap the same', or Hosea 8:7, 'they have sown the wind, and they shall reap the whirlwind', are still familiar today, if only as catch-phrases rather than verses from the Bible. The garnering references are no longer familiar in the same way, but their point is the same: 'Alas for the day! for the day of the Lord is at hand . . . the seed is rotten . . . the garners are laid desolate' (Joel 1:15–17). One such passage, that Dickens would certainly have known familiarly, is especially to the point: 'that our *sons* may be as plants grown up in their youth; that our *daughters* may be as corner-stones . . . that our garners may be full . . . happy is that people, whose God is the Lord' (Psalms 144:12–15; my italics). This is one of the small handful of 'proper' psalms which in most months of the year are said twice, not once only like the others, in the Anglican Church to which, of course, Dickens belonged.

These miscellaneous points, and others like them such as the implicit reference to the 'Arabian Nights Tales' at the end of Book I, Chapter 7 ('[he read] about the Fairies, Sir, and the Dwarf, and the Hunchback, and the Genies'), or the repeated likening of the Coketown mills to fairy palaces, and indeed quite a deal else of the kind, are far from trivialising *Hard Times*. If they are thought about together, though, they may help one not to expect, in a work that has so much of the traditional and legendary and fabulous in its raw material, overmuch by way of close treatment of contemporary intellectual or political movements. At the same time, there is no need to rely upon indirect evidence of that kind in order to reach such an understanding of the nature of the book. A simple, straight look at its detail is enough to show that it is far from a close and analytical study. This, though, has not always been recognised. One critic has seen *Hard Times* as a critique of 'the World of Bentham' and the 'Utilitarian calculus', and singles out for special praise, as 'a triumph of ironic art',[2] the passage where Gradgrind puts Bounderby's proposal of marriage before Louisa:

> 'Louisa', returned her father, 'it appears to me that nothing can be plainer . . . the question of Fact you state to yourself is: Does Mr Bounderby ask me to marry him? Yes, he does. The sole remaining question then is: Shall I marry him?'

That strikes me as a witty picture of how the muddled Gradgrind might perhaps have thought, along 'practical' and to that minimal extent Benthamite lines; but it hardly begins to contribute to real discussion of how Bentham, or the Utilitarians more generally, thought that problems of conduct should be reflected upon. Dickens's treatment of Utilitarianism in this book is not easy to see as any more close and informed than his treatment of early trade unionism.

The same critic rejects that view I expressed in an earlier discussion, that Dickens does not endow Sleary's horse-riders with a profound, poetic quality. 'All that we see of the Horse-riding', he wrote, 'evokes for us spontaneous and daring vitality disciplined into skill and grace'. Is that true? It is not, perhaps, over-difficult to write in that eloquent vein; but turn back to Dickens's text, and we read of 'Signor' Jupe's 'highly novel and laughable hippo-comedietta of the Tailor's Journey to Brentford' (I, ch. 3: this is another folk-tale or street-ballad association); or the same Jupe, driven by failure and ridicule into viciously angry despair and into deserting his beloved daughter. (Dickens had his reason for stressing the toil, hardship and drab squalor that went to make up the horse-rider's life, and we shall see what it was.) Nor does the critic's '*All* that we see . . .' fit the horse-riding as we see it towards the close of the book: 'The Emperor of Japan, on a steady old white horse stencilled with black spots, was twirling five wash-hand basins at once, as it is the favourite recreation of that monarch to do'; or the Children-in-the-Wood turn, 'both a goin' a blackberyin' on a horthe – and the Robinth a coming in to cover 'em with leavth, upon a horthe'. It is useless to deny that a large part of what interested Dickens in Sleary's circus in general, and in the horse-riding in particular, was how it offered relaxation and light entertainment. 'People mutht be amuthed. They can't be alwayth a learning, nor yet they can't be always a working' (III, ch. 8). This is in fact also the note upon which Louisa's future life actually ends the book: 'thinking no innocent and pretty fancy ever to be despised; trying hard to know her humbler fellow-creatures, and to beautify their lives of machinery and reality with those imaginative graces and delights.'

This emphasis on lightness, relaxation and play (which one can argue against by reference to the word 'imaginative' in the previous quotation only by ignoring the rest of the sentence) runs throughout the book, and is an essential part of what Dickens wishes to mean by the book. But there is also another part to its meaning which is quite different from that. This becomes clear if one compares the two discussions between Louisa and her father about the marriage with Bounderby (I, ch. 15; II, ch. 12). In the first of these, Louisa does indeed ask whether Bounderby is thought to love her, or she is thought to love him; though she does so, one might say, a little baldly. But when she begins to dilate upon her inner life, or her lack of that, what she speaks of is 'tastes and fancies . . . aspirations and affections . . . all that part of my nature in which such light things might be nourished . . . I never had a child's heart'.

One notices that word 'light' as the one which sums up all that she has been thinking about; but is it not the case that the last phrase of that quotation strikes another note? Perhaps it is a little like some words which, deliberately, I omitted at the end of the quotation which concludes the previous paragraph: 'those imaginative graces and delights . . . without which the heart of infancy will wither up, the sturdiest physical manhood will be morally stark dead'. And then, when Louisa escapes home in the storm, it is this note, altogether stronger, altogether more impassioned and agonised, that she strikes almost all the time. Once or twice she lapses into phrases like 'exercise my fancy somewhat', but in the main she is now simply not concerned with some part of her nature that might have accommodated 'light things'. Now, she speaks for its deep and vital core, with what brings the individual soul out of living death and into life. 'Where are the graces of my soul? Where are the sentiments of my heart?' 'This great wilderness here . . . the void in which my whole life sinks . . . with a hunger and thirst upon me . . . that have never for a moment been appeased.' 'If you had only neglected me, what a much better and much happier creature I should have been this day!' And when Dickens writes, 'Would you have robbed me . . . only for the greater desolation of this world – of the immaterial part of my life, the spring and summer of my belief', he is not only speaking in generally religious terms, but is actually echoing the key idea, and the key word also, of Newman's great sermon on the regeneration of the soul from the inadequacy of the material world: the sermon he entitled 'The Second Spring'.

We know, of course, and certainly Dickens also knew, that those two languages, the language of lightness, grace and 'amuthment', and the language of the desolation and renewed springtime of the soul, stand in a relation. But if what is at issue is whether those two strands of thought and feeling truly become one in the novel, my own opinion is that on the whole they do not. The novel does not convince that the transition from the one to the other is a simple gradation that makes no particular demand on the attention; yet that is how Dickens seems repeatedly to treat the matter. Other characters besides Louisa, however, know that second and more urgent language, the ranges of emotion it conveys and the great primal efforts of life, like Louisa's own journey through the storm, that it can lead to:

> he cried out that the very dog knew he was failing, and had no compassion on him. Then he beat the dog and I was frightened, and said 'Father, father! Pray don't hurt the creature who is so fond of you . . .' and he stopped, and the dog was bloody, and father lay down crying on the floor with the dog in his arms, and the dog licked his face. (I, ch. 9)

In that passage (I find its horrendous echoes not only of the beggar Lazarus, in Luke 16, but of the Passion itself, buried just deep enough to leave it moving and not embarrassing) 'Signor Jupe' does not stand in need of innocent and pretty fancy. His running away so as no longer to hurt the one creature he loved was like Louisa's tortured and terrible cry for life, not death. His daughter saw this. When she records what she sees, she speaks it in that same language, again almost biblical in its sternness and plainness:

> When he left me for my own good – he never would have left me for his own – he was almost broken-hearted with the trial. He will not be happy for a single moment until he comes back . . . he used to come home despairing . . . he felt himself to be a poor, weak, ignorant, helpless man (those used to be his words. (I, ch. 9)

Sissy also wants no 'graces', no 'little more play'; and Jupe was like Louisa, he lived in a 'great wilderness' before he 'morrithed'.

It would be appropriate now to turn to the case of Stephen, but before I do so I should like to raise a more general question. Is there anything, other than simple critical intuition, that might guide the reader towards a sense of how substantial, how central, such passages as those two set out above actually are for the novel as a whole? I believe that there are two matters regarding the novel's *form*, which do so. By a matter of form, in this context, I mean a feature of such a level of generality that it could be traced, equally easily, in any number of fictions, fictions between the 'stories' of which there would be no similarity at all. Such features of high generality can be important to a fiction because they can pervade it – they can be present more or less continually, from beginning through to end. Two such features of *Hard Times* may be stated, in each case briefly.

The first is a remarkable feature of the *dialogue* in this novel. Save for one or two short passages in Book I, Chapter 6, at Sleary's circus, the *dialogue* of the novel is almost invariably *duologue*. Only two characters (A and B, say) speak to each other, then their interchange is replaced by another dual interchange, sometimes between C and D, but more often between, say, A and C. Throughout *Hard Times* there is virtually no variation on this pattern, and on several occasions Dickens writes so as to underline its presence. Thus in Book I, Chapter 11, when Stephen calls on Bounderby and the two of them talk, Mrs Sparsit interjects a query; but Bounderby forestalls the possibility that Stephen should answer her direct by repeating that query himself. The same sort of thing happens on Stephen's second visit: ' "Here's a gentleman from London present," Mr Bounderby said . . . "I should like him to hear a short bit of *dialogue* between you and me" ' (II, ch. 5). 'Pray don't speak to me, nor yet take any notice of me', Mrs Pegler is made to say to Stephen and Rachael when she hears that Louisa has called (II, ch. 6). 'You can't get it out, ma'am . . . leave me to get it out', Bounderby says to Mrs Sparsit – thus preventing her from speaking – when they call (III, ch. 3) on Gradgrind. Admittedly, most of these excerpts rely on Bounderby's officious garrulity. But what they draw attention to is a mode of presenting conversation that is almost uninterrupted in the book, that goes on whether Bounderby is present or absent.

Unless there is something else prominent in a book, to negate the effect of this mode of presentation (and in *Hard Times* there surely is not), then the effect must be to convey that in the world of the book, *there is nowhere any true social group*. Save briefly and indeed minimally among the circus people, human communication is at a nadir below which no novel, certainly no nineteenth-century novel, could be sustained. Human communion is atomised to the last degree. What is in itself a device of form is making a powerful contribution to material, and is reinforcing what Dickens's material is already, and explicitly, telling us to be the case.

What is the other matter of form that, as I suggested, contributes significantly to content? It is that the novel has what might be called a 'type-act'; and this type-act, over and over again, for one character after another, is to *quit*; to break away from an environment which has become more or less of a living death. 'Oh give me my clothes . . . and let me go away before I break my heart', says Sissy when she leaves the circus (I, ch. 6). 'There's one thing to be said of it', Tom tells Louisa about going into the bank, 'it will be getting away from home' – the 'Jaundiced Jail' of home (I, ch. 8). Tom's only subsequent act of any moment (apart from the robbery, which we never see and only have reported to us) is once again to break away from a life where 'I can't be more miserable anywhere . . . than I have been here, ever since I can remember' (III, ch. 7). When Louisa is leaving home to marry Bounderby, she too sees home as a desert: she is indifferent to the date proposed – 'What does it matter?' she says.

In Book II, Chapter 11, Mrs Sparsit quits the bank to spy on Louisa after she had 'sat at her window all day long', looking out, watching and nursing her frustrated vindictiveness. Even Gradgrind, in his culminatory act, quits Coketown and goes on a hurried clandestine journey, to end up on the clown's chair in the middle of the circus ring. Harthouse ('All up at Coketown. Bored out of the place', III, ch. 2) quits England altogether; and Mrs Sparsit's final act is to quit the Bounderby household which has become impossible for her. In fact, we may go so far as to exclaim:

'How *little* happens in the book save variations on this one basic and recurrent action!'

In detail, the instances of the type-act vary much. Sometimes the departure is voluntary, sometimes enforced from outside. It is not always undertaken for the same reason – far from it. But, if we think of what actually happens in the book as against what nearly happens (the robbery, Mrs Pegler going home), this recurrent event in which the individual quits a hostile environment virtually *is* the 'what happens' of the novel.

Perhaps this recurrence, along with the direct qualities of these crisis-scenes, helps one to see a particular weight and centrality in the cases where this type-act is most deeply charged with emotion and meaning. Two of these, Louisa's flight from Bounderby and Jupe's from the circus, were mentioned earlier. A third is Stephen's departure from Coketown (II, ch. 6). Here, as in the two other cases, humour and sentimentality are alike absent, the writing is severe and plain and intense, the minor or peripheral needs of the psyche are far away. What we are shown is an authentic act of the individual struggling against almost crushing difficulty to retain what matters as much as life (Louisa's case, and Jupe's) or indeed simply to retain life itself, which is Stephen's need:

> It was barely daybreak when . . . he went out. . . . Everything looked wan at that hour. . . . By the place where Rachael lived, though it was not in his way . . . by the great silent factories, not trembling yet . . . by coal-dust paths and many varieties of ugliness; Stephen got to the top of the hill, and looked back. Day was shining radiantly upon the town then, and the bells were going for morning work . . . some of the many windows were golden, which showed the Coketown people a sun eternally in eclipse, through a medium of smoked glass . . . Stephen took his attentive face along the high road.

Here, and in Louisa's marvellously depicted and symbolised journey through the storm and later meeting with her father, the type-act of the book seems focused into its fullest reality.

In these scenes, Dickens is not passing us any message which we could verbalise and thematise without almost total loss. His work is operating at a far deeper level than in the passages about play and fancy and graces, or indeed about wonder and imagination, or Sleary's parting 'It theemth to prethent two thingth to a perthon, don't it, Thquire. . . . I never thought before . . . that I wath so muth of a Cackler!' and along with those words, his references to love and to the need of it, such as are near enough to hand in all these scenes. Certainly one recalls Mrs Pegler's moving outburst, 'I can love for love's own sake' in Book III, Chapter 2; but (leaving aside the rhetorical prophecies of the book's concluding page) in this novel Dickens, as always, praises love; but he does not show it, in itself, to *avail*. It suffers, it seems almost to be punished by events. Jupe's love for his daughter avails nothing until he leaves her. Louisa's for Tom, Mrs Pegler's, that between Rachael and Stephen, Gradgrind's for his daughter, all are real but ineffective or destructive. Where the reader senses primal energy and power, fundamental strength and likelihood of success, as Dickens presents the world of this novel, is elsewhere.

Perhaps – if one allows oneself to speculate – Rachael's lifelong self-abnegation, or Louisa's, after the close of the novel as we have it, could have brought them unutterably great rewards. Dickens hints at this; perhaps he would like us to believe it (though not for Louisa – 'Such a thing was never to be'). But where Dickens actually *shows* us primal energy and power, fundamental strength and likelihood of success, it is somewhere else. He brings before the reader an ultimate reality of the Self, and an ultimate question about that reality, which is, what is the nature of the final effort that the self will make, when self-perpetuation is the reward and self-disintegration the penalty? That is what the great, central scenes of the book tell us about. First, they do so through their intrinsic qualities as the reader directly receives them in the act of reading, scene by scene. But also, we are helped to recognise these fundamentals through the two formal qualities that I have referred to. The dialogue-form as exclusively duologue warns us that ultimately the Self must make such a supreme effort, because in the world of this work there is *no* human society for it to belong to; and the constant recurrence of the type-act, even when one of its major potentialities are in question, focuses our attention upon the places where those potentialities are decisively in question.

These two formal aspects of *Hard Times* help us, I believe, to a more exact comprehension of Bounderby as a character. They both point out that the novel is depicting a world in which society does not provide for the individual, but preys on him. That is why the individual, to remain such, must break away. At the same time, we have seen that *Hard Times* does not present its understanding of experience realistically and analytically, but after the manner of a folk-tale or legend. What then (in what I am inclined to speak of as this *masque* of trapped individual and social colossus) may be the role of a character like Bounderby, so clearly endowed with a fabulous, more-than-individual dimension, and so clearly lacking in the humanities that make an individual nature?

I have already indicated that I found Bounderby 'interesting', and that perhaps Dickens did not err in giving him that disquieting excess of power and self-perpetuation, as against the other characters; but I did not say why. Bounderby stands wholly apart over the type-act of the book. He never even begins to find his position unbearable and so is never ready to give it up and to quit. So far from that, his last act (I referred to it early on, and said that it would have to come up again) is more than one further superb representation of his egotism, though Dickens doubtless saw it as that. His last act is to pullulate his personal Selfhood twenty-five times over and in perpetuity. Bounderby the individual, by his own will, becomes a Bounderby-society. What then does this individual really represent? – an individual immune to the crushing life-inimical burden that society seems to impose, irresistably, upon all its other individuals?

But we have already seen, early on, how Bounderby is other than an individual like the rest of the characters in the book. He is something of the Bear, of the Giant, of the Monster. I believe that Bounderby's full function and purpose in the novel is to begin to be an incarnation, a symbolisation, of all-acquisitive, all-subjugating Victorian society itself. He is the Apollyon, the Giant Despair, of the book. He embodies, not at all in social or intellectual analysis but in legendary and nightmarish fashion, that social juggernaut which, in novel after novel over his later years, Dickens showed almost no one as able to escape or evade. Here, incidentally, is why Dickens was so careful to stress the drabness and grinding hardship even of the 'Horse-riding'. And hence Bounderby's inhumanity, hence his indestructibility, hence his immunity to what I have called the type-act of desperate escape which circumstances – no, which Bounderby himself, whether we look at his individual role or his social-incarnation role – sooner or later oblige every individual character to perform in one way or another.

With one exception: though a minor as well as a repellent one –

Bitzer. He is the very pale 'light porter' who becomes Bounderby's 'rising young man': the odious little ferret, one could say, destined to assume in time the role, fairy-tale-wise, of the fabulous mortal–immortal Bear.

NOTES

1. Katherine M. Briggs, *A Dictionary of British Folk-Tales in the English Language* (London, 1970) Part A, I, p. 536.
2. F. R. Leavis in F. R. and Q. D. Leavis, *Dickens the Novelist* (London, 1970). Leavis added a note in this book to his chapter on *Hard Times*, contradicting an earlier discussion of it by myself in *Dickens and the Twentieth Century*, ed. J. Gross and G. Pearson (London, 1962). In 1970, it seemed to me that what he said did not need a reply from me; on re-reading him now, I find myself thinking along the same lines. It should be noted, though, that the present essay is a substantial extension of what I argued in detail about *Hard Times* in 1962, and so, it may justly be said, is a substantial modification of that.

4

The Choir-master and the Single Buffer: an Essay on *The Mystery of Edwin Drood*

W. W. ROBSON

In the setting of the old cathedral town is placed the main character of *The Mystery of Edwin Drood* and the centre of the Mystery, John Jasper the choir-master. His part in the story has been a matter for controversy ever since Dickens died leaving the novel without its denouement. Jasper is a man with a secret life, his time divided between his duties in the cathedral and the opium den. 'Religion', said Karl Marx, 'is the sigh of the oppressed creature, the soul of soulless circumstance, the heart of a heartless world. It is the opium of the poor.' But this opium has ceased to work for the choir-master, and he has turned to the literal variety as an escape from ennui. He tells Edwin:

> The echoes of my own voice among the arches seem to mock me with my daily drudging round. No wretched monk who droned his life away in that gloomy place before me, can have been more tired of it than I am. He could take for relief (and did take) to carving demons out of the stalls and seats and desks. What shall I do? Must I take to carving them out of my heart?[1]

The mystery of Jasper is heightened by the external way in which he is (usually) presented.

> Jasper turned that perplexed face to the fire. Mr Crisparkle continuing to observe it, found it even more perplexing than before, inasmuch as it seemed to denote (which could hardly be) some close internal calculation.

He bears a family resemblance to Bradley Headstone, the schoolmaster in *Our Mutual Friend*, who,

> in his decent black coat and waistcoat, and decent white shirt, and decent formal black tie, and decent pantaloons of pepper and salt, with his decent silver watch in his pocket and its decent hair-guard round his neck, looks a thoroughly decent young man.

Compare this with the description of Jasper in Chapter 2:

> a dark man of some six-and-twenty, with thick, lustrous, well-arranged black hair and whiskers. He looks older than he is, as dark men often do. His voice is deep and good, his face and figure are good, his manner is a little sombre. His room is a little sombre, and may have had its influence in forming his character. It is mostly in shadow.

G. K. Chesterton remarks on the effective 'piece of artistic mystery' of the fact that Jasper always keeps his eyes fixed on his nephew's face with a dark and watchful tenderness: 'The thing is so told that at first we really take it as only indicating something morbid in the affection; it is only afterwards that the frightful fancy breaks upon us that it is not morbid affection but morbid antagonism.' The likeness to Bradley Headstone is very marked in the melodramatic Chapter 19, when Jasper reveals to Rosa his passion for her – perhaps an artistic mistake, unless Felix Aylmer is right in thinking that it is a deliberate parody of Headstone. Aylmer believes in Jasper's innocence, but the references to *Macbeth* in the novel have been often noticed, and in Chapter 14, significantly entitled, in a near-quotation from that play, 'When Shall These Three Meet Again?' there are *Macbeth*-like ironies; for example we hear that Jasper

> is early among the shopkeepers, ordering little table luxuries that his nephew likes. His nephew will not be with him long, he tells his provision-dealers, and so must be petted and made much of.

Compare this with Lady Macbeth's 'He that's coming / Must be provided for'. We hear that

> Mr Jasper is in beautiful voice this day. His nervous temperament is occasionally prone to take difficult music a little too quickly; to-day, his time is perfect.

Mr Crisparkle, noticing a change in him, says:

> 'One would think, Jasper, you had been trying a new medicine for that occasional indisposition of yours.'
>
> 'No, really? That's well observed; for I have.'
>
> 'Then stick to it, my dear fellow,' says Mr Crisparkle, clapping him on the shoulder with friendly encouragement, 'stick to it.'
>
> 'I will.'

Richard M. Baker suggests that the 'new medicine' is the opium, but he had taken that before. Is it not likely that it is the decision to murder Edwin?

> In his opium dreams he had often done the murder.
>
> 'I did it over and over again. I have done it hundreds of thousands of times in this room.'
>
> 'It's to be hoped it was pleasant to do, deary.'
>
> 'It *was* pleasant to do!' . . .
>
> '. . . I did it so often, and through such vast expanses of time, that when it was really done, it seemed not worth the doing, it was done so soon . . .'
>
> 'No struggle, no consciousness of peril, no entreaty – and yet I never saw *that* before.'

Baker may be right to interpret this as meaning that in his dreams before the murder Jasper could not visualise the actual appearance of a dead body.

> 'Look at it! Look what a poor, mean, miserable thing it is! *That* must be real. It's over.'

There is a suggestive parallel with another novel of Dickens. When the Dean and Minor Canon Crisparkle and the rest look towards Jasper's window,

> a fire shines out upon the fast-darkening scene, involving in

> shadow the pendent masses of ivy and creeper covering the building's front.

On the Christmas Eve when Drood disappears,

> the red light burns steadily all the evening on the margin of the tide of busy life.

Through the terrible wind storm the red light in Jasper's window burns on steadily. The parallel is with Mrs Clennam, another victim of suppressed passion, and *her* windows, in *Little Dorrit*.

> The varying light of fire and candle in Mrs Clennam's room made the greatest change that ever broke the dead monotony of the spot. In her two long narrow windows, the fire shone sullenly all day, and sullenly all night. On rare occasions, it flashed up passionately, as she did; but for the most part it was suppressed, like her, and preyed upon itself evenly and slowly. Strange, if the little wickroom fire were in effect a beacon fire, summoning someone, and that the most unlikely someone in the world, to the spot that *must* be come to.

Mrs Clennam's windows summon Rigaud to his death; did Jasper's do the same for Edwin?

The final tableau in the cathedral gives a glimpse of the demons that Jasper has carved out of his heart, as Mr Datchery and Deputy watch the Princess Puffer watching Jasper.

> She is behind a pillar, carefully withdrawn from the Choir Master's view, but regards him with the closest attention. All unconscious of her presence, he chants and sings. She grins when he is most musically fervid, and – yes, Mr Datchery sees her do it! – shakes her fist at him – behind the pillar's friendly shelter.
>
> Mr Datchery looks again to convince himself. Yes, again! As ugly and withered as one of the fantastic carvings on the under brackets of the stall seats, as malignant as the Evil One, as hard as the big brass eagle holding the sacred books upon his wings (and, according to the sculptor's presentation of his ferocious attributes, not at all converted by them) she hugs herself in her lean arms, and then shakes both fists at the leader of the choir.

And at that moment, outside the grated door of the choir, having eluded the vigilance of Mr Tope by shifty resources in which he is an adept, Deputy peeps, sharp-eyed, through the bars, and stares astounded from the threatener to the threatened.

If we assume the guilt of Jasper, it is possible to trace plausibly the development of the story down to the point where *The Mystery of Edwin Drood* breaks off. The case against Jasper is clear. He has a motive in his jealousy of Edwin over Rosa. There is his warning – is it a threat? – to Edwin (ch. 2). Why is he so polite to Sapsea? (No doubt for the same reason why Datchery is, later on; they both want to use him.) Why does Jasper take up Durdles, and why is he interested in his keys? (ch. 4). He overhears Edwin and Neville quarrel in the street, revives the quarrel, drugs the wine. The way he looks from one to the other suggests that he knows that the presence of a third person will aggravate the quarrel (ch. 8). He tells Crisparkle that night about the quarrel and tells Mrs Crisparkle next day, apparently in case Crisparkle kept it from her. There is his peculiar choice of words, insisted on: 'God *save* them both!' (ch. 9; my italics). Jasper wants everyone to know of Neville's animosity towards Edwin. He is at first perplexed by the proposal that he should make peace between Edwin and Neville, but agrees to it, realising that a meeting at his house could be to his advantage. He shows his diary entry to Crisparkle (ch. 10).

Then there is the matter of the quicklime. How much did Jasper (or Dickens) know about quicklime? Did they both 'entertain the common but entirely erroneous belief that quicklime was capable of completely destroying a body'? (Baker, 1951). Compare Forster's account of the plot as Dickens sketched it to him, which refers to a gold ring which had resisted the corrosive effects of the lime. And here I will cite a passage I have not seen referred to, from *Great Expectations* (Chapter 53), when Orlick says to Pip:

> 'I won't have a rag of you, I won't have none of you, left on earth. I'll put your body in the kiln – I'd carry two such to it, on my shoulders – and, let people suppose what they may of you, they should never know nothing.'

On the other hand, as M. Saunders (1914) points out, Dickens lived near the Medway cement works and might well have known that quicklime (without water) would not destroy a body. Could it be that, while *Dickens* knew that, *Jasper* did not, and the discovery of the murder was to depend on it?

But this is to anticipate a part of the novel that was never written. Returning to the actual story, we read of Jasper's 'Night with Durdles' (ch. 12). He apparently drugs Durdles into a long sleep till 12 a.m. His rage at Deputy seems to be due to his not wanting a witness. Then there is the business of the ring, clearly to be important. (Edwin did not mention it to Rosa.) Their parting kiss, really a brother-and-sister farewell, is mistaken by Jasper ('He saw us as we took leave of each other', says Edwin) for a lovers' parting. From then on Edwin is doomed (ch. 13). Jasper makes much of his affection for Edwin to shopkeepers, and prejudices Sapsea against Neville, but tells Crisparkle he has overcome his fear of Neville and will burn this year's diary at the year's end – the purpose of this being to prevent the Minor Canon from suspecting Jasper (ch. 14).

What happened on the night of Edwin's disappearance? We are not told, but the obvious inference is that Jasper drugged Edwin and then strangled him with 'that great black scarf'. How did he dispose of the body? Again we do not know. The crypt is not indicated, for Durdles delights in making discoveries there. But Durdles always carries his dinner bundle, and on one occasion it contained the key to Mrs Sapsea's tomb. Perhaps it does on this occasion. Jasper may have substituted another key for it. The tomb would not be opened till Mr Sapsea's death, and by then he thought all traces of Edwin's body would have disappeared. His activities covered by the wild stormy night, he put the body in the tomb, went to Cloisterham Weir and saw to it that the watch-chain was caught in the interstices of the timbers, and flung the shirt-pin into the water. It was his scheme to bring about that Crisparkle should find the watch, so that he becomes a chief witness against Neville.

None of this was suspected. What drew suspicion to Jasper was his collapse at Grewgious's news, in a sort of proleptic hanging (ch. 15).

> Mr Grewgious heard a terrible shriek, and saw no ghastly figure, sitting or standing; saw nothing but a heap of torn and miry clothes upon the floor.

Compare this with Fagin's meditations on hanging in *Oliver Twist*, Chapter 52:

> With what a rattling noise the drop went down and how suddenly they changed from strong and vigorous men to dangling heaps of clothes!

How was Jasper brought to justice? Datchery, an enigmatic character, appears to be playing the part of a detective watching Jasper. (Perhaps he is employed by Grewgious.) We note his look of interest when Deputy points to part of the gatehouse and says 'That's Jarsper'. Like Jasper he is excessively polite to Sapsea. His white hair is unusually thick and ample, and he has black eyebrows (ch. 18).

More than half a year passes. Jasper reveals to Rosa his love for her, admitting that but for his affection for Edwin he would have swept him from his path. Rosa suspects Jasper, but she hides her suspicion. Neville and Helena may suspect Jasper, but they say nothing, and the open and frank Crisparkle suspects no one. Grewgious admits he dislikes Jasper, but nothing more.

As the extant story draws to a close there are signs that Jasper will be brought to justice. We see him again in the opium den. Her Royal Highness the Princess Puffer had overheard his broken sentences, devoted herself to learning his secret. She had tricked him that Christmas Eve and warned Edwin of his danger. When Jasper leaves her house she exclaims: 'I'll not miss ye twice!' She follows Jasper to Cloisterham and falls in with Datchery, who extracts information from her that astonishes him. He bargains with Deputy to find out where she lives in London. In the cathedral next day he sees her threatening gestures at Jasper, and later hears from her own lips that she recognises him. Datchery goes home.

> Mrs Tope's care has spread a very neat, clean breakfast ready for her lodger. Before sitting down to it, he opens his corner-cupboard door; takes his bit of chalk from its shelf; adds one thick line to the scores, extending from the top of the cupboard door to the bottom; and then falls to with an appetite.

These words were written by Dickens in his little Swiss chalet on 8 June 1870, only hours before he died. They are the conclusion of Chapter 23. (It is clear that this is the end of a chapter because below the last line in the manuscript there is a flourish.) What was to follow? No one knows.

Forster says in his *Life* of Dickens:

> Nothing had been written, however, of the main parts of the design excepting what is found in the published chapters; there was no hint or preparation of the sequel in any notes of chapters in advance. . . . The evidence of matured designs never to be accomplished, intentions planned never to be executed, roads of thought marked out never to be traversed, goals shining in the distance never to be reached, was wanting here. It was all a blank.

A would-be solver of the mystery must confront the testimony of Forster about Dickens's plans for his last novel. Forster says the story

> was to be that of the murder of a nephew by his uncle; the originality of which was to consist in the review of the murderer's career by himself at the close, when its temptations were to be dwelt on as if not he the culprit, but some other man, were the tempted. The last chapters were to be written in the condemned cell, to which his wickedness, all elaborately elicited from him as if told of another, had brought him. Discovery by the murderer of the utter needlessness of the murder for its object, was to follow hard upon the commission of the deed; when by the means of a gold ring which had resisted the corrosive effects of the lime into which he had thrown the body, not only the person murdered was to be identified but the locality of the crime and the man who committed it. So much was told me before any of the book was written; and it will recollected that the ring, taken by Drood to be given to his betrothed only if their engagement went on, was brought away by him from their last interview. Rosa was to marry Tartar, and Crisparkle the sister of Landless, who was himself, I think, to have perished in assisting Tartar finally to unmask the murderer.

Two comments from a couple of other people close to Dickens may be mentioned as confirming Forster's account. Charles

Dickens junior, the novelist's eldest son, said that his father told him Jasper murdered Edwin. And Luke Fildes, the novelist's illustrator, said that Dickens told him: 'Can you keep a secret? I must have the double necktie. It is necessary, for Jasper strangles Edwin Drood with it.' (In the novel it is a black scarf.)

But Forster's account did not go unchallenged. The general reliability of the *Life* was soon questioned. This takes us into the thick of the controversy about Dickens's private life, which is still a matter of dispute among scholars. And apart from this background of uncertainty, specific doubts have been expressed about Forster's account of *Edwin Drood*. There is one worrying problem for those who believe Forster. He says that in July 1869 Dickens wrote to him:

> What should you think of a story beginning in this way? – Two people, boy or girl or very young, going apart from one another, pledged to be married after many years – at the end of the book. The interest to arise out of the tracing of their separate ways, and the impossibility of telling what will be done with that impending fate.

Forster says this idea was discarded, and that in a letter dated Friday 6 August 1869 Dickens wrote:

> I laid aside the fancy I told you of, and have a very curious and new idea for my new story. Not a communicable idea (or the interest would be gone) but a very strong one, though difficult to work.

Forster then says: 'I learnt immediately afterward' that 'the story . . . was to be that of the murder of a nephew, &c.'

The problem here is that the first idea for *Edwin Drood* which Forster says Dickens wrote to him about has been shown to appear in Dickens's Memoranda Book, kept by him between 1855 and 1865, in an entry which cannot be dated later than 1862.

What are we to make of this? It is agreed that Forster is not such a good witness for Dickens's last years as he is for 1840–60. Things had happened in the lives of both men to diminish their intimacy, and Forster disapproved of Dickens's public readings. So it has been suggested that when Forster wrote his biography he was anxious to show that he had been on intimate terms with

Dickens to the end, and so he copies out a plot from the old Memoranda Book and claims that Dickens had sent it to him. As Angus Wilson has said, this is not a charge of faulty memory but of bad faith. It throws doubt on the whole of the *Life*. If Forster had been capable of it surely he would have been capable of what is also alleged, that he based his account of *Edwin Drood* not on what Dickens told him but merely on inferences from his reading of what was published.

If Forster's account is rejected, the recollections of Fildes (recorded long afterwards and partly discrepant) and Charles Dickens junior (which appeared many years after his own death) cannot carry great weight. The essential truth of Forster's account is clearly the crucial question. Can it be defended?

Not all the considerations that can be urged against it are equally strong. There is no evidence of estrangement between Forster and Dickens at this time, and some evidence against it. As for the fact that Forster's account of the continuation of *Edwin Drood* could have been deduced from what was published of the novel, this makes no difference one way or the other. *Any* account would have to be consistent with what was published.

The real difficulty is the business of the Memoranda Book. Of course it could be that Dickens, considering a new story, himself consulted it. And there is no doubt that many modern scholars are convinced of Forster's general reliability and good faith, even if there are minor distortions of fact in the *Life*. All the same, this business seems fishy, and Forster's account of *Edwin Drood* must for the present remain problematic. If his word is doubted, this account becomes only one more attempt to describe the 'trajectory' of the story (such as the one I have already attempted in outlining the plot on the assumption of Jasper's guilt).

One puzzling aspect of what Forster says is the apparent inconsistency between Dickens's statement that his new idea was 'not . . . communicable' with Forster's statement that Dickens 'immediately' communicated it to him. A little joke? or a contradiction? Charles Forsyte (1980) has argued that there need be no contradiction. It is surely probable that Dickens told Forster *something* about *Edwin Drood*; not all the details, as that would have spoilt the plot for him, but a vague outline of the story, which did not give away the real secret of the mystery; and it was *this* that Forster 'learnt immediately afterward'. It is not certain that Forster even meant to imply that Dickens revealed the incommunicable secret to him.

Even if he did mean to imply that, we do not have to believe that Dickens actually did so.

Can we find out what it was? Sylvère Monod is sceptical. He thinks the 'new idea' was destined never to be communicated. And he points out that in any case, whatever the novelist may have told Forster, it is by no means certain that Dickens would not have introduced significant modifications at the last moment and departed from any intentions he may have had before June 1870. These are wise words. All the same it is hard to believe that Dickens had no idea what was to be the solution to his mystery when he embarked on *Edwin Drood*, even if he may not have decided on all the details. There is in fact reason to think that he did know. The first sketch for the cover was made by Dickens's son-in-law and was approved by Dickens on 5 December 1869. It includes a dramatic scene with a man holding a lantern, which does not correspond to anything in the text as we have it. Surely Dickens already had in mind, while still writing the early part of the novel, a scene that was to occur in the later part?

There have been many guesses about the new idea. A popular theory is that Edwin Drood was not really murdered but was to reappear in the denouement. And it is true that Dickens's list of possible titles for the novel, which has survived, does include some which leave open the question of what happened to Edwin. But as Margaret Cardwell points out in her admirable edition of the novel for the World's Classics, Dickens was prepared in 1869, while still planning his own story, to print in *All the Year Round* a serial by Robert Lytton, for which Dickens suggested the title *The Disappearance of John Acland*, as it would 'leave the reader in doubt whether he was really murdered, till the end'. If Dickens was prepared to print such a story, the 'curious *and new* idea . . . strong . . . though difficult to work' (my italics), cannot be the question of whether or not Drood was murdered.

Nor is it likely that the new idea was the innocence of John Jasper, maintained by Felix Aylmer (1964) in his Agatha Christie-type solution. This kind of solution, elaborately ingenious, is open to the serious objection that Sherlock Holmes did not make his first bow till 1887, seventeen years after the publication of *Edwin Drood*. If it is hard to believe that Dickens anticipated him, it is even harder to believe that he could have anticipated the sophistication of detective and mystery stories which has occurred since the days of Conan Doyle. The Victorian Agatha Christie was not

Dickens but Wilkie Collins, and in a letter to Collins of 6 October 1859 Dickens seems to deny any interest in that kind of plotting.

> I think the business of art is to lay all that ground carefully, not with the care that conceals itself – to show, by a backward light, what everything has been working to – but only to suggest, until the fulfilment comes. These are the ways of Providence, of which ways art is but a little imitation.

There *is* a mystery in *Edwin Drood*, but not that kind of mystery.

The truth is that for the modern connoisseur of mystery stories *Edwin Drood* must be very disappointing. There is almost nothing to find out. Every clue indicates that Jasper is the murderer. As a detective story it is a primitive, like Mark Twain's *Pudd'nhead Wilson* (1894). Yet the effect of the novel is anything but feeble. We feel all the time that it is full of meaning. Dickens had never written in this pregnant and intense way before. The sense of deep mystery that pervades the novel does not derive from the whodunit but from undisclosed personal secrets and from the haunting figure of Jasper – a man not only leading a double life, but deeply divided within himself. He is a brother under the skin of some other Dickens figures, among them Sydney Carton, Arthur Clennam, Pip and Bradley Headstone. He can also be readily related to other examples in nineteenth-century literature of the divided self or *âme damnée*, in books such as Hogg's *Justified Sinner* (1824), Balzac's *Illusions Perdues* (1837), Poe's *William Wilson* (1839), Dostoyevsky's *Crime and Punishment* (1866) and, after Dickens's time, Stevenson's *Dr Jekyll and Mr Hyde* (1886) and Wilde's *Picture of Dorian Gray* (1891). Jasper is placed in Cloisterham, and on the old cathedral city there falls both light and shadow, alternating suggestions of what is life-giving and holy, and what is sinister and corrupt and makes for death. The appropriate culmination of the novel would have been a dramatic confrontation of good and evil. It has been suggested that this might have come about through a revelation of the 'Jekyll' and 'Hyde' aspects of Jasper. (Forster's account of the projected scene in the condemned cell may support this.) Or there might have been a final confrontation between Jasper, the symbol of evil, and an opponent from among the 'good' characters.

Supposing that this were in fact to have been the story, it seems plausible that the opponent might have been Datchery, that mysterious personage whom we leave (for ever) eating his breakfast at the end of Chapter 23. Many critics agree with S. C. Roberts that what we are told of him is 'the beginning of a new element in the narrative'. There are one or two straws in the wind here. In a letter to James T. Fields of 14 January 1870 Dickens wrote:

> There is a curious interest working up to No. 5, which requires a great deal of art and self-denial. . . . So I hope at Nos. 5 and 6 the story will turn upon an interest suspended until the end.

Datchery first appears in Number 5 (ch. 18) and again in Number 6 (ch. 23). Was he the 'curious interest', 'suspended until the end'? Modern scholarship lends support to the view that he was to be a key figure. The manuscript, says M. Cardwell (1982), 'confirms the importance to Dickens of Datchery or of a character playing Datchery's role'. And in her Clarendon Press Edition (1974) she points out an interesting difference between Charles Collins's sketch for the wrapper of the monthly parts and the drawing by Fildes, who replaced him.

Collins's sketch showed 'the second and third of three figures rushing up the staircase, with a glimpse of the fourth in the background', to be police officers, but this is not the case in Fildes's drawing. It looks as if Dickens had decided that the mystery and detection were to have remained completely private. This is the point at which to note that several leading literary critics, including V. S. Pritchett (1946) and Humphry House (1947), lay stress on the 'private' character of the whole of *Edwin Drood*. They imply that it contains secrets. At any rate the police are absent from the story, as Philip Collins (1965) has noted, though the fictional action is usually thought to take place at a time when policemen were on their beats. We hear at one point that the search for the missing Edwin was 'pressed on every hand', yet the only collector of clues we see is Datchery.

Could Datchery be a policeman? Dickens had introduced the professional police detective into English fiction in *Bleak House* (1852) – Inspector Bucket. But Datchery, unlike Inspector Bucket, is a gentleman. It seems more probable that he is an amateur. Philip Collins remarks on the frequency of the motif of shadowing and pursuing in Dickens's novels: Monks follows Oliver Twist, Quilp follows Nell, Dombey chases Carker. In *Bleak House* itself, Bucket the professional is reinforced by the amateurs Tulkinghorn and Guppy, all in search of secrets. Dickens is fond of amateur investigators – no doubt because they enjoy the fictional advantage of being emotionally involved with the victim or the villain. There may be a hint of this towards the end of Chapter 23 of *Edwin Drood*.

> John Jasper's lamp is kindled, and his Lighthouse is shining when Mr Datchery returns alone towards it. As mariners on a dangerous voyage, approaching an iron-bound coast, may look along the beams of the warning light to the haven lying beyond it that may never be reached, so Mr Datchery's *wistful* gaze is directed to this beacon and beyond. (my italics)

That Datchery was to be a *deus ex machina* may be suggested by a conversation in Chapter 17, which Dickens deleted, between Neville Landless, who is suspected of the murder of Edwin, and Crisparkle. Neville says: 'It seems a little hard to be so tied to a stake and innocent; but I don't complain.' 'And you must expect no miracle to help you', says Mr Crisparkle compassionately. 'No, sir, I know that. The ordinary fulness of time and circumstance is all I have to trust to.' At the end of the chapter, lawyer Grewgious is looking up at the stars 'as if he would have read in them something that was hidden from him'. The next chapter (18) begins: 'At about this time a stranger appeared in Cloisterham' – Datchery. Is he the 'miracle'?

Who is Datchery, of the white (or grey) hair and black eyebrows? He may be a new character. But there seem to be hints that he is in disguise, and it has been usually thought that he is a character who has already appeared. Two of the proposed identifications are sensational. The first is that he is Edwin Drood himself in disguise. This was cleverly argued for in an early study, *Watched by the Dead* (by Richard A. Proctor, 1887), but it contradicts Forster, Fildes and a son of Dickens, three men who in different ways were close to him, and who all affirm that Dickens told them that Edwin was murdered. The *John Acland* business also makes against it. The other exciting suggestion is Helena Landless, supported by Edmund Wilson in his influential essay in *The Wound and the Bow*. 'The plausibles', as Alfred Hitchcock called them, will not like this idea. Helena is a lady known in Cloisterham, yet she walks about disguised as a retired buffer in broad daylight. Would a young girl be likely to know about 'the old tavern way of keeping scores'?

– as likely as the Dean, one would think, or less. The Helena idea does not appear to be in Dickens's style. We learn from his letter to W. H. Wills (30 June 1867) that he was relieved to find in *The Moonstone* 'nothing belonging to disguised women or the like' (a reference to Collins's *No Name*).

Other identifications are less interesting. On Grewgious as Datchery, G. K. Chesterton has surely said the last word; 'There is something pointless about one grotesque character dressing up as another grotesque character actually less amusing than himself.' Recent books on *Edwin Drood* have favoured Bazzard, amateur dramatist and author of the *Thorn of Anxiety*. His character seems to be quite different from Datchery's, but of course it might also be a pose; as Aylmer says, his theatrical manner may conceal deep motives. But in that case we have to invent a 'real' Bazzard about whom we know absolutely nothing. Equally uninteresting is the suggestion that Datchery is Neville Landless, or Lieutenant Tartar. Tartar knows nothing of Jasper.

One more suggestion may be mentioned, as 'getting warmer'. This is the young man named Poker, who does not actually appear in *Edwin Drood*, but who teases 'the old Tory jackass' in the enigmatic 'Sapsea fragment', discovered by Forster. Forster thought that Dickens had used up his material too quickly and was trying to invent some more, but it is not credible that the business of Poker could have been introduced as it stands into the novel: it is too similar to the business of Datchery. Charles Forsyte suggests that the Sapsea fragment may have been an earlier unpublished sketch which Dickens kept by him as something that might be worked into *Edwin Drood*. Or (an attractive suggestion) it may be a tentative first sketch of the Datchery idea. Once again we do not know.

Philip Hobsbaum (1973), after listing the various hypotheses about Datchery, concludes: 'Clearly, this is stalemate. The critics should confess themselves baffled.'

But I believe there is an explanation. I think that Dickens was planning to wind up the story with a spectacular final coup not to be equalled in detective fiction until Agatha Christie's *The Murder of Roger Ackroyd*, and I base this belief on three considerations.

1. *The period of Dickens's life during which 'Edwin Drood' was concocted*. In his readings Dickens had achieved a direct contact with his public which meant a great deal to them and to him. In April 1869 his health broke down and his doctors insisted that he should stop. But he was allowed to give twelve farewell performances in 1870. He took his last leave of his audience at St James's Hall with a little joke:

> In but two short weeks from this time I hope that you may enter, in your homes, on a new series of readings at which my assistance will be indispensable; but from these garish lights I vanish now for evermore with a heartfelt, grateful, respectful, affectionate farewell.

Dickens could not know that *Edwin Drood* was to be a farewell performance in fiction, but he may well have guessed it. If so, it would be surprising if he had not considered some way of making his last bow in the novel itself. At any rate there is little doubt of the influence of the readings on *Edwin Drood*: it is full of 'stage directions'.

2. *The personal significance of 'Edwin Drood'*. While we need not accept the whole of Edmund Wilson's theory about the novel, it is easy to agree with him that John Jasper and Charles Dickens have affinities. Whether or not Dickens had a divided personality like Jasper, Jasper like Dickens is an artist, a gifted musician with a beautiful voice. His use of opium can be regarded as a symbol for the life of imagination which he leads apart from other men. He is apparently a skilful mesmerist (compare Dickens and Mrs De La Rue) with a potentially dangerous power over his fellow men and women. He seems an alien from another world, yet he is accepted in the conventional English community, where he passes for a man of kindly feelings and good spirits. But his hymns to the God of Christianity in the decaying cathedral are false – whether or not, as Wilson thinks, his real object of worship is Kali, goddess of destruction.

We must be wary of identifying Dickens (or any other great novelist) with any one character. As Taylor Stoehr says, 'Dickens seems to be in all his characters.' This seems to prevent him taking any one role and identifying himself with it. We never have the impression, Stoehr feels, that the author himself is the hero, as we do in *Middlemarch* or *Evelina* or *The Sun Also Rises*. Critics have remarked on the thin, 'distant' quality of Dickens's first-person narrators – David, Esther, Pip. 'Dickens's people are nearly all flat', says E. M. Forster, adding that 'Pip and David Copperfield attempt roundness, but so diffidently that they seem more like bubbles than solids.' Yet it is hard not to feel a strong personal engagement in one character – Jasper. 'His own temptations and imaginings', says House of the 'macabre Dickens', 'isolated and heightened by the peculiar, narrowing intense quality of his imagination, fed daily by the immense power he felt himself to possess over others' personalities – these were the authentic sources of his great criminal characters.' We should avoid the kind of interpretation Monod calls 'effroyablement sérieux', but there does seem to be a serious centre of interest in this book, and it is Jasper.

But if Jasper represents an aspect of Dickens, he cannot be the puppet in whose costume Dickens would have made his 'positively last appearance'. He is a bad man in disguise; is it not likely that he will be defeated by a good man in disguise, and *that* is the part that Dickens himself would play? In both life and art Dickens loved the incognito and was fascinated by role-playing. 'There had always been something vaguely theatrical about his style of dress', says Ellen Moers, who gives him a place in the line of dandies from Beau Brummell to Max Beerbohm. He could dress up to attract attention, as a Heavy Swell. But he could also, says John Reed, derive a deep satisfaction from moving secretly about the low districts of London, 'like Haroun al-Raschid in disguise'.

3. *Dickens's lifelong fascination with 'The Arabian Nights'.* Angus Wilson has written convincingly about the profound significance of Jasper's 'oriental dream' under the influence of opium. 'Dickens is identifying the world of *The Arabian Nights* with the erotic and the violent, those parts of it which we may suppose he was conscious of when as a child he so loved it.' There are many references to *The Arabian Nights* in Dickens's work – for example in *Martin Chuzzlewit* (Chapter 5), *David Copperfield* (Chapters 3 and 59) and *American Notes* (Chapter 9). They are frequent in the *Christmas Stories.* There is the detailed account in 'A Christmas Tree' of the hold these stories had over his childish imagination. In another story he speaks of the 'sweet memories' with which the name of 'the good Caliph Haroun Alraschid' is 'scented'. Of yet another passage Michael Slater in his recent *Dickens and Women* says: 'As always with Dickens, *The Arabian Nights* allusions are a sure sign that his emotions are deeply stirred.' 'Under the lightest of fictional disguises he enjoys . . . that pleasure so dear to him, of exposing his deepest feelings to his beloved public without that public at all suspecting what it is that he is doing.'

We must keep in mind the possibility that if Philip Collins is right Dickens had composed a mystery plot in the real world at this time – the house at Slough, the assumed name, the double life. But psychological explanations are quite speculative. The solution I suggest does not depend on them. It is a simple one. *Edwin Drood* turns out to be an 'Arabian Nights expedition' (Dickens once invited Wilkie Collins to one in real life). Datchery is Charles Dickens himself, moving like Haroun al-Raschid in disguise among the subjects of his fictional kingdom.

This would explain why Dickens was so secretive in the notes for *The Mystery of Edwin Drood*, intended for his private use. 'They are curiously cryptic', says Arthur J. Cox, 'as if the author wished to conceal, even at the privacy of his desk, the solution to his Mystery.' All the other suggested solutions are either 'difficult' in an un-Dickensian, Agatha Christie way, or they are not credibly 'difficult' for a genius like Dickens. This solution gives a reason why Dickens played his cards close to his chest. The secret would have been uniquely exciting while it was kept, but anti-climactic if it had got out prematurely. It would also explain his reference to the 'self-denial' required in writing the Datchery numbers, and the curious phrase 'the Datchery assumption' quoted by Forster as used by Dickens. It would explain the deleted reference to 'a mircale'. A miracle is a direct intervention of God, and in a novel the novelist himself is God. There are anticipations of the idea in Dickens's earlier work. The teller of the tale of the Baron of Grogzwig in *Nicholas Nickleby* is clearly a persona of the author. There is the revelation of Master Humphrey as himself 'the single gentleman' at the end of *The Old Curiosity Shop*. There is the peculiar character 'The Shadow' which intrigued Dickens at one time. In his later years we have the sketches collected as *The Uncommercial Traveller*, in which Dickens goes about as 'Mr Uncommercial'. If Hitchcock could appear in his own films, why not Dickens in his own novel?[2]

Of course it is impossible to say how the Dickens/Datchery figure would have been finally explained. I suspect that he would have turned out to be the person referred to by Grewgious in Chapter 20: 'a Firm down stairs with which I have business relations, lent me a substitute' – that is for Bazzard, who is 'off duty at present'. This would give a reason for the mention of this 'substitute', otherwise unexplained. It would also give some relevance to the mystery about Grewgious's career and the unknown help he received in it. Would he have been the 'Agent' and the 'Receiver' of the author in the Datchery role?

Whoever Datchery is, it seems probable that he would have played a leading part in the unmasking of Jasper. Jack Lindsay suggested that his name may have come from an unconscious reminiscence of 'Datchet' in *Cheveley* (1839), Lady Lytton's *roman-à-clef*, in which Datchet is the instrument for the exposure of a wicked novelist who had treated his wife cruelly. (This is a novel Dickens is sure to have read with interest, as besides Lytton it contains portraits of other figures from his own milieu, including Forster.) Who knows? A more reliable inference is that there is no reason to believe that the process of detection would have been very ingenious or elaborate. Those who know Dickens's work well will not hesitate to agree with Kate Perugini, his daughter, when she said of *Edwin Drood*:

> It was not, I imagine, for the intricate working out of his plot alone that my father cared to write this story; but it was through his wonderful observation of character, and his strange insight into the tragic secrets of the human heart, that he desired his greatest triumph to be achieved.

NOTES

1. All references are to the works listed below as works consulted. The place of publication is London, unless otherwise stated.
2. I tried this idea out in an article in *The Times Literary Supplement* (11 November 1983), which was followed by some correspondence in succeeding issues. So far as I could learn from this and from private letters it convinced no Dickens specialists, but was attractive to some general readers of Dickens.

WORKS CONSULTED

New Oxford Illustrated Dickens (Oxford, 1947–8).

The Mystery of Edwin Drood, ed. Margaret Cardwell (Oxford, 1972) and her edition for the World's Classics (Oxford, 1982).

The Letters of Charles Dickens, Nonesuch Edition (1938), and Pilgrim Edition (Oxford, 1965–).

The Speeches of Charles Dickens, ed. K. J. Fielding (Oxford, 1960).

All the Year Round (1859–70).

Felix Aylmer, *Dickens Incognito* (1959), and *The Drood Case* (1964).
Richard M. Baker, *The Drood Murder Case* (1951).
R. Bulwer-Lytton, *Cheveley* (1839).
G. K. Chesterton, *Criticisms and Appreciations of Dickens* (1911).
Agatha Christie, *The Murder of Roger Ackroyd* (1926).
Philip Collins, *Dickens and Crime* (2nd edn, 1965).
Wilkie Collins, *No Name* (1862), and *The Moonstone* (1868).
Arthur J. Cox, *The Mystery of Edwin Drood* (Harmondsworth, 1974).
C. G. L. Du Cann, *The Love Lives of Charles Dickens* (1961).
E. M. Forster, *Aspects of the Novel* (1927).
John Forster, *Life of Charles Dickens* (1872–4).
Charles Forsyte, *The Decoding of Edwin Drood* (1980).
Leon Garfield, Conclusion to *The Mystery of Edwin Drood* (1980).
George Gissing, *Charles Dickens* (1898).
Philip Hobsbaum, *A Reader's Guide to Charles Dickens* (1972).
Humphry House, *All in Due Time* (1955).
William R. Hughes, *A Week's Tramp in Dickensland* (1891).
Jack Lindsay, *Charles Dickens: A Biographical and Critical Study* (1950).
Karl Marx, *Selected Writings* (Harmondsworth, 1970).
Sylvère Monod, *Dickens the Novelist* (Norman, Oklahoma, 1967).
Ellen Moers, *The Dandy: Brummell to Beerbohm* (New York, 1960).
V. S. Pritchett, *The Living Novel* (1946).
Richard A. Proctor, *Watched by the Dead* (1887).
John R. Reed, *Victorian Conventions* (Athens, Ohio, 1975).
S. C. Roberts, *The Mystery of Edwin Drood* (Oxford, 1955).
Montagu Saunders, *The Mystery in the Drood Family* (1914).
Michael Slater, *Dickens and Women* (1983).
Taylor Stoehr, *Dickens: The Dreamer's Stance* (1965).
Angus Wilson, Introduction to *The Mystery of Edwin Drood* (Harmondsworth, 1974).
Edmund Wilson, *The Wound and the Bow* (1941).
Robin Wood, *Hitchcock's Films* (1965).

5

'I must keep in good health, and not die': the Conception of the Self in an Unorthodox Victorian Novel

MIRIAM ALLOTT

'Who in the world cares for you? *or who will be injured by what you do?'*

Still indomitable was the reply – 'I *care for myself. The more solitary, the more friendless, the more unsustained I am the more I will respect myself'. . . . Mr Rochester . . . seemed to devour me with his flaming glance: physically, I felt, at the moment, powerless as stubble exposed to the draught and flow of a furnace – mentally I still possessed my soul. . . .*

I broke from St John. . . . It was my *turn to assume ascendancy.* My *powers were in play, and in force . . . I desired him to leave me: I must and would be alone. He obeyed at once. Where there is energy to command obedience never fails.*

(Charlotte Brontë, *Jane Eyre*)

The conception of the self, its interests thus fervently defended in Jane Eyre's spirited refusals of her two suitors, as indeed they are throughout her story, seems to have more in common with European rather than English romantic traditions. Its tremendous *amour de soi* struggles towards something approaching the Goethian notion of 'renunciation' – *Entsagen* – which, as Carlyle came to see in his own dealings with the idea, has little to do with orthodox notions of self-denial. 'God wants only a separation of spirit from flesh to crown us with a full reward', says Jane Eyre's pious school friend Helen Burns, but *Entsagen* does not entertain this kind of dualism. Carlyle's reading of *Wilhelm Meister*, that major document of the romantic sensibility, appears to have left him initially with the notion that Goethe's *Entsagen* did indeed imply a certain degree of asceticism. He argues in *Sartor Resartus* that 'Love of happiness is but a kind of hunger at best: a craving because I have not enough of sweet provision in the world', and makes his Teufelsdroch proclaim in the 'Everlasting Yea' after his emergence from despair, 'Foolish soul! what Act of Legislation was there that *thou* shouldst be happy. . . . Close thy Byron, open thy Goethe.' In other words, avoid self-indulgence and strive to see life steadily and whole. The 'self' in Goethe's *Entsagen* may be 'the self as object, not the self as subject . . . matter considered as an end in itself, personal happiness as "appetite" alone – these, not the individual consciousness or spirit, were the elements of our nature to be repressed'.[1] But the best gloss is perhaps to describe it as in effect an aesthetic ideal, pointing 'to the harmonious outflowering of all one's energies, the lower subordinated to the higher. . . . It has no similarity to the ascetic ideal; it is fundamentally a creative act, an effort at a constant engaging of the whole.' This romantic aspiration towards unity of being does begin to emerge as a striking feature in the movement of European thought and feeling at the beginning of the nineteenth century. *Sartor Resartus* is of the 1830s, the decade before the Brontës published their work and were reading voraciously as well as being engrossed in compiling their chronicles of Gondal and Angria. They would certainly know Carlyle's writings on German literature from *Blackwood's Magazine*, and it may well be, as some have suggested, that *Wuthering Heights* was affected by Emily Brontë's knowledge of the German literature to which she was introduced by his articles and translations there. Jane Eyre's cousins, Diana and Mary Rivers, are reading Schiller and practising their German when she first catches sight of them through the windows of Moor House.

Whether or not we can make out any direct influence, it is clear that Charlotte Brontë's own 'propensities' – she makes her St John Rivers use the word in *Jane Eyre* – lead her along a path which runs parallel to the path which led Carlyle to recognise that *Entsagen* when properly understood made for the sentiments and the predilections of the artist, literature itself becoming the avenue which could open on to the self's 'higher regions'. The promotion of the aesthetic self, we see at once, cannot go ahead if the senses are either repressed or inharmoniously ordered. Charlotte Brontë struggles from the exciting self-indulgences of her Angrian tales, through the relentlessly pared-down style of *The Professor*, to the freely moving and exuberant *Jane Eyre*. In *Villette*, her last and perhaps most complex effort to confront the problem, Lucy Snowe has her own comment to make about the aesthetic sensibility. 'Of the artistic temperament, I deny that I am', she says, 'yet I must possess something of the artist's faculty of making the most of present pleasure: that is to say, when it is of the kind to my taste.'[2]

The family resemblance to Jane Eyre is immediately apparent, in spite of Lucy being rather glum and Jane Eyre not at all so. Jane Eyre is a creature of quick senses and healthy appetites which are at first thwarted, then given sufficient head to risk a troubling imbalance and finally allowed to approach balance and harmony. Rochester himself, necessarily portrayed in less detail, is discovered in the end to have undergone a similar process. In both, it is the ordering, not the nature, of the propensities that has been altered.

The heroine's story unfolds in the five stages of childhood at Gateshead with the Reeds; schooldays at Lowood; young womanhood at Thornfield with Rochester; life with her cousins at Moor House; and reunion with her lover at Ferndean. It is in the fourth stage that St John Rivers makes his first entrance, acting as a counterpart to Rochester at Thornfield. 'Propensities and principles must be reconciled by some means', he says at a moment of unusual discomfort at finding these at odds in himself, and the Moor House sequence opens with Jane Eyre apparently stoically set to repress 'propensities' for ever. This turns out to be far from the case. Her individual history makes us think in some ways of her Irish successor Stephen Dedalus, whose portrait – 'of the artist as a young man' – is also presented, as it happens, in five sequences, and who in growing from childhood to youth preserves throughout the same keen response to the physical world. Taste, touch, smell, the sound of words, delight and quicken him, and his assent to the beauty of the girl on the shore, celebrated in youthfully heady style in the fourth part of his story, is in keeping with the child's response to his father's 'hairy face', the boy's to the evening sounds and smells as he stands by himself on the Clongowes cricket field and the adolescent's to the girl in the dingy room in Dublin's night town. His changes of mood are also in keeping, shifting through happiness, boredom, despair, exhilaration. By the time of *her* fourth phase, that is the Moor

House sequence, Jane Eyre has come to accept as unreservedly as Stephen that she is a creature who enjoys the pleasures of the physical world. She likes company, talk, food, the sights and smells of the country, and has no inhibitions about proclaiming that happiness in this world, here and now, is her good. She takes flight from the alien vision of St John Rivers, who summons her to a life of self-sacrifice with reward in Heaven. Happiness here and now includes sexual passion and its fulfilment. There is no trace of the *contemptus mundi* encouraged by disenchanting experiences of life which seems in the end to possess Isabel Archer, Henry James's daughter of the Puritans, or of the self-denial which obliges Maggie Tulliver to subdue her passionate nature in the interests of the powerful missionary sense which informs her history. 'I must indulge my feelings', Jane Eyre tells St John Rivers when arranging to share her legacy with her cousins – characteristically she has no intention of giving all of it away. 'I want to enjoy my own faculties', she tells him, 'as well as to cultivate those of other people.' It is much to the point that, once she has the money to help her, she enjoys the pleasures of everyday life in the world even more than in the period of her most excitingly passionate time at Thornfield. She thrives on prosperity and loves spending money: 'Dark handsome new carpets . . . curtains . . . mirrors . . . dressing-cases for the toilet tables . . . a spare parlour and bedroom I furnished entirely, with old mahogany and crimson upholstery' (III, ch. 8, p. 396).[3]

Everything she does in Moor House at this stage is consistent with her propensities as a child. She is miserable and ill-treated then, but not subdued or overcome by guilt. She may be sick with terror when immured in the red room, but arrives there because of a characteristic act of defiance. The opening paragraphs of her story show her working hard to preserve her already pronounced sense of personal identity inside the group that threatens to destroy it. She sits cross-legged in the window seat, absorbed in a book she has chosen for its pictures, not for its sober print, and finds protection behind the scarlet moreen curtains. Many readers have noticed the play which the narrative makes with the colour red, and it does indeed signal certain perils and attractions pertinent to the present discussion, as in the associations gathered around the red room at Gateshead Hall and the fire at Thornfield Hall, and in the contrasted associations of warmth and happiness in the crimson upholstery bought for Moor House (as Charlotte herself in later years bought red curtains to make the room at Haworth welcoming for guests). Christmas at Moor House, again, is less a season of pious observance than cheerful festivity:

> a sort of merry domestic dissipation. The air of the moors, the freedom of home, the dawn of prosperity, acted on Diana's and Mary's spirits like some life-giving elixir. . . . They could always talk; and their discourse, witty, pithy, original, had such charm for me, that I preferred listening to, and sharing in it, to doing anything else. (III, ch. 8, p. 399)

St John, we learn, 'did not rebuke our vivacity; but he escaped from it'.

We may well feel that Jane's creator speaks through her heroine in much of this, expressing something of her own and her sisters' life and longings. We may be led to notice too that Jane's narrative does not mention the figure in whose name the religious festival is celebrated. If not noted earlier, it may now dawn on the reader that the figure of Christ, though the narrative records references by others, is conspicuous by its absence from Jane Eyre's interior commentary. This too is in keeping with her early self. Her native attachment to this world rather than the next gets its first defiant expression when she confronts Mr Brocklehurst, the schoolmaster at Lowood whither she is bound on the next stage of her journey.

> 'And what is hell. Can you tell me that?'
> 'A pit full of fire.'
> 'And should you like to fall into that pit and to be burning there for ever?'
> 'No, sir.'
> 'What must you do to avoid it?'
> I deliberated a moment; my answer when it did come, was objectionable: 'I must keep in good health and not die.'
> (I, ch. 4, p. 32)

When cross-examined about the Bible, it transpires that she prefers the Old Testament to the New. She rejects the gospels for the visionary exhilaration of Revelations (*sic*) and for Daniel, Genesis, Samuel, 'a little bit of Exodus . . . some parts of Kings and Chronicles, and Job and Jonah. . . . Psalms are not interesting' (I, ch. 4, p. 33). Once at Lowood, her friendship with Helen Burns confirms this want of affinity with Gospel teaching. 'When we're struck without a reason', she says, 'we should strike back very hard . . . to teach the person . . . never to do it again. I *feel* this Helen. . . . It is as natural that I should love those who show me affection or submit to punishment when I feel it is deserved.' Her 'I feel', 'it is natural', look forward to her adult responses to Rochester and St John Rivers. Helen Burns finds her incomprehensible. 'Observe what Christ says . . . love your enemies; bless them that curse you; do good to them that hate you', she tells her, for 'we are burdened with faults in this world', but in the next will 'put them off in putting off our corruptible bodies' (I, ch. 6, pp. 58–9). At one end of the orthodox 'axis' in the story is Helen Burns, mild but firm in faith; at the other is St John Rivers, harshly intransigent and spiritually ambitious. What they have in common is their certainty that what happens here and now is important only in so far as it affects the there and then of the next world. The point about Jane Eyre in relation to these two is her total want of natural sympathy with either. She has much in common, though, with whoever it is that speaks in Emily Brontë's poem, 'I see around me tombstones grey',

> We would not leave our earthly home
> for *any* world beyond the tomb,

and indeed with Catherine Earnshaw in the ninth chapter of *Wuthering Heights*, whose frightening dream it is that she will die and go to Heaven, for there she can only feel herself to be an outlaw. Angry angels cast her out and she wakes up 'sobbing for joy'. This is a remarkable conception for a clergyman's daughter to place at the centre of her tale, but no much more so than her sister's creation of so unorthodox a heroine. *Wuthering Heights* suggests a higher degree of daring in its moral and metaphysical speculation, but there is considerably more of such speculation in *Jane Eyre* than its absorbing narrative verve sometimes allows us to see.

Indeed the narrative *élan* in both novels can disguise the studiedly patterned structure which they also share. Few readers come away from a first reading of *Wuthering Heights* with a sharp sense of the division of space given to the story of the two generations (the ending of one and the beginning of the other occurs almost exactly half-way through: there are thirty-four chapters and the first Catherine dies in childbirth at the start of the sixteenth); within this division is elaborated a series of still other meticulously patterned contrasts, each deriving its meaning from conjunction with the rest. The symmetrical structure in both books is the means by which the major themes operate on the understanding. In the five-part structure of *Jane Eyre*, each part sets up its own contrast with the others to contribute to the total statement which the narrative makes.

Of the two passages quoted at the beginning of this essay, the first is part of the long soliloquy in Chapter 27 which follows the interrupted wedding ceremony, the second occurs in Chapter 35. The first marks the close of the third 'act', set at Thornfield Hall. The second marks the close of the fourth, set in Moor House. After this there come the closing five chapters, set in Ferndean manor-house, scene of the reunion between Rochester and Jane and the flowering of 'propensities' in harmony with certain 'principles'. So these ardent utterances belong to the culminating stages of the heroine's history; they and the events precipitating them are organised to heighten tension and excitement at crucial, and climactic, points of the narrative, especially as these derive from the clashing egotisms of the three characters concerned, St John Rivers having been introduced late on in order to stand to the Moor House element in the book as Rochester stands to that of Thornfield Hall. Each focuses a type of powerful egotism against which the heroine's equally powerful *amour de soi* has to test itself. It is not merely the question of who will win that keeps the reader on the qui vive, but also the question of whom and what is to be cheered for, and why.

The physical contrast between the two men indicates in part this novel's affinity with *Wuthering Heights*, but the effects are different. Rochester is stocky and barrel-chested, with 'square brow' and dark 'speaking eyes', his general physique in keeping with his passionate temperament, and bearing, then, some resemblance to Heathcliff, though the characters are by no means identical. St John Rivers is tall, fair and pale, with high austere brow, and cold blue eyes used 'as instruments to search other people's thoughts' rather than as 'agents to reveal his own'; a man, he says, for whom 'Reason, and not Feeling, is my guide', so he has even less resemblance to the fair Edgar Linton, Heathcliff's counterpart in *Wuthering Heights*, than Rochester has to Heathcliff. Rochester and Jane are, like Catherine and Heathcliff, bound by strong mutual passion, but again the difference is marked since their passion is physical as well as emotional and as such is quite untroubled (the sensuous is notably absent from Emily Brontë's lovers but they are surrounded by the troubling atmosphere of cosmic outlawry powerfully conveyed in Catherine's dream).

St John Rivers, on the other hand, wants Jane as a fellow labourer in the service of God, but with absolutely no thought of her as a passionately loved companion. There is no such passion for him on her side either. Her initial decision is to refuse marriage but accept the role of fellow-worker in the parching worlds of the Indian sub-continent. He sternly insists on marriage, the issue being suddenly and dramatically complicated by the revelation in him of an extraordinary passion, albeit of a different order from Rochester's. Pressed home in the heroine's struggle with 'laws and principles' as she tears herself away from Rochester are the power and intensity of his passion and her response to it:

> Not a human being that ever lived could wish to be loved better than I was loved; and him who thus loved me I absolutely worshipped . . . my veins running fire . . . my heart beating faster than I can count its throbs . . . he crossed the floor and seized my arm, and grasped my waist. He seemed to devour me with his flaming glance. (III, ch. 1, pp. 320–2)

It turns out that St John Rivers can be equally impassioned. As he conducts family prayers one moonlit May evening after her refusal, his coldness drops away, he prays fervently for those in jeopardy and directs all this force and energy at Jane Eyre, the victim, as he sees it, of a passion as unsanctified as it is powerful: 'he was in deep earnest, wrestling with God, and resolved on conquest. . . . He asked, he urged, he claimed the boon of a brand snatched from the burning.' The effect is devastating and, in a scene which is to mark a temporary parting between them but becomes final, she relives the emotional storm at Thornfield.

> I felt veneration . . . so strong that its impetus thrust me at once to the point I had so long shunned. I was tempted to . . . rush down the torrent of his will into the gulf of his existence, and there lose my own. I was almost as hard beset . . . as . . . before, in a different way, by another . . . I stood motionless under my hierophant's touch. My refusals were forgotten – my wrestlings

> paralyzed. The Impossible – *i.e.* my marriage with St. John – was fast becoming the Possible. All was changing utterly. . . . Religion called – Angels beckoned – God commanded – life rolled together like a scroll. . . . The dim room was full of visions . . . I sincerely, deeply, fervently, longed to do what was right . . . 'Shew me – shew me the path!' I entreated of Heaven. I was more excited than I had ever been. (III, ch. 4, pp. 423–5)

It is at this moment that she feels her 'heart beat fast and thick: I heard it throb', as in the last encounter with Rochester; but now 'it stood still to an inexpressible feeling that thrilled it through' and Rochester's voice is mysteriously heard calling her name. Thereupon it becomes '*my* turn to assume ascendancy' and St John leaves the scene for ever.

All this has made powerful reading since the novel broke into literary history in 1847 and started, among other things, the long debate about the rights and wrongs and plausibilities of these larger-than-life events. Latter-day argument tends to take it for granted that the 'principles' with which her creator endows Jane Eyre – the word is constantly on her lips in times of crisis – must refer to the moral and religious conventions which are still held to be characteristically 'Victorian'. Jane Eyre's 'principles' have in fact nothing to do with conventional notions of what is sexually permissible or with allegiance to the idea of personal renunciation as in itself desirable and good. They have little in common with the moral impulses behind the creation of Maggie Tulliver or Dorothea Brooke or Dickens's Little Emily. They have everything to do with *amour de soi* of the sort which finds such striking expression in Emily Brontë's *Wuthering Heights* and does so here in the fashioning of Jane, Rochester and St John Rivers, who demonstrate its power, its peril and its avid determination to wrest from circumstance the opportunity to have one's strong-flavoured cake and eat it too.

If this fact is overlooked, the author's originality in creating St John Rivers may be overlooked with it. Experience in classrooms and seminars shows that response to this figure is usually one of total condemnation, distaste for the qualities displayed making against the play of literary judgement. And if any sympathy is still felt for a heroine who retreats from Rochester and love simply for want of a wedding ring, there is some suspense lest she succumb to this dreadful representative of male chauvinism, with his domineering manner, terrifying ideals of self-abnegation, crushing of natural feeling and choice of a woman he finds physically undesirable but requires to serve as a life companion in his work for God. A major source of the heroine's anxiety is sufficiently explicit to win favour with a contemporary reader. 'Can I', she wonders when weighing his unenticing offer, 'endure all the forms of love (which I doubt not he would scrupulously observe) and know that the spirit [is] quite absent?' (III, ch. 8, p. 410). The powerful animus so successfully aroused by his creator when she places him in the foreground of this penultimate stage of her narrative, distracts attention from his signal role in her choreography of the self's diverse forms of 'ineradicable ambition'. This is the phrase which she makes Jane Eyre apply to her cousin – the cousinship should not be overlooked – as she wakes up to the fact that he is 'erring as I . . . I was with an equal – one with whom I might argue – one whom, if I saw good, I could resist.' His creator makes him, on his side, capable of chilling self-analysis. 'I am simply, in my original state – stripped of that blood-bleached robe with which Christianity covers human deformity – a cold, hard, ambitious man' (III, ch. 6, p. 379). His life of dedication clearly has little in common with the renunciation on high moral grounds which provided much staple material for nineteenth-century writers of improving fiction. The words 'I', 'my', 'me', 'myself' pulsate with equal strength in everything he, Rochester and Jane Eyre have to say. St John Rivers, 'acutely sensible' to the charms of Rosamund Oliver, tells Jane Eyre, 'Rosamund a sufferer, a labourer, a female apostle? Rosamund a missionary's wife? No!' Then why not, he is asked, relinquish that scheme?

> Relinquish! What – *my* vocation? *my* great work? *My* foundation laid on earth for a mansion in heaven? . . . It is what *I* have to look forward to. (III, ch. 6, p. 378; my italics)

As for Rochester, every utterance is instinct with a sense of self owing much to a tradition inspired by enthusiasm for Byron. His looks would suit Lara or the Giaour; so would 'Mesrour', his black horse on which in the Yorkshire wilds he rides into the heroine's life. His self-absorption can make him absurd, aided at times by his creator's want of experience in handling her otherwise compelling material. 'You examine me, Miss Eyre', he says early on, 'do you think me handsome? . . . Young lady I am disposed to be gregarious and communicative tonight.' Nevertheless she brings vividly off the page the impression of alert self-centredness, wilfully, at times quizzically, absorbed in its own doings. Although it is no part of her business to seek with Arnold for the 'buried self', she differentiates forcefully between various self-driving impulses, each character being possessed by a totally individual set of obsessions. Jane Eyre contemplates St John Rivers unbelievingly as he first indulges, and then rejects as evil, his fantasies about Rosamund Oliver. His 'mauvais quart d'heure' lasts literally for fifteen minutes by his watch, at the end of which he replaces it and rises to speak:

> 'that little space was given to delirium. I rested my temples on the breast of temptation, and put my neck voluntarily under her yoke of flowers: I tasted her cup. The pillow was burning: there is an asp in the garland: the wine has a bitter taste: her promises are hollow – her offers false: I see and know all this.'
>
> I gazed at him in wonder. (III, ch. 6, p. 378)

As well she might. Her own needs are diametrically opposed, and what is particularly impressive in bringing this out is the manner in which the cousins are made to share a particular kind of rage when the self is threatened. St John sees that Jane would find it no more possible to remain in the meagre world of the village school than he to 'keep the narrow and narrowing – the tranquil, hidden office of English country incumbent: for in your nature is an alloy as detrimental to repose as that in mine; though of a different kind'. He is startled by her shrewd rejoinder, 'I am not ambitious', which prompts his also shrewd analysis:

> 'What made you think of ambition? Who is ambitious? I know I am, but how did you find it out?'
>
> 'I was speaking of myself.'
>
> 'Well, if you are not ambitious, you are –' He paused.
>
> 'I was going to say, impassioned: but perhaps you would have misunderstood the word, and been displeased. I mean, that human affections and sympathies have a most powerful hold on you . . . you cannot long be content to pass your leisure in solitude, and to devote your working hours to a monotonous labour . . . any more than I can be content,' he added, with emphasis, 'to live here, buried in morass, pent in with mountain

> – my nature, that God gave me, contravened; my faculties, heaven-bestowed, paralyzed – made useless. You hear now how I contradict myself. I, who preached contentment with a humble lot . . . in God's service – I, his ordained minister, almost rave in my restlessness. Well, propensities and principles must be reconciled by some means.' (III, ch. 4, pp. 360–1)

These images of imprisonment and constriction – 'pent', 'buried', 'paralyzed', 'contravened' – are familiar in the work of the Brontë sisters, along with their emphatic references to freedom and release as necessary imperatives. But it is the qualities thought to be imprisoned and those that seek release which matter here. There is a strong moral pull in Jane Eyre and St John Rivers towards the belief that to obey one's 'propensities' is in fact a 'principle'; in his case the principle requires a chilling of the senses, in hers their nourishment and celebration. Both rebel if their nature, felt to be 'God-given', is contravened, and if their faculties, said to be 'heaven-bestowed', are paralysed. 'How I contradict myself', says St John nevertheless, having preached forbearance. He fails to acknowledge his other contradiction, which is to claim to understand his cousin's 'propensities' while requiring her to act against them.

What the author is less accomplished in handling, understandably given her want of worldly experience and, of course, her concentration on her heroine, is the movement of Rochester's 'principles' and 'propensities' in the period between the broken-off wedding and his reappearance at Ferndean. But she gives us enough to go on, and her shaping of other principal figures is a help. Mainly, though, we have her confident direction of the movement of feeling and event at Thornfield Hall to demonstrate the self's essential need for a balanced ordering of its most powerful drives.

Jane Eyre arrives at Thornfield with her 'propensities' established but not yet brought into harmony, a fact which helps to precipitate the crisis and ensure its outcome. From her years of growing out of Gateshead and childhood into maturity at Lowood she has become conscious of her wide range of sensuous needs and is delighted when they are met. She has a healthy appetite for food, which was in short supply at Lowood, where tea with Miss Temple is Lucullan – 'How fragrant was the steam of the beverage, and the scent of the toast' – and where her dreams are of 'hot roast potatoes, or white bread and new milk'. She has a taste for 'racy, pungent gossip', which she has shared at school with Mary Wilson, as later she will share it with her cousins Diana and Mary. She appreciates pretty faces and clothes, having admired Miss Temple's dress and jewellery, her 'shining curls' and 'becoming dark eyes', as later she appreciates in Rosamund Oliver her beauty, health and charm. She likes looking good herself and regrets not looking better. She wishes to appear more sexually attractive, as we find in the passage describing her preparation for the first meal at Thornfield:

> I dressed myself with care: obliged to be plain – for I had no article of attire that was not made with extreme simplicity – I was still by nature solicitous to be neat. It was not my habit to be disregardful of appearance, or careless of the impression I made . . . I ever wished to look as well as I could, and to please as much as my want of beauty would permit. I sometimes regretted that I was not handsomer: I sometimes wished to have rosy cheeks, a straight nose, and small cherry mouth; I desired to be tall, stately, and finely developed in figure. . . . And why had I these aspirations and these regrets? It would be difficult to say . . . yet I had a reason, and a logical, natural reason too. However . . . I . . . brushed my hair very smooth, and put on my black frock – which, Quaker-like as it was, at least had the merit of fitting to a nicety. (I, ch. 11, p. 99)

'Logical, natural reason' errs on the side of discretion but still puts in its place the novelistic convention that the heroine should be pretty but keep silent about wanting to be physically attractive to men. Jane Eyre's frock 'fits to a nicety', and if 'plain' is revealing. We learn later from her cousin Diana that she is 'much too pretty, as well as too good, to be grilled alive in Calcutta'. We have learnt from the preceding Lowood chapters other matters, such as her craving for love and for excitement, and the fact that she is captivated by romantic chiaroscuro and the huge pagan forms she pictures in her drawings, where titanic figures associated with powers of light and darkness testify to the fascination for her of the idea of vast preternatural forces at work in the world.

What so dramatically comes about at Thornfield is that these propensities, kept out of common view by the *bien rangée* little governess, find themselves magically fulfilled, even to the desire for violent action and the thrilling frisson of the supernatural, at least until the Gothic atmosphere surrounding Rochester's wife is drastically dispelled. Once this is understood, it is clear that the outcome can be no other than it is. Some stay, some shock, some redirecting of the energies is essential if the self is not to succumb to the tyranny of its own appetency. The moral and aesthetic self in Jane Eyre's creator knew that arson, bloodshed, madness, all these heady Angrian delights, were too rich a diet for the healthy sensibility, the most potentially dangerous ingredients being present in the passionate love-affair at the centre of the story.

From the first, playing in and out of the exchanges between Rochester and Jane Eyre, are hints of what is exorbitant, lawless and unsanctioned, by which is not of course meant the idea of sexual passion *per se*. In one of their early encounters, Rochester speaks of his will and his motives:

> 'I don't count myself: I know what my aim is, what my motives are; and at this moment I pass a law, unalterable as that of the Medes and Persians, that both are right.'
>
> 'They cannot be, sir, if they require a new statute to legalize them.'
>
> 'They are, Miss Eyre, though they absolutely require a new statute.' (I, ch. 14, p. 139)

The dangers inherent in such an exaltation of the self are immediately recognised by his listener:

> 'The human and fallible should not arrogate a power with which the divine and perfect alone can be safely trusted.'
>
> 'What power?'
>
> 'That of saying of any strange, unsanctioned line of action, – "Let it be right." '
>
> ' "Let it be right" – the very words: you have pronounced them.' (III, ch. 14, p. 139)

The tone is familiar for it chimes in with the mood of the age's *l'homme revolté*, from Byron's metaphysical rebels, especially in 'Cain' and *Manfred*, through Heathcliff, Raskolnikov and Stavrogin, and beyond them to the *actes gratuits* performed by heroes in Gide and Camus. The claim, as with the Dostoevskyan rebels, is that 'all is lawful', which paradoxically invites a sanction.

Rochester says 'let it be right' and the paradox points to the inevitable concomitant of this satanic (as distinct from Promethean) rebellion, the troubled sense that by violating the normal, 'natural', social and moral sanctions, one altogether cuts oneself off from one's kind, Raskolnikov being the classic instance. Emily Brontë focuses this in that atmosphere of cosmic outlawry with which she surrounds Heathcliff and Cathy in her own effort to explore the conflict between an overpowering *amour de soi* and the natural rhythms of ordinary life, which struggle to reassert themselves in the second half of her narrative.

It is to such an order that Rochester and Jane also repair in the end. But to move in that direction is impossible until the disruptive, the discordant, the excessive, the anarchic 'all is lawful', are transmuted and dissipated. These violences and excesses find one of their imaginative embodiments in Bertha's derangement and the alarming events it generates, but are also focused in the nature and quality of the lovers' attachment to each other. Rochester becomes Jane Eyre's 'idol', her 'whole world' and, as Heathcliff for Cathy, transcends whatever 'hope of heaven' she may still possess:

> He stood between me and every thought of religion, as an eclipse intervenes between man and the broad sun. I could not, in those days, see God for his creation: of whom I had made an idol. (II, ch. 9, p. 277)

The chapter closes impressively on this confession. 'I am a free human being with an independent will which I now exert to leave you', she had declared when Rochester appeared to be on the point of marrying Blanche Ingram. But 'free' is exactly what she is not once that fear is removed and she finds herself basking coyly in his 'sultan' smiles and favours. He is as much in thrall, incarcerated in his role of 'master' and the solipsistic world where 'all is lawful', including the deceptions attendant on his planned *modus vivendi*. A breaking-out of these constraints there has to be, for the more lavish this indulgence of the self the narrower its chances of happiness and harmony.

I have described Bertha, whom we see finally as the wild figure on the roof engulfed in flames, as one embodiment of these violent discordances. Objects and events in this novel, as everyone has seen, assume such emblematic qualities at moments of crisis: the tree sundered by lightning allegorising the imminent disaster, Rochester's mysterious cry, the frequent metaphorical references to fire and ice, and Jane Eyre's revealing paintings. The first of these depicts a shipwreck in 'a swollen sea', with a cormorant on the broken mast holding in its beak a jewelled bracelet 'washed or torn' from the arm of a drowned girl; the second, less sombre but equally mysterious, depicts the Evening Star as a vast female figure rising above a hill against a dark blue sky; and the third shows another colossal form, its sombre aspect inspired by Milton's Death (I, ch. 13, pp. 126–7).

The drawings owe something to John Martin's Gothicism, that powerful source of imaginative stimulus for the Brontë children; the Evening Star also has qualities in common with the outsize female fantasy figures found in George Macdonald's *At the Back of the North Wind* and Kingsley's *The Water Babies*. But more importantly there is a resemblance to the pantheistic figure of Nature conjured up by Shirley, Charlotte Brontë's attempt to portray her sister Emily, had she been prosperous and happy:

> Nature is now at her evening prayers; she is kneeling before those red hills. I see her prostrate on the great steps of her altar, praying for a fair night for mariners at sea, for travellers in deserts, for lambs on moors and unfledged birds in woods.[4]

She is like Eve, not Milton's but the mother of the Titans, 'from her sprang Saturn, Hyperion, Oceanus; she bore Prometheus'. 'Pagan that you are', is Caroline's comment and Jane Eyre's deities are equally pagan and Titanesque, like the figures of Moneta or Saturn or Oceanus as Keats depicts them in his two *Hyperions*. Her drawings illustrate aspects of the world which Nature, the Great Mother, seeks to protect in Shirley's vision. This is the 'Mother' who manifests herself to the heroine at Thornfield:

> the roof resolved to clouds, high and dim; the gleam was such as the moon imparts to vapours she is about to sever. . . . She broke forth . . . a hand first penetrated the sable folds and waved them away . . . a white human form shone in the azure, inclining a glorious brow earthward. It gazed and gazed on me. It spoke to my spirit: immeasurably distant was the tone, yet so near, it whispered in my heart –
>
> 'My daughter, flee temptation!'
>
> 'Mother, I will.' (III, ch. 1, pp. 323–4)

Nature intervenes again when Jane Eyre hears Rochester's voice in her high state of 'excitement' and breaks free from St John Rivers. With calm restored, she reflects that, mysterious as it had seemed, it was 'the work of nature. She was roused, and did – no miracle – but her best' (III, ch. 9, p. 425). What St John Rivers had urged was unnatural and thus inimical to the powerful natural law with which her essential self, whatever its temporary 'madness', is basically in harmony. When she learns that Rochester had in fact called out to her that night, she is awed and remains silent about it. She would have understood Carlyle's 'natural supernaturalism' and assented, we imagine, to Auden's 'we are lived by powers we do not understand' or Yeats's 'Man cannot know truth, he can only embody it.' The irreducible surd element indicates the obedience of the natural order of human life to laws governing the vaster and still more mysterious order of the larger reality.

The function of the story's dominant natural imagery is in keeping with this conception of the natural law. Fire is good when regulated, bringing warmth, light, comfort; when unregulated it destroys; at the same time, if destructive it can be purgative, the burning of Bertha and Thornfield Hall being also the condition of a new beginning. So with cold. This imagery is particularly associated with St John Rivers, even in less fraught moments. 'I am cold: no fervour infects me', he declares when bringing Jane Eyre news of her legacy, 'whereas I am hot', she replies, 'and fire dissolves ice. The blaze there has thawed all the snow from your cloak (III, ch. 7, p. 388). In other words, a balance of natural forces is aimed for at the lighter as well as the more intense levels of the narrative. The children of the union with Rochester are strong, healthy and attractive, being the children of love, like the second generation children in *Wuthering Heights* (Linton Heathcliff, perverse and sickly, is the child of hate). Rochester loses a hand and his sight is impaired (like old Patrick Brontë's it is not finally lost) and when Jane returns they promptly resume what has always been their rather cheerfully physical love-making. Above all, the effects of the accident, which propels Rochester out of his dangerous *amour de soi* to act selflessly at last, dissipates their sultan–slave behaviour and makes for a different balance of forces. Equal emphasis is laid on his unimpaired physical strength and her supportive verve and resource. (That she still displays her rather jarring flirtatiousness is partly owed to a general want of sophistication in the author's handling of the external 'manners', so to speak, of an adult love-affair, and is connected with her own experience of the master–pupil relationship to which her novels constantly revert.) This, then, is not a Lawrentian union, whose equipoise is found in conflict, the Lion and the Unicorn for ever fighting for the crown, but a similar importance is attached to reciprocity and equipollence.

At the last, aesthetic balance, just recognition of difference and the customary need of the novelist to tie up ends, leads the author to close the narrative with recollections of St John Rivers, a salute to his dedication and, significantly, an acknowledgement of his short sojourn in this world. He is about to depart this life, far away in the distant land, while Rochester and Jane are still vigorously in the middest. Moreover he is happy to be leaving a world which to him, as to the gentler Helen Burns, is a place *en route*, one in which to suffer and, through suffering, to move in an orthodox Pilgrim's Progress across the threshold and so to the other side where all the trumpets will sound. Between Jane and Rochester on the one side and Helen Burns and St John Rivers on the other is a line which, in terms of our ordinary human temperaments and predilections, is virtually uncrossable. Each kind looks at the other across the divide more or less uncomprehendingly even if also sympathetically and perhaps longingly (in the case of the artistic sensibility, also empathically). Their existence side by side in this novel testifies to the importance for the author of a debate no less essential for her than the debate between opposing values is for her sister. Emily Brontë in *Wuthering Heights* seemingly eats her cake and has it too, for she destroys Heathcliff in one way while keeping him alive in another in order that his spirit and Cathy's may survive in the unregulated region outside the normal social order. In *Jane Eyre* a great deal more organisational and creative energy is devoted to establishing the means and justification for eating one's cake here and now than to ensuring that it will also be had, in orthodox Christian fashion, there and then. Whatever her own references to conventional piety (and it must be said that there are precious few in this novel, even allowing for Rochester's prayerful self-criticism at the close), Jane Eyre's 'Mighty Spirit' and the 'Mother' guiding her *amour de soi* at times of crisis remain in feeling, like Shirley's Nature, stubbornly pantheistic and pagan.

NOTES

1. A. Abbot Ikeler, *Puritan Temper and Transcendental Faith, Carlyle's Literary Vision* (London, 1972) p. 187.
2. Charlotte Brontë, *Villette*, Haworth Edition (London, 1899) Chapter 7, p. 67.
3. This and subsequent *Jane Eyre* references are to the World's Classics Edition (Oxford, 1980).
4. *Shirley*, opening of Chapter 18.

6

Love and the Aspiring Mind in *Villette*

JOCELYN HARRIS

Dale Spender's thesis in *Mothers of the Novel: One Hundred Good Women Writers before Jane Austen* (London, 1986) that fiction is predominantly the creation of women cries out to be tested.[1] Charlotte Brontë is one of the female tradition's heroines, and yet in *Villette* her obsessive exploration of the conflict for a woman between romantic love and intellectual aspirations seems to have been resolved, as far as it ever could be, with the help of three male authors, one of them a poet. To judge from the likenesses, Tennyson's poem *The Princess* provided the impossible Utopian ideal, Bernardin de Saint-Pierre's *Paul et Virginie* a warning and a drastic solution and the fifteenth-century story of Abélard and Héloïse a powerful and actual precursor.

Women, especially clever ones, have not always wanted to marry. Their dream of a Protestant nunnery would eventually result in the foundation of women's colleges, but until then women joined communities where they could pool their resources and educate one another in poverty and chastity. Sir Thomas More's household was such, the community at Little Gidding another. Indeed Haworth Parsonage itself might be said to have been a community of mutual learning.

Jane Eyre too is attracted to what is in essence a Protestant nunnery after the wreck of her relationship with Rochester. The black-clad Rivers sisters, named from two chaste goddesses, Mary and Diana, invite her into their clean and spartan room to seek shelter and to study German. She is content – until the loveless request of St John Rivers to accompany him to India makes her recognise her true sexual needs. Determined that the relationship with St John remain fraternal, and fortuitously enriched by an inheritance, she returns to a lover who respects both her passion and her mind. *Villette* is, rather, the reverse: Lucy Snowe rejects sexual relationship with her 'brother' John Bretton because of his sexual tyranny (Jane Eyre resists Rochester for the same reason), and when a growing passion for Paul Emmanuel threatens their intellectual relationship, Charlotte Brontë obliterates him, leaving Lucy happy in possession of a school, her Protestant nunnery.

From Mary Astell's *A Serious Proposal to the Ladies for the Advancement of their True and Greatest Interest* (1694 and 1697) to Tennyson's *The Princess* (1847), attempts were often made in the eighteenth and nineteenth centuries to replace the lost nunneries of Catholicism. Some of the plans, like Mary Astell's or Sarah Scott's in her novel of 1762, *Millenium Hall*, were mainly spiritual, even millenial; others were largely pragmatic, as in Samuel Richardson's thoughtful presentation of Astell's scheme as an alternative to marriages without love in *The History of Sir Charles Grandison* and in *Clarissa*.

The idea was often satirised. Swift in *The Tatler* (Number 9) argued that nunneries were fatally vulnerable to the incursions of men, and Tennyson a century later, though celebrating the feats and achievements of women in *The Princess*, still forces the traditional female role of nursing on to his intellectual women. Learning and love, that is, are usually set in opposition, for women. In practice, of course, aspiring minds in women have generally been overwhelmed by the prompt assumption into motherhood consequent upon sexual experience. *Wuthering Heights* proves it, when Emily Brontë's ardent, Faustian Catherine leaps quickly from unfettered child to imperilled child-bearer. So does Charlotte Brontë's own death, caused by a pregnancy she was not fit for. Since sex, until recently, could destroy any woman attracted to a man by his mind, the sole solution is a protective taboo, the brother–sister relationship. This is what Charlotte Brontë resorts to in her last complete novel, published in 1853.

Villette is far more pessimistic than *Jane Eyre* about the chances of a woman reconciling love and learning. The deaths of two precious sisters and a less precious brother doubtless shadow the book, but still, Charlotte Brontë is no longer sanguine about being afflicted with an aspiring mind. Already in December 1836 Robert Southey had told her, 'literature cannot be the business of a woman's life, and it ought not to be'. She had pitifully replied, 'I have endeavoured to . . . observe all the duties a woman ought to fulfil . . . I don't always succeed, for sometimes when I'm teaching or sewing, I would rather be reading or writing.'[2] Lucy Snowe never attains to Jane Eyre's fortune and free choice: her relationship with Dr John Graham Bretton never moves beyond friendship and the brother–sister relationship to sexuality; her second with Professor Paul Emmanuel is muted to that of brother and sister before it ends in death.

The conventual life offered to Jane Eyre is frequently held out to Lucy Snowe as an alternative to her impossible craving for love and learning combined, but she rejects the Catholic institutions of Villette in favour of a Protestant nunnery, the school given her by Paul Emmanuel. It may be symbolic that at crucial times in the novel her attraction to a man is 'answered' by the apparition of a nun. Although eventually revealed to be a man in disguise, the nun represents in *Villette* the call to poverty, chastity and discipline, to a life of mind free from emotion and pain.

The house in Villette where Lucy teaches has actually been a convent, and at her lowest point she is tempted to become a Carmelite nun.[3] Thinking that 'school solitude, conventual silence and stagnation, anything seemed preferable to living embroiled with Dr John' (p. 171), she soon, however, finds that she is little suited to the self-sacrificing life of a nurse, such as Tennyson portrayed as the appropriate career for intellectual women in *The Princess*, which Charlotte had bought in December 1847 for Emily.[4] To Paul's masculine jibes she returns sharply, 'Could Monsieur do it himself?' (pp. 183–4). Like him, she wants a sphere for her passionate blood and her intelligent brains together.

Lucy Snowe's first happy friendship with Dr John is soon answered by the apparitions of 'A NUN' (p. 222): as if defying it, Dr John immediately makes much of her, in order he says 'to keep away the nun' (p. 231). Alone at the concert with Dr John, Lucy may seem 'a sister with a brother' (p. 232), but her pink dress departs significantly from sobriety. At once the nun reappears as if in challenge: Lucy ignores it. At Vashti's concert (a name perhaps caught from *The Princess*, III, l. 212) she surrenders herself utterly to the singer's genius, her passionate feelings imaged in the fire that promptly breaks out in the theatre. Dr John, however, is a man attracted to beauty, not intelligence. He who played the Grand Turk to little Polly as his Odalisque (pp. 19, 23), or the slave to Ginevra Fanshawe 'to gain the tyranny', as Tennyson wrote (*The Princess*, IV, l. 114), here meets pretty Polly-Paulina, his future wife, when he rescues her masterfully from the flames. Grand Turk to the last, for Mrs Bretton's posing of the turban on his head is no joke (p. 248), he proves to Lucy that attraction by outward appearance inevitably leads to inequality. He and Lucy could only have been good friends, he says, if she had been a boy (p. 287). 'Nobody in the world but you cares for cleverness', says the sneering flirt Ginevra (p. 130); drearily agreeing, Lucy buries her letters from Dr John in the nun's pear-tree (p. 269). The nun, as if to approve this sacrifice of earthly love, appears to her once more.

Lucy's relationship with Paul Emmanuel begins in friendship; she cannot bring herself to use 'mon ami', with its 'sense of domestic and intimate affection', but willingly allows him the English 'friend' (p. 292). Even better, he offers her the valuable (and safe) relation of brother:

> He asked whether, if I were his sister, I should always be content to stay with a brother such as he. I said I believed I should; and I felt it. Again, he inquired whether, if he were to leave Villette, and go far away, I should be sorry; and I dropped Corneille, and made no reply.
>
> 'Petite soeur,' said he: 'how long could you remember me if we were separated?'
>
> 'That, monsieur, I can never tell, because I do not know how long it will be before I shall cease to remember everything earthly.' (pp. 348–9)

The brother–sister relationship offers the security of friendship and more, for here there is no dependence, no love game, no slavery. It is an ideal sketched by Tennyson's Princess, who argues that since women are not 'pretty babes / To be dandled' but 'living wills, and sphered / Whole in ourselves and owed to none' (IV, ll. 129–30), they should not be treated as 'Odalisques' and 'stunted squaws' (II, ll. 63–4). In the openness and freedom of the brotherly relation, Paul Emmanuel can recognise Lucy's passion and her intellect. What he see as 'la flamme à l'âme', she swiftly acknowledges: 'Oui; j'ai la flamme à l'âme, and je dois l'avoir!' (p. 290). Others may call her the 'learned and blue' Madame Minerva Gravity, chaste Goddess of Wisdom (pp. 274–5), but this clever man appreciates her completely. Paul expands her intellectually and emotionally by offering 'mental wealth' from the 'library' of his mind (p. 346), and pushes her into the 'show-trial' of an intellectual test before two scoffing professors. Stung to excellence by the realisation that 'those two faces looking out of a forest of long hair, moustache, and whisker' belong to the men who terrified her the night she arrived in Villette (pp. 364–6), she sees, however, that even in the moment of her triumph, she is sexually vulnerable.

Charlotte Brontë's fear that sexuality is unleashed by knowledge is Milton's: Paul hisses sharply in Lucy's ear like a boa constrictor (p. 290), and his sweet apples only make her feverish and thirsty (p. 326). They are indeed 'Eve's apples' (p. 333) forced upon her by Paul playing the part of Satan, because mentor and pupil are rapidly falling in love. 'Could it be that he was becoming more than a friend or brother? Did his looks speak a kindness beyond fraternity or amity?', she asks anxiously (p. 402). She is being punished for her 'pride of intellect', for 'trespass[ing] the limits proper to my sex', says Paul. She has conceived 'a contraband appetite for unfeminine knowledge', he tells her (p. 320):

> 'Women of intellect' was the next theme: here he was at home. A 'woman of intellect,' it appeared, was a sort of *lusus naturae*, a luckless accident, a thing for which there was neither place nor use in creation, wanted neither as wife nor worker. Beauty anticipated her in the first office. He believed in his soul that lovely, placid, and passive feminine mediocrity was the only pillow on which manly thought and sense could find rest for its aching temples; and as to work, male mind alone could work to any good practical result, hein? (p. 323)

But Lucy's revulsion from the four stages of women stereotypically portrayed in the 'Musée des Beaux Arts' proves that his demand is intolerable to her.

Their relationship can therefore develop no further. It had moved inevitably and dangerously from gladly accepted fraternity (p. 371) to encroaching sexuality: 'I called myself your brother', says Paul, 'I hardly know what I am – brother – I cannot tell. I know I think of you – I feel I wish you well – but I must check myself; you are to be feared' (p. 380). At this crucial point the Church intervenes, as in the earlier story, to separate the lovers.

Frenzied by loss, Lucy turns on the habit of the nun which has been placed tauntingly in her bed: 'I tore her up – the incubus! I held her on high – the goblin! I shook her loose – the mystery! And down she fell – down all around me – down in shreds and fragments – and I trode upon her' (p. 429). Lucy rejects chastity; the nun is seen no more in the Rue Fossette. Unexpectedly, though, Paul comes to her again in the 'amity' which guarantees equality even within romantic love; she loves him in return 'with a passion beyond what I had yet felt' (pp. 437–9). To her long-suppressed anxiety that men prefer beauty to cleverness, he gives 'a short, strong answer . . . which silenced, subdued, yet profoundly satisfied' (p. 440). His gift of a school, clean, spare and her own, grants her the financial and emotional advantages of a Protestant nunnery, softened by colours and flowers (p. 441), and free both from invasive sexuality and the dangers of Catholicism.

Now they return to Eden before the Fall, for here they share a simple, paradisal meal (p. 444), here she kisses his hand as her king and benefactor. They walk back to Rue Fossette

> by moonlight – such moonlight as fell on Eden – shining through the shades of the Great Garden. . . . Once in their lives some men and women go back to these first fresh days of our great Sire and Mother – taste that grand morning's dew – bathe in its sunrise. . . . 'Lucy, take my love. One day share my life. Be my dearest, first on earth.' (p. 447)

In a paradisal house and garden destined to be a community of women,

> a jet rose from a well, and a pale statue leaned over the play of the waters. M. Paul talked to me. His voice was so modulated that it mixed harmonious with the silver whisper, the gush, the musical sigh, in which light breeze, fountain, and foliage intoned their lulling vesper. (p. 444)

In Tennyson's university of women a 'woman-statue' similarly overlooks a scene 'half garden and half house' where clocks chime 'like silver hammers falling / On silver anvils', and the 'splash and stir / Of fountains spouted up and showering down / In meshes of the jasmine and the rose' (*The Princess*, I, ll. 206–16). Here the Prince consoles the defeated Princess with the hope that women and men will one day be equal in a chaste millenial world:[5]

And so these twain, upon the skirts of Time,
Sit side by side, full-summed in all their powers,
Dispensing harvest, sowing the To-be,
Self-reverent each and reverencing each,
Distinct in individualities,
But like each other even as those who love.
Then comes the statelier Eden back to men:
Then reign the world's great bridals, chaste and calm:
Then springs the crowning race of humankind.
(VII, ll. 271–9)

But not yet, says Tennyson. Charlotte Brontë seems also to despair of equality now, for she separates Lucy from her lover before he can destroy her.

Significantly she uses a nun to do so, a young woman pictured in nun's dress who is the lost fiancée of Paul Emmanuel (p. 356). For her sake he has vowed eternal constancy, chastity and poverty in a 'monkish' life, with a 'hard, cold, monkish' heart (pp. 368, 370). Lucy realises that their relationship is at an end: 'Was the picture of a pale dead nun to rise, an eternal barrier? . . . what of his heart sworn to virginity?' (p. 362).

Paul offers her instead an asexual friendship such as the maimed priest Abélard once offered to the cloistered nun Héloïse, an intellectual passion communicated only in letters. Charlotte Brontë refers at least twice to Pope's influential and luscious *Eloisa to Abelard* in Chapters 24 and 35 of *Jane Eyre*:[6] both Paul Emmanuel's temporary blindness (p. 297) and Rochester's more permanent injuries may owe something to the example of Pope's poem.

The original story of Abélard's misfortunes together with the lovers' personal letters had, however, been reprinted in English many times during the eighteenth century, and if Charlotte Brontë knew Pope's version she might well have read the original. It is at times remarkably similar to her own experience at Brussels, the story that formed the basis for *Villette*. To paraphrase what Pope says of Eloisa's woes, 'She best can paint 'em, who shall feel 'em most.'

The medieval monk Abélard, shabby, quarrelsome, proud, but an inspiring teacher (like Paul) was appointed to teach Héloïse, a young woman with a brilliant mind (like Lucy). 'To avert suspicion', he wrote, 'I sometimes struck her, but these blows were prompted by love and tender feeling rather than anger and irritation, and were sweeter than any balm could be.'[7] Paul too is 'bien dur, bien exigeant' (p. 349), his 'reconcilement . . . always sweet' (p. 321). Like Abélard he forces the best from his pupil:

> 'Prove yourself ere I cherish you,' was his ordinance; and how difficult he made that proof! What thorns and briars, what flints, he strewed in the path of feet not inured to rough travel! He watched tearlessly ordeals that he exacted should be passed through fearlessly. He followed footprints that . . . were sometimes marked in blood – followed them grimly, holding the austerest police-watch over the pain-pressed pilgrim . . . he tried the temper, the sense, and the health; and it was only when every severest test had been applied and endured, when the most corrosive aquafortis had been used, and failed to tarnish the ore, that he admitted it genuine and, still in clouded silence, stamped it with his deep brand of approval. (p. 319)

Abélard and Héloïse rapidly fell in love, and had a son. Héloïse disguised herself unsuccessfully as a nun (Paul Emannuel courted Justine Marie when she was dressed in the costume of a nun) and her uncle had Abélard castrated. Héloïse took the veil, but twelve years later when the story of his calamities was published she wrote three despairing, passionate, nostalgic letters accusing him of coldness and failure to write. These accusations and revelations, with their imagery of cold, stone, fire and storm, bear extremely close comparison not only with Charlotte Brontë's own poems[8] and her highly literary letters to Héger, picked out of the waste-paper basket and stitched together by the watchful Mme Héger, but to the imagery and relationships of *Villette* and *Jane Eyre*.

Eventually Héloïse proved an efficient and inspiring abbess, teaching nuns, novices and children, as Lucy did. Abélard provided her pupils with his own oratory as their home, just as Paul Emmanuel provides Lucy Snowe with a school out of his own purse. Even the name 'Lucy Snowe' may derive from the old story, for Abélard's mother was Lucy, and snow or the 'Frost' Brontë originally chose for her heroine's name, is often used by Héloïse to describe the restraints placed upon youthful passions.

At one time, however, Héloïse declared to Abélard that she preferred chastity to wedlock: she wished to remain his mistress, she said, so that he could realise his true self as a philosopher. She and Abélard would be bound simply by *gratia*, love freely given, since marriage could add nothing of significance to the relationship ideally described in Cicero's *De Amicitia*: true friendship is 'disinterested love', the sublimation of physical feeling.[9] Since marriage merely legalises the weaknesses of the flesh, their life should be one of love, not lust. Héloïse therefore addresses her one-time lover Abélard by the safer titles of 'master, or rather her father, husband, or rather, brother', calling herself his 'handmaid, or rather his daughter, wife, or rather sister' (Letter 1). These are the very terms which characterise the relationship of Paul Emmanuel and Lucy Snowe. Rebuffed by his coldness, Héloïse lured Abélard into writing by asking instructions for her order, just as Charlotte Brontë would lure M. Héger: his warnings about the corruptions of flattery brought about when women live with women seem to echo frequently in *Villette*, and his remark that it would be unseemly 'for those holy hands which now turn the pages of sacred books to have to perform degrading services in women's concerns' (p. 93) might well be reflected in Lucy Snowe's impatience and coolness towards the children and young women in her book. 'One thing is pretty clear', wrote Charlotte Brontë to a friend in 1850, '*Women*, must give up living an artist's life, if home duties are to be paramount.'[10] Abélard died years before Héloïse; so does Paul, before Lucy. Abélard's closing appeal to Héloïse to submit to Providence perhaps consoled the author of the providentially-controlled *Jane Eyre*, for it is couched in the very language of *Villette*'s conclusion: 'The storm may rage but I am unshaken, though the winds may blow they leave me unmoved; for the rock of my foundation stands firm.' Real wind and actual storm destroy Lucy's love, but she herself survives. The forerunner to her new life was John, but its rocky foundation is Paul. Jane Eyre like Héloïse had erred when she idolised Rochester rather than God: Lucy Snowe, however, finds in Emmanuel an Immanuel, a Messiah, whose sacrifice endows her with a life.

Winifred Gérin's biography shows how closely *Villette* was based on the relationship of Charlotte Brontë and M. Héger, her beloved teacher at Brussels. Because he was already married and unable to return her affection, his letters were as heartbreakingly cool as Abélard's to Héloïse. But when he presented to her the works of Bernardin de Saint-Pierre,[11] he may have provided her with an ending. The *Paul et Virginie*, named for Saint-Pierre's most famous novel, is the ship that carries Paul Emmanuel to his doom, and names of ships are always significant in *Villette*. For instance Lucy passes the *Ocean*, the *Phoenix*, the *Consort* and the *Dolphin* on her way to her own ship, the *Vivid* (p. 42). A voyage by sea represents spiritual pilgrimage, and her bourn will be the consort that she craves; the phoenix and the dolphin inhabit the dangerous and stormy elements of fire and water, as she herself longs for the vivid and the story in life. To reach her ship she glides down a 'sable flood' that reminds her of the Styx, of Charon rowing some solitary soul to the Land of Shades. Stimulation and death force her to a romantic testing of limits. She is of the proud elect of suffering: 'some must deeply suffer while they live, and I thrilled in the certainty that of this number I was one' (p. 141).

Ships in *Villette* constantly image the pilgrim's life, Lucy's life: typically she pictures herself as a ship perishing in a tempest (p. 28). Whereas her godmother, Mrs Bretton, is 'a stately ship cruising safe on smooth seas' (p. 162), she, like a lifeboat, chooses to go to sea in storm. She needs to be painfully 'stimulated into action. I must be goaded, driven, stung, forced to energy' (p. 31); fire and water, rebellion and storm, are her natural elements, as Paul Emmanuel sees (p. 210). Dr John she dismisses: 'for what belonged to storm, what was wild and intense, dangerous, sudden, and flaming, he had no sympathy, and held with it no communion' (p. 236). She prefers the 'storm' of her master, who excites her emotionally and intellectually (p. 218). He is a 'salamander', who like the phoenix survives the hottest fire (p. 322). Even the most ordinary of lessons proves 'a vessel for an outpouring, and [he] filled it with his native verve and passion like a cup with a vital brewage' (p. 298). He gives her the vividness she hungered for on that symbolically named ship.

M. Héger's gift may have supplied Charlotte Brontë with more than just a name. One can imagine her reading *Paul et Virginie* with almost obsessional interest, and certainly it is very similar to *Villette*. In both novels an idyllic prelapsarian relationship between two people calling themselves brother and sister is shattered by the intervention of the outside world just as it is about to become sexual. Both books end in drowning, of Virginie as she returns to Paul, of Paul Emmanuel as he returns to Lucy. Two Pauls, two virgins who love them.

Paul et Virginie may have provided Charlotte Brontë with a solution to her novel and an explanation for her life: she was anguished that Mme Héger should think her more than a friend to M. Héger.[12] Her draconian solution is death for Paul; Lucy herself, the learned, chaste, moonlit frost-piece, will survive. By losing Paul she keeps him for ever. The greatest fear of Lucy Snowe, as it was of her creator, was that love, once gained, could be taken away. Lucy dreams that 'the well-loved dead, who had loved *me* well in life, met me elsewhere, alienated' (p. 143), and writes later, 'I thought I loved him when he went away; I love him now in another degree; he is more my own' (p. 450). Happy, she fears loss, and might well say with Othello that if it were now to die, ' 'twere now to be most happy'.

Saint-Pierre's Paul and Virginie, though unrelated by blood, are reared as brother and sister in a Rousseau-esque state of nature. Their virginal innocence allows of ardent passion together with absolute purity, but when they become adult and sexual, a kind of incest threatens. Close similarities to *Villette* seem to exist. For instance their paradisal island home is Mauritius, an island 'sur la route des Indes' (VI, p. 45): Paul sets sail for an 'Indian isle'. The sunsets which flame over Villette mimic their spectacular counterparts in Mauritius, while the 'simple' paradisal meal of chocolates, rolls, fresh summer fruit, cherries and strawberries bedded in green leaves shared by Lucy and Paul (p. 444) is very like the lavish pastoral meals served on leafy plates in the Edenic island. Ideas of Eden inform both narratives: 'Au matin de la vie, ils en avaient toute la fraîcheur: tels dans le jardin d'Eden parurent nos premiers parents, lorsque, sortant des mains de Dieu, ils se virent, s'approchèrent, et conversèrent d'abord comme frère et soeur.'[13] Virginie sends Paul a purse she has embroidered herself (VI, p. 129); Lucy embroiders a watch guard for Paul. Virginie embarks on her fatal voyage for financial reasons, driven to it by an older, rich, domineering woman; Paul Emmanuel sets sail under similar circumstances.

The most striking correspondence between the two books is, however, the episode when Lucy, drugged and delirious with unrealised lust, roams solitary through Villette's 'moonlit, midnight park'. Leaving the 'oppressive heat' of the dormitory, she seeks out

> a huge stone basin . . . deep-set in the tree-shadows, brimming with cool water, clear, with a green, leafy, rushy bed. . . . My vague aim, as I went, was to find the stone basin, with its clear depth and green lining: of that coolness and verdure I thought, with the passionate thirst of unconscious fever. . . . I still

secretly and chiefly longed to come on that circular mirror of crystal, and surprise the moon glassing therein her pearly front.

I saw the thick-planted trees which framed this tremulous and rippled glass. . . . The effect was as a sea breaking into song with all its waves. (pp. 410–14)

Virginie plunges into that pool. Wandering 'ça et là dans les lieux les plus solitaires de l'habitation', she is disturbed by 'un mal inconnu' (VI, p. 95), her awakening passion for Paul:

C'était vers la fin de décembre, lorsque le soleil, au Capricorne, échauffe pendant trois semaines l'Ile-de-France de ses feux verticaux.

Le vent du sud-est, qui y regne presque toute l'année, n'y soufflait plus.

. . . Aucun nuage ne venait du côté de la mer. Seulement, pendant le jour, des vapeurs rousses s'élèvaient de dessus ses plaines, et paraissaient, au coucher du soleil, comme les flammes d'un incendie. La nuit même n'apportait aucun rafraîchissement à l'atmosphère embrasée. L'orbe de la lune, tout rouge, se levait, dans un horizon embrumé, d'une grandeur démesurée. . . .

Dans une de ces nuits ardentes, Virginie sentit redoubler tous les symptômes de son mal. Elle se levait, elle s'asseyait, elle se recouchait, et ne trouvait dans aucune attitude ni le sommeil ni le repos. Elle s'achemine, à la clarté de la lune, vers sa fontaine. Elle en aperçoit la source qui, malgré la sécheresse, coulait encore en filets d'argent sur les flancs bruns du rocher. Elle se plonge dans son bassin. . . . Elle se rappelle . . . que Paul . . . reservant ce bain pour elle seule, en avait creusé le lit, couvert le fond de sable, et semé sur ses bords des herbes aromatiques. Elle entrevoit dans l'eau, sur ses bras nus et sur son sein, les reflets des deux palmiers plantés à la naissance de son frère et à la sienne, qui entrelaçaient au-dessus de sa tête leurs rameaux verts et leurs jeunes cocos. Elle pense a l'amitié de Paul, plus douce que les parfums, plus pure que l'eau des fontaines, plus forte que les palmiers unis; et elle soupire. (VI, pp. 96–7)

The heat, the moon, the pool, the verdure, the rambling, the longing to cool oneself in water, and the pure friendship are all the same. Even such details as the overarching and interweaving trees, a traditional image for love, find their counterparts in *Villette* (p. 418).

Virginie dies in a shipwreck after an absence of three and a half years; Paul Emmanuel drowns after an absence of three years. Both are on their way home. Saint-Pierre's narrator reflects from the vantage point of old age that 'après le rare bonheur de trouver une compagne qui nous soit bien assortie, l'état le moins malheureux de la vie est sans doute de vivre seul' (VI, pp. 131–2): Lucy too spends the three happiest years of her life while Paul is away, and even when he is dead, can be productive in her work and life. Lucy Snowe survives, for she has work, an income and responsibility in the real world. Paul's legacy of the school liberates her mind and powers; here in her humanised convent she will thrive. Denied sexual experience with her 'brother', Lucy, like Héloïse, like Charlotte Brontë herself, turns instead to a life of mind. She inhabits a Protestant nunnery.

For her last scene Charlotte Brontë was, I think, inspired by Tennyson's 'Ulysses', which she read in 1849,[14] for like that poem, *Villette* ends in the prospect of new voyages and a determination not to yield. Tennyson's poem was written 'under the sense of loss and all that had gone by, but that still life must be fought out to the end',[15] a statement very like the final message of *Villette*. Lucy Snowe, like Ulysses 'For always roaming with a hungry heart', and making his Faustian discovery that 'all experience is an arch wherethrough / Gleams that untravelled world, whose margin fades / For ever and for ever when I move', sees striding 'from north to south a God-bent bow, an arch of hope', and knows that exertion, peril and conflict will be hers on the morrow (pp. 48–9). Ulysses seeks out the cities of men; Lucy seeks adventure in the streets of London, finding 'elation and pleasure' in all she sees. 'Prodigious was the amount of life I lived that morning . . . in a still ecstacy of freedom and enjoyment' (p. 40). Both have drunk life to the lees, enjoyed greatly and suffered greatly, both with those who loved them and alone. Both Ulysses and Lucy hunger for an infinity of knowledge: Ulysses is 'yearning in desire / To follow knowledge like a sinking star, / Beyond the utmost bound of human thought'; Lucy admires in Paul 'the noble hunger for science in the abstract – the godlike thirst after discovery' that releases her own aspiring mind (pp. 320, 138).

The only solution for these inchoate desires is work. To

repudiate the domestic chores of government, Ulysses employs an image found in both *Hamlet* and *Troilus and Cressida*:

> How dull it is to pause, to make an end,
> To rust unburnished, not to shine in use.
> As though to breathe were life.

Lucy Snowe says the same: who but a coward, she asks, 'would pass his whole life in hamlets, and forever abandon his faculties to the eating rust of obscurity?' (p. 39). She rejects the tameness of 'sitting twenty years teaching infants the hornbook, turning silk dresses, and making children's frocks' (p. 66), and once a teacher, finds herself 'getting on; not lying the stagnant prey of mould and rust, but polishing my faculties and whetting them to a keen edge with constant use' (p. 71). Lucy, like Ulysses, has drunk delight of battle with Paul Emmanuel her peer, and won honour from her opponents (p. 325). Her aspiration to Ulysses' 'work of noble note' is fulfilled by the school; she has a 'wonderfully changed life . . . such a thought for the present, such a hope for the future, such a motive for a persevering, a laborious enterprise, an enterprising, a patient and brave course – I *could* not flag' (p. 449). Charlotte Brontë's friend Mary Taylor called her 'a coward and a traitor' for not declaring in *Jane Eyre* that work, 'this great necessity', is the first duty of a woman's life: 'you seem to think that *some* women may indulge in [it] – if they give up marriage and don't make themselves too disagreeable to the other sex', she wrote angrily from her pioneer life in New Zealand; 'a woman who works is by that alone better than one who does not'.[16] Charlotte Brontë seems to be persuaded, in *Villette*.

Finally, the inexplicitness of Paul's death is paralleled by that of Ulysses. Do the gulfs wash them both down, or do they meet Achilles in the Happy Isles? No more than Tennyson will Charlotte Brontë say outright whether her hero lives or dies in the tempest. Her father and George Smith begged her not to kill him, and perhaps it was Tennyson who helped her to a compromise. But both accounts speak suggestively of gathering darkness, moaning, sunset, danger, and the possibility of death. 'Death closes all' in 'Ulysses'. Surely it does so too in *Villette*. Lucy is alone, but from Paul Emmanuel's brotherly friendship she has gained strength, as Tennyson wrote, to 'strive, to seek, to find, and not to yield'.

Though much is taken from her, much abides. She has been loved and befriended as a sister, though cursed with an aspiring mind.

NOTES

1. Pat Rogers raises a rare protesting voice at a 'tradition' that excludes for instance Richardson, in *The London Review of Books*, 7 August 1986, 11–13.
2. Margot Peters, *Unquiet Soul. A Biography of Charlotte Brontë* (London, 1975) pp. 55–6.
3. Charlotte Brontë, *Villette*, Everyman's Library Edition (London, 1969) pp. 93, 146. Subsequent references are to this edition.
4. Winifred Gérin, *Charlotte Brontë: The Evolution of Genius* (Oxford, 1967) p. 368.
5. Nina Auerbach also links the two works in *Communities of Women: An Idea in Fiction* (Cambridge, Mass., 1978) p. 106.
6. See Jean Hagstrum, *Sex and Sensibility: Ideal and Erotic Love from Milton to Mozart* (Chicago, 1980) p. 131.
7. *Abelard and Heloise: 'The Story of his Misfortunes' and the Personal Letters*, trans. and ed. Betty Radice (London, 1977) p. 25.
8. Peters, *Unquiet Soul*, pp. 160, 170–1.
9. Radice, *Abelard and Heloise*, p. 11.
10. Peters, *Unquiet Soul*, p. 304.
11. Ibid., p. 131.
12. Gérin, *Charlotte Brontë*, pp. 284, 240–1. John N. Ware's 'Bernardin de Saint-Pierre and Charlotte Brontë', *MLN*, 40 (1925) 381–2, remarks on Brontë's allusions to Saint-Pierre in *Shirley*, *The Professor* and the ending of *Villette*. Robert A. Colby, in '*Villette* and the Life of the Mind', *PMLA*, 75 (1960) 410–19, suggests additional influences from Bunyan, the Bible, *The Arabian Nights*, Coleridge, de Quincy, Balzac, Sand, Mrs Radcliffe and Maturin, as well as from Rousseau and Saint-Pierre.
13. *Oeuvres complètes de Jacques-Henri-Bernardin de Saint-Pierre*, nouvelle edition révue, corrigée et augmentée par L. Aimé-Martin, 12 vols (Paris, 1825) VI, p. 93.
14. See Peters, *Unquiet Soul*, p. 249.
15. *Complete Poems*, ed. Christopher Ricks (London, 1977) p. 560.
16. Joan Stevens, *Mary Taylor, Friend to Charlotte Brontë: Letters from New Zealand and Elsewhere* (Auckland and Oxford, 1972) pp. 93–4.

7

The Historic Imagination in George Eliot

IAN MILNER

History was the seed-bed of George Eliot's creative imagination: as the objective process and register of human actions and events, and as the subjective 'remembrance of things past'. In her earlier writing the sense of the past is the primary impetus. As she wrote soon after publishing *Adam Bede*: 'my mind works with the most freedom and the keenest sense of poetry in my remotest past, and there are many strata to be worked through before I can begin to use *artistically* any material I may gather in the present'.[1] The accent is personal, the voice tinged with nostalgic remembrance for Shepperton Church or Dorlcote Mill bridge. The evocation of familiar scene and occasion in *The Mill on the Floss* won praise from Proust. The backward glance induces the pastoral colour and rhythms of *Adam Bede*.

Increasingly the viewpoint of personal reminiscence is blended with an historical awareness. Indications of period, social context and their specific shaping influences belong to the narrative structure. The 'author's introduction' to *Felix Holt, the Radical* begins in nostalgic vein which counterpoints the Shepperton Church opening of *Amos Barton*: 'Five-and-thirty years ago the glory had not yet departed from the old coach-roads'. But the next paragraph introduces what becomes a sustained piece of closely observed social and political reportage, organically linked with the plot. As George Eliot put it to R. H. Hutton: 'the habit of my imagination [is] to strive after as full a vision of the medium in which a character moves as of the character itself'.

Her 'medium' was not intended as a passive back-drop for the fiction. She sought to show a constant interrelation and interaction between the public and private life. The individual might be a 'free spirit' but did not take the stage as a desocialised free agent. As she remarked authorially: 'I like to mark the time, and connect the course of individual lives with the historic stream'.[2]

History in her mature art means process rather than chronicle; continuous flow, not static registration. She was the daughter of her age, preoccupied with concepts of development, progress, historical continuity. The opening of the Prelude to *Middlemarch* sets the key: 'Who that cares much to know the history of man, and how that mysterious mixture behaves under the varying experiments of Time, has not dwelt, at least briefly, on the life of Saint Theresa.' She takes us back three centuries to reinforce her vision of the present joining hands with the past: 'these later-born Theresas'. In her review of Riehl's *The Natural History of German Life* she cites Ruskin to her purpose (perhaps had the passage in mind when she composed the Proem to *Romola*):

> Abroad, a building of the eighth or tenth century stands ruinous in the open street. . . . No one wonders at it, or thinks of it as separate, and of another time; we feel the ancient world to be a real thing, and one with the new; antiquity is no dream; it is rather the children playing about the old stones that are the dream. But all is continuous; and the words 'from generation', understandable [here].[3]

Carlyle's view of history 'stretching dimly into the remote Time . . . the end of it enveloping *us* at this hour, whereof we at this hour, both as actors and relators, form part!'[4] struck the same chord that she found 'fundamental' in Riehl: 'He sees in European society *incarnate history*.'[5]

In the years between the publication of *Middlemarch* and that of *Theophrastus Such* in 1879, George Eliot wrote a reflection on the place of history in fiction under the title 'Historic Imagination', which merits more critical attention than it has had:

> The exercise of a veracious imagination in historical picturing seems to be capable of a development that might help the judgment greatly with regard to present and future events. By veracious imagination, I mean the working out in detail of the various steps by which a political or social change was reached, using all extant evidence and supplying deficiencies by careful analogical creation. How triumphant opinions originally spread

– how institutions arose – what were the conditions of great inventions, discoveries, or theoretic conceptions – what circumstances affecting individual lots are attendant on the decay of long-established systems, – all these grand elements of history require the illumination of special imaginative treatment.[6]

To that end one must reject 'the vulgar coercion of conventional plot'. Having perhaps in mind past urgings that she compose a positivist novel, she goes on:

> Utopian pictures help the reception of ideas as to constructive results, but hardly so much as a vivid presentation of how results have actually been brought about, especially in religious and social change. And there is the pathos, the heroism often accompanying the decay and final struggle of old systems, which has not had its share of tragic commemoration. What really took place in and around Constantine before, upon, and immediately after his declared conversion? Could a momentary flash be thrown on Eusebius in his sayings and doings as an ordinary man in bishop's garments? Or on Julian and Libanius?[7]

The conclusion of her clearly well-considered credo follows:

> There has been abundant writing on such great turning-points, but not such as serves to instruct the imagination in true comparison. I want something different from the abstract treatment which belongs to grave history from a doctrinal point of view, and something different from the schemed picturesqueness of ordinary historical fiction. I want brief, severely conscientious reproductions, in their concrete incidents, of pregnant movements in the past.

The emphases in this aesthetic of historical fiction are revealing. The individual psyche responding by introspection, motivation and action to the pressures of history – 'What really took place in and around Constantine' – is the central interest. Not the historical process as such, nor its local colour, but the human act is what matters. And the artist requires a selective view of history, not its undiscriminated aggregate of facts and events. Art has an elective affinity for 'the great turning-points', the 'pregnant movements in the past': 'the times that try men's souls'. Such contexts can throw 'a momentary flash' on the mind, feelings and actions of the characters. Gwendolen Grandcourt has her illumination from contemporary history as metaphor:

> There comes a terrible moment to many souls when the great movements of the world, the larger destinies of mankind, which have lain aloof in newspapers and other neglected reading, enter like an earthquake into their own lives – when the slow urgency of growing generations turns into the tread of an invading army or the dire clash of civil war.[8]

George Eliot's one conventionally historical novel might seem to contravene her theory of the 'historic imagination'. She worked so hard at her 'medium' that history, quantitatively treated, crowds out art. The reader is aware of the immense effort to provide an elaborate design of Florentine period costume, custom and colour. The weight of detail makes the back-cloth inert, faithful diagram rather than living picture. Yet for the setting she selected Florence between 1492 and 1498, years which included the upsurge of popular agitation leading to the forcible temporary ending of Medici rule in November 1494 and restoration of the Republic. At the centre of the storm stood the charismatic figure of Girolamo Savonarola, calling for reform of a corrupt Church and swaying the popular party, which he did much to form, to demand the moral, political and social regeneration of Florence. It was a 'great turning-point' whose consequences reached far beyond the city-state, involving the intervention of Charles VIII of France, counter-measures by the Papacy, and finally the fall and execution of Savonarola and restoration of the Medicis.

Within this context Romola and Tito live their personal story. The opening of Book 2 (ch. 21) links the public and private lot:

> It was the 17th of November 1494: more than eighteen months since Tito and Romola had been finally united in the joyous Easter time. . . .
>
> Since that Easter a great change had come over the prospects of Florence; and as in the tree that bears a myriad of blossoms, each single bud with its fruit is dependent on the primary circulation of the sap, so the fortunes of Tito and Romola were dependent on certain grand political and social conditions which made an epoch in the history of Italy.

> In this very November, little more than a week ago, the spirit of old centuries seemed to have re-entered the breasts of Florentines. The great bell in the palace tower had rung out the hammer-sound of alarm, and the people had mustered with their rusty arms, their tools and impromptu cudgels, to drive out the Medici.

The linkage here is laboured, mechanically overt: in *Middlemarch* and *Daniel Deronda* less obtrusive means would be found. But the passage is faithful to her notion of the 'great turning-point': the placing of characters on the eve or in the midst of convulsive change. The story of Romola turns upon her disillusion with her marriage as her insights into Tito's character and deeds accumulate. These insights, while expressed in personal relations touching her father, Baldassarre, Tessa, her godfather Bernardo del Nero and others, proceed from the intermingling of Romola's and Tito's lives with public events.

At one thematic level *Romola* enacts a drama of moral and social commitment. The early Romola follows duty and habit in a life of solitary devotion to her blind father-scholar. Unlike Dorothea Brooke she didn't yearn 'after some lofty conception of the world'. She had little social awareness. Tito arouses her feelings and idealising tendency. Her growing commitment involves his rejection. But only as part of a much wider change of moral and social allegiance. The change is not sought: history compels it in the shape of Savonarola and the political crisis.

The narration of Fra Girolamo's influence is discontinuous, episodic. At the outset Romola has to overcome her aversion to 'monkish' associations and Church dogma. The intermittently registered appeal of the Frate grows as her personal life brings bitterness instead of fulfilment, and as social awareness is forced upon her not only by Savonarola's preaching but by her husband's political intriguing. The turning-point comes when, in despair at Tito's breaches of faith, she is confronted and stopped by the Frate while fleeing from Florence. The force of his moral challenge transforms her initial anger to an awakened sense of mission. He demands her commitment:

> See, then, my daughter, how you are below the life of the believer who worships that image of the Supreme Offering, and feels the glow of a common life with the lost multitude for whom

> that offering was made, and beholds the history of the world as the history of great redemption in which he is himself a fellow-worker, in his own place and among his own people! . . . If you forsake your place, who will fill it? (ch. 40)

Returning to Florence she devotes herself to the relief of plague victims and the needy, and earns the title of Madonna. But her sense of commitment went beyond charity. The authorial voice is raised, in place of scenic portrayal, to confirm why:

> His [Savonarola's] burning indignation against the abuses and oppression that made the daily story of the Church and of States had kindled the ready fire in her too. His special care for liberty and purity of government in Florence, with his constant reference of this immediate object to the wider end of a universal regeneration, had created in her a new consciousness of the great drama of human existence in which her life was a part; and through her daily helpful contact with the less fortunate of her fellow-citizens this new consciousness became something stronger than a vague sentiment. (ch. 44)

Accepting that 'her lot was vitally united with the general lot', Romola, despite the failure of her marriage, was now woman militant in the common cause:

> She was marching with a great army; she was feeling the stress of a common life. If victims were needed, and it was uncertain on whom the lot might fall, she would stand ready to answer to her name. (ch. 56)

The persistent and elaborate interweaving of private and public life is not always mediated by the authorial voice. In Chapter 24, 'Inside the Duomo', both Romola and Baldassarre, unknown to each other, listen along with the 'multitude' to Savonarola, crucifix uplifted in his hand, declaring: 'The day of vengeance is at hand! . . . For the sword is hanging from the sky; it is quivering; it is about to fall!' (The French king and army, believed to be the instrument of God's vengeance, were at the gates of Florence.) Like the populace, Romola is buoyant with hope. Baldassarre reacts more passionately than any other to the preacher. But the public cause is turned to private feeling:

> The thunder of denunciation fell on his passion-wrought nerves with all the force of self-evidence: his thought never went beyond it into questions – he was possessed by it as the war-horse is possessed by the clash of sounds. No word that was not a threat touched his consciousness; he had no fibre to be thrilled by it.

The responses are dramatically contrasted: Romola's assent to social responsibility and Baldassarre's mission of private vengeance.

It has been objected that the 'stiffness' of Savonarola creates imbalance: 'Historically valid as the portrait may be, it fails to give the novel a core of equally vivid characters, for the Frate has neither sufficient mystery nor sufficient blood.'[9] The 'historic imagination' was felt by George Eliot to be able to throw 'a momentary flash on Eusebius . . . as an ordinary man in bishop's garments'. If such was her intention, the light failed in Savonarola's case. Did she wish to individualise him? His role is to be the prophet of the 'great turning-point', the herald and partisan of social regeneration. His natural stance is that of the pulpit. He is a supra-personal but not a stucco figure.

The weakness of focus in his portrayal is that though he inspired, and helped to form, a popular party, we know little about its aims and activities or his part in its leadership. George Eliot makes most of his religious and moral fervour. But his cause, in the circumstances, is more secular than ecclesiastical, requiring political and social specification in the narrational design. She didn't here live up to her principle: 'I want brief, severely conscientious reproductions, in their concrete incidents, of pregnant movements in the past.'

Towards the end, the authorial voice ascribes to Savonarola a scheme of inner intellectual and emotional cross-currents that have not previously been disclosed or hinted at. Fantasies of power are imposed on him: a 'marble rigidity' ousts his humanity. His involvement in the political crisis arising from Medicean intrigues coincides with his sudden dehumanisation. Ideological displacement is at work here, induced by George Eliot's increasing conservative distrust of popular and working-class action to obtain the franchise during the 1860s. In the novel that followed *Romola*, her would-be 'radical' leader, Felix Holt, tells the working men (who erupt into 'mob' violence on election day) that political means will get them nowhere: only moral reform can help.

The final confrontation between public and personal claims comes in Chapter 59 when Romola intercedes with Savonarola to allow an appeal against the sentence of execution passed on her godfather. A crescendo of tension is built up between total commitment to political ends and individual suffering. As he rejects her plea, Savonarola speaks with the accents of revolutionary justice, familiar to the twentieth century as to his own:

> '*You* see one ground of action in this matter. I see many. I have to choose that which will further the work intrusted to me. The end I seek is one to which minor respects must be sacrificed. The death of five men – were they less guilty than these – is a light matter weighed against the withstanding of the vicious tyrannies which stifle the life of Italy, and foster the corruption of the Church; a light matter weighed against the furthering of God's kingdom upon earth, the end for which I live and am willing myself to die.'

Romola's response has an equally strong modern resonance when in reply to Fra Girolamo's authoritarian assertion, 'The cause of my party *is* the cause of God's kingdom', she says:

> 'I do not believe it! . . . God's kingdom is something wider – else, let me stand outside it with the beings that I love.'

Ironically her very commitment to the Frate's cause, her marching with his army, had given her the moral assurance now to defy him in the name of the human heart's affections.

She suffers a despairing disillusion, not only regarding Savonarola, but as to any meliorist action: 'that political reform which had once made a new interest in her life seemed now to reduce itself to narrow devices for the safety of Florence' (ch. 61). The emotive stylistic register of her revulsion against political and social movements again suggests ideological intrusion. Yet the authorial voice enters to right the balance between the impersonal law of commitment and the right of personal affective judgement:

> In that declaration of his that the cause of his party was the cause of God's kingdom, she heard only the ring of egoism.

> Perhaps such words have rarely been uttered without that meaner ring in them; yet they are the implicit formula of all energetic belief. And if such energetic belief, pursuing a grand and remote end, is often in danger of becoming a demon-worship, in which the votary lets his son and daughter pass through the fire with a readiness that hardly looks like sacrifice; tender fellow-feeling for the nearest has its danger too, and is apt to be timid and sceptical towards the larger aims without which life cannot rise into religion. In this way poor Romola was being blinded by her tears. (ch. 61)

Her sense of fellowship lost, Romola 'drifts away' by boat at night; 'she had freed herself from all claims' (ch. 61). Alienation falls heavily on her:

> Romola felt orphaned in those wide spaces of sea and sky. She read no message of love for her in that far-off symbolic writing of the heavens, and with a great sob she wished that she might be gliding into death.

The recovery is moral fable. In a legendary land afflicted by the plague she reverts to her Madonna role, symbolically enacting George Eliot's version of the 'religion of humanity' and Christian *caritas*. She has turned her back on history and its causes. All that matters is individual feeling and judgement. Appropriately she recalls the Frate at the close of the Epilogue in purely personal terms:

> 'There are many good people who did not love Fra Girolamo. Perhaps I should never have learned to love him if he had not helped me when I was in great need.'

The action of *Middlemarch*, spanning the period from September 1829 to the end of May 1832 (the eve of the first Reform Act) most richly and subtly provides the fictional picturing of one of history's 'pregnant movements'. If the bare historical facts do not usually enter the narration directly, as Jerome Beaty argued,[10] the manifestations of the Reform movement, and varied forms of resistance to it, permeate the complex interwoven tissues of the novel.

'Reform' and anti-Reform are in the air the characters breathe, reaching far beyond parliament and hustings to at first sight disconnected strata of social experience like the medical profession, housing conditions of poor tenants, industrial progress and the agricultural labourer, the place of women in society, marriage prospects, the scientific and the artistic temperament, xenophobia and the workings of the provincial mind. Even in historical *Romola* George Eliot didn't rely on the mere insertion of dates and facts (fictionally obtrusive or no) to create the sense of response to a 'great turning-point'. The more so in *Middlemarch*, where the historical struggle for Reform is refracted, directly, metaphorically, analogically, implicitly, in a myriad narrational facets of aspiration, endeavour, professional politicising, unawareness, indifference, traditional prejudice, snobbery, frustration, disillusion, resignation, commitment and fulfilment.

Arguing that '*Middlemarch* is the first English novel to analyse the psychology of historical consciousness', Barbara Hardy has perceptively illustrated the variety of means by which George Eliot 'emphasizes Dorothea's historical consciousness, her sense of the past, and its relation to her needs in the present, and for the future'.[11] Many readers have seen in Dorothea's final authorial assessment as having achieved 'unhistoric acts', a 'foundress of nothing', a reductive disenchantment with her earlier ideal of leading 'a grand life here – now – in England'. There was exalted aspiration and idealism in Dorothea as a latter-day St Theresa. But Barbara Hardy makes a vital point when she remarks that Dorothea 'wants to reconstruct the past in order to know how to live in the present'.[12]

In the end Dorothea may be thought to settle for domesticity, motherhood and a whiff of radicalism vicariously. It is a relativist reading, coloured overmuch by the contrast with the fervour of her early idealistic questing. Within the limited and limiting 'provincial life' context, we can hardly underestimate the quality of her 'unhistoric arts'. According to Sir James Chettam's estate manager she has 'the best notion in the world of a plan for cottages' for poor tenants and labourers. And she is emphatic about it: 'I think we deserve to be beaten out of our beautiful houses with a scourge of small cords – all of us who let tenants live in such styes as we see around us' (ch. 3). She supports Lydgate in his hospital project when he is opposed and vilified by his fellow professionals and Middlemarch's business and propertied interests, offering to free him of his debt to Bulstrode so that he may go on with his medical research. Released from the Casaubon marriage, she ignores the deprivation codicil to his will and marries Ladislaw, the Polish outsider of 'rebel' ancestry and a political Radical, earning the gentry's scorn, and ostracism from Sir James Chettam.

A muted authorial voice in the Finale affirms that, despite appearances, domesticity was not enough: 'Dorothea could have liked nothing better, since wrongs existed, than that her husband should be in the thick of a struggle against them, and that she should give him wifely help.' She is conscious, looking back at her first marriage, of a 'convulsive change' within her mind and feelings. Hers too, within a reductive tonal framework, is a story of an acquired sense of social commitment growing from her efforts to understand history as a continuous process of 'vital connection'.

The flowing rhetoric of the Proem to *Romola* most amply expresses George Eliot's view of history as incessant onward movement from past to related present:

> The great river-courses which have shaped the lives of men have hardly changed; and those other streams, the life-currents that ebb and flow in human hearts, pulsate to the same great needs, the same great loves and terrors. As our thought follows in the slow wake of the dawn, we are impressed with the broad sameness of the human lot, which never alters in the main headings of its history – hunger and labour, seed-time and harvest, love and death.

Like act and consequence in personal life, the past, above all in its 'pregnant movements', reaches into the present, directly or analogically. The 'great bell in the palace tower' which Romola heard ringing out 'the hammer-sound of alarm' for the people to arm themselves and drive out the Medicis sounded again for George Eliot in 1860 when Garibaldi's men liberated Sicily and routed the Neapolitan forces. Within two years of *Romola*'s publication, Florence became temporary capital of an independent Italian kingdom.

By an irony that surprises and persuades, George Eliot's single novel of contemporary life was centred a decade back from the time of writing, precisely in those momentous years 1864–6 which showed the Austro-Prussian War, the consequent liberation and prospective reunification of Italy and the American Civil War as 'great turning-points'. As in *Middlemarch*, a primary theme is the quest for historical awareness and understanding: 'a mind consciously, energetically moving with the larger march of human destinies' (ch. 42).

Daniel Deronda is perhaps the most consciously elaborate, though not the most aesthetically satisfying, exercise of the 'historic imagination'. Deronda's personal quest for ancestry leads him to explore, at varied levels, the objective history of the Jewish people and their religious and cultural heritage. A widening historical understanding, and eventual discovery of his Jewish origin, bring him a growing sense of 'fellowship' and 'partisanship', in George Eliot's terms, in place of his early 'social neutrality'. His commitment to restoring his people's national existence takes him away to Palestine. His moral and social attitudes have distanced him from contemporary upper-class English society, shown with a wealth of sharp irony to be in need of improvement. His withdrawal from the English scene has been taken as further example of ideological influence, reflecting George Eliot's now marked distrust of political and social action.[13]

Thematically his role, not adequately made real throughout its long stretches, is to be the man who seeks historical understanding and so finds his own identity and a social mission. He acts within an ambience of contemporary history that is shown to be emancipatory and charged with momentous change. He arrives in Genoa to learn about his origin from his mother on the eve of the decisive battle of the Austro-Prussian War:

> Day after day passed, and the very air of Italy seemed to carry the consciousness that war had been declared against Austria, and every day was a hurrying march of crowded time towards the world-changing battle of Sadowa. (ch. 50)

The 'link with the onward movement of history adds a dimension to the drama of Deronda's personal crisis: fact serves as symbolic overtone of the fiction. The outcome of Sadowa was the liberation of Venice from Austrian domination and a decisive step towards fulfilment of Mazzini's vision of a free and united Italy.'[14] Deronda is freed from his burden of doubt and his life's perspective changed. This is a particular instance of a general textural policy. The historical event is used again and again, in varied ways, to intensify the fictional experience.

The stylisation, at high points of tension, is itself strongly coloured by images and figurative terms drawn from contemporary political and social history. As I have remarked elsewhere:

> The historical references and analogues in *Middlemarch*, and especially Dorothea's slow-growing consciousness of the historical process, enrich the novel's compositional framework and thematic expression. But they do not enter into the stylistic register as significant image clusters or verbal motifs. *Daniel Deronda* is concerned with the search for personal identity and the conditions of moral growth in a world of mercenary values, social privilege, and coercive state and imperial power structures, which in turn generate emancipatory movements. The history of the day makes its presence felt not only by way of metaphoric connections in the fiction but is also reflected in the novel's distinctive imagery and figurative modes.[15]

Gwendolen Grandcourt, by contrast, is 'the spoiled child' (the title of Book 1) who continues to believe she can ignore history, which bores her as it does even more her husband. Walled in her self-assured egocentricity she thinks herself a born 'empress of luck', at roulette or in marriage. The family fortune lost by act of history (the fictional Grapnell & Co. collapse was paralleled by the sudden failure of Overend and Gurney, the most important London banking house),[16] Gwendolen married into wealth and outward gentility. Her disillusion is counterpointed with her growing friendship with Deronda and dependence on him for guidance and moral solace. History in the shape of his insistence that the personal must take account of the social life, and assume obligation to non-personal ends, finally breaks into her selfhood. Images of the American Civil War ironically point to the gap between unhistorical and historical consciousness. The shock of recognising Deronda's commitment to the Jewish cause at last forces on her 'a sense that her horizon was but a dipping onward of an existence with which her own was revolving' (ch. 69).

George Eliot's abiding concern with the 'historic imagination', coloured in early years by the impulse to evoke personal recollection of the past, proceeds from her basic moral and aesthetic views. As artist she wished to explore and reveal human character in act and consequence. Character was inseparable from history, its formative matrix. And in the varied fictional responses to the 'great turning-points' of history, subtly elaborated as medium, she achieved her most searching and moving illuminations.

NOTES

1. G. S. Haight (ed.), *The George Eliot Letters* (New Haven, Conn., 1954–5) III, pp. 128–9.
2. *Daniel Deronda*, ch. 8.
3. Thomas Pinney (ed.), *Essays of George Eliot* (New York and London, 1963), pp. 288–9. The original reads 'there'.
4. Thomas Carlyle, 'On History Again' (1833); cited by Barbara Hardy in '*Middlemarch*: Public and Private Worlds', *English*, 25 (1976), reprinted in *Particularities: Readings in George Eliot* (London, 1982) p. 108.
5. Pinney, *Essays of George Eliot*, p. 287.
6. 'Leaves from a Note-Book', in ibid. pp. 446–7.
7. Pinney comments: 'George Eliot's reference to these figures from church history in the fourth century recalls her youthful interest in the development of early Christianity' (ibid., p. 447n.).
8. *Daniel Deronda*, ch. 69.
9. Andrew Sanders, *The Victorian Historical Novel 1840–1880* (London, 1978) p. 179.
10. Jerome Beaty, 'History by Indirection: the Era of Reform in *Middlemarch*', *Victorian Studies*, 1 (1957) 173–9.
11. Barbara Hardy, *Particularities*, pp. 108, 106.
12. Ibid., p. 118.
13. Graham Martin, '*Daniel Deronda*: George Eliot and Political Change', in Barbara Hardy (ed.), *Critical Essays on George Eliot* (New York, 1970) pp. 140ff.
14. Ian Milner, '*Daniel Deronda* and Contemporary English Society', in *Centenary Essays on George Eliot*, collected by M. Wahba (Cairo, 1981) p. 73.
15. Ibid., p. 80.
16. The fall of Overend and Gurney in May 1866 occurred about a year later than that of the fictional Grapnell & Co. But the suddenness, scale and coincidental features of fact and fiction would have been in many readers' minds: history underwrote the fiction.

8

Physicians in Victorian Fiction

PHILIP COLLINS

My title is snappily alliterative rather than slavishly accurate, for I shall be mentioning some fictional apothecaries and surgeons too – thus, as the physicians of the period would have thought, lowering the social tone of my survey. Physicians were a touchy lot, and not only when they were resenting the 'new-fangled notions' being introduced by such enterprising young men as George Eliot's Mr Lydgate or Charles Kingsley's Tom Thurnall. There were also strong professional and social jealousies within the old tripartite system; the physicians regarded themselves as gentlemen, much superior to the surgeons and apothecaries. When it does not matter to which branch of the profession a practitioner belongs, I shall use the term 'doctor' though strictly speaking that title could only be used by physicians (Fellows and Licentiates of the Royal College of Physicians).

Many of the 42,000 novels published in Britain during the reign of Victoria contained doctors, I would guess from the sample I have read, but one cannot list or discuss them all. One is tempted to go to the other extreme and concentrate entirely on George Eliot's *Middlemarch* (1872). As the distinguished medical professor Sir William Osler reported, near the end of the century, 'Ask the opinion of a dozen medical men upon the novel in which the doctor is best described, and the majority will say *Middlemarch*.' Certainly George Eliot knew more about medicine and could imagine more deeply than any other novelist of the period the multiplicity of roles of a doctor – clinical, scientific, social and domestic. To quote Osler again: 'Writers of our times, like George Eliot, have told for future generations in a character such as Lydgate the little everyday struggles and aspirations of the profession in the nineteenth century, of which we find no record whatever in the files of the *Lancet*.'[1] This is so, and one would add only this qualification to Osler's statement, that there are no novelists on this topic '*like* George Eliot' nor other fictional doctors '*such as* her Lydgate'. The uniqueness of her contribution here, and the reasons why she alone was able to make it, have been excellently demonstrated by Patrick J. MacCarthy, and the historian Asa Briggs has given impressive endorsement to Osler's claim that fiction – and eminently *Middlemarch* – can provide invaluable evidence for the historian of medicine. *Middlemarch*, says Lord Briggs, tells us 'a great deal more than most academic monographs' about the significance of medical reform, and George Eliot is 'far more successful than [the great medical and health Reports of the 1840s] were in making the worst abuses sound plausible'.[2] We shall return, several times, to *Middlemarch*.

One reason for the doctor's frequent appearance in Victorian fiction is the popularity then of death-bed scenes. Many doctors in these novels are indeed only bit-players, incidental attenders on sick-beds or death-beds, as inevitable but hardly more personally significant than the mutes at the funerals which resulted from their failures – though doctors, of course, came more expensive than mutes. Novelists were fond of portraying doctors' bedside manners. From a well-paid physician, a certain orotundity was expected, proceeding from a deep chest housed in a capacious waistcoat – such a figure as Dickens's Doctor Parker Peps, for instance, 'who speaks in a round, deep, sonorous voice, but muffled for the occasion, like the door knocker' (*Dombey and Son*, 1848, ch. 1), or his more bogus Mr Jobling (in *Martin Chuzzlewit*, 1844, ch. 27), Medical Officer of the fraudulent Anglo-Bengalee Disinterested Loan and Life Insurance Company, who 'had a portentously sagacious chin, and a pompous voice, with a rich huskiness in some of its tones that went directly to the heart, like a ray of light shining through the ruddy medium of choice old burgundy'. One other description of the pattern physician may be quoted, from Dickens's friend Wilkie Collins:

> The doctor . . . was one of those carefully constructed physicians in whom the public – especially the female public – implicitly trust. He had the necessary bald head, the necessary double eyeglass, the necessary black clothes, and the necessary blandness of manner, all complete. His voice was soothing, his ways were deliberate, his smile was confidential. (*Armadale*, 1866, III, ch. 3)

Such passages (and there are many of them) give mildly enjoyable glimpses of contemporary stereotypes, but there is not much to be learnt, historically, from them – nor from fictional doctors with such appellations as Dickens's Doctor Soemup, Doctor Payne, Doctor Slasher, Mr Knight Bell, Dr Kutankumagen (from Moscow) or Mr Sawyer, or from Trollope's exercises in this kind, Doctor Fillgrave, Doctor Rerechild and Doctor Pullbody. Here, of course, we are in the region of stereotype jokes about the profession: uneasy jokes, for we all fear pain and death, and must provide ourselves with some protective facetiousness about those medical dignitaries who will preside over our humiliation and extinction.

The popularity of death-beds in Victorian fiction – *Pickwick Papers*, a predominantly comic and even farcical novel, contains thirteen deaths – is only one reason for the high incidence of doctors. Another is that the doctor, particularly in the provincial and rural communities which often provided the settings for novels in this period, was commonly a prominent citizen, likely to be both dining at genteel tables and to be involved in local affairs and controversies. Moreover he was a uniquely privileged figure – and in ways highly convenient to a novelist – in that he had a potentially intimate relationship with his patients at crisis points in their lives, and that his patients might plausibly include both rich and poor. Both points are made forcibly by Dickens in a passage about the unnamed but illustrious Physician in *Little Dorrit*. (F. R. Leavis has made effective use of it in his essay on this novel.) It is through Physician's eyes that we discover the suicide of Mr Merdle, which has such consequences for everybody in the story, and that episode is preluded by a dinner-party at Physician's house, at which the absent Mr Merdle's seat is an empty 'Banquo's chair':

> Few ways of life were hidden from Physician, and he was oftener in its darkest places than even Bishop. There were brilliant ladies about London who perfectly doted on him, my dear, as the most charming creature and the most delightful person, who would have been shocked to find themselves so close to him if they could have known on what sights those thoughtful eyes of his had rested within an hour or two, and near to whose beds, and under what roofs, his composed figure had stood. But Physician was a composed man, who performed neither on his own trumpet, nor on the trumpets of other people. Many

> wonderful things did he see and hear, and much irreconcilable moral contradiction did he pass his life among; yet his equality of compassion was no more disturbed than the Divine Master's of all healing was. He went, like the rain, among the just and unjust, doing all the good he could, and neither proclaiming it in the synagogues nor at the corners of streets.
>
> As no man of large experience of humanity, however quietly carried it may be, can fail to be invested with an interest peculiar to the possession of such knowledge, Physician was an attractive man. Even the daintier gentlemen and ladies who had no idea of his secret, and who would have been startled out of more wits than they had by the monstrous impropriety of his proposing to them 'Come and see what I see!' confessed his attraction. Where he was, something real was.[3]

'Where he was, something real was': of no other professional group could this so confidently be said (as Dickens implies by his comparisons with Bar and Bishop, representing the other two traditional learned professions). Also Physician, unlike them, has moved, a familiar figure, among the just and the unjust, in the darkest places as well as in the most brilliant and affluent circles.

Partly because it was generally lengthy, and partly for more estimable artistic and ideological reasons, the mid-nineteenth-century novel tended towards the panoramic, whether in the metropolis or in a regional setting, and the doctor could be useful as the reader's guide to disparate households, ranging from the grand to the squalid, and particularly the latter. To quote Dickens again, where he is making (in *Dombey and Son*, ch. 47) a plea for 'the unnatural outcasts of society': 'But follow the good clergyman or doctor, who, with his life imperilled at every breath he draws, goes down into their dens, lying within the echoes of our carriage wheels and daily tread upon the pavement stones.' Or the doctor could serve as the novelist's linkman, helping to create some feeling of unity in the crowded, heterogeneous scene. Thus Allan Woodcourt, the doctor in Dickens's *Bleak House* (1853), tends upon a variety of characters, mostly unknown to one another (Miss Flite, Captain Hawson, Jenny, Jo, Richard and Caddy) besides playing an heroic part (off-stage) as a ship's surgeon, studying when back in England the 'miserable by-ways' of London (such slums as Tom-All-Alone's), and finally marrying the heroine and taking her off to a Yorkshire industrial town where he works as 'a medical attendant for the poor' (chs 46, 60). The much-esteemed Mr Gibson, in Mrs Gaskell's *Wives and Daughters* (1866), moves with similar freedom through county society:

> There were not many surgeons in the county who had so wide a practice as he; he went to lonely cottages on the borders of great commons; to farmhouses at the end of narrow country lanes that led to nowhere else. . . . He attended all the gentry within a circle of fifteen miles round Hollingford; and was the appointed doctor to the still greater families who went up to London every February – as the fashion then was – and returned to their acres in the early weeks of July. (ch. 5)

Such an ubiquitous figure has obvious technical advantages for a novelist, especially if social exploration of the 'Two Nations' theme is part of his intention. Q. D. Leavis, in her discussion of 'The Symbolic Function of the Doctor in Victorian Novels', remarks that novelists still find doctors useful in this way – witness *Dr Zhivago* and Camus's *La Peste*.[4]

But the doctor was a yet more crucially important member of his community then than now, because his functions included many later taken over by other specialist professions which were only just emerging. Notably, the local general practitioner was – or could and should be – at the centre of that basic reformist activity, 'the Sanitary Question' (the provision of better housing, better means of sewage disposal and purer water). The necessity of these reforms was most vividly demonstrated, of course, by the major outbreaks of cholera and typhus which periodically swept the country, and it is no surprise that such epidemics often occur in novels. George Eliot's Lydgate, fresh from his medical studies in Paris, with new ideas about diet and ventilation, is particularly anxious to get control of the local Fever Hospital. He establishes his reputation in Middlemarch by correctly diagnosing Fred Vincy's illness as typhoid (and thus comes to know, and marry, Fred's sister Rosamond) – but, since the old-fashioned local physician Mr Wrench had misdiagnosed Fred's condition, and had prescribed the wrong medicines, this case exacerbates Lydgate's uneasy relationship with the medical fraternity. Fever is important in *Bleak House* too, involving several characters: 'And dying thus around us every day', Dickens ends the chapter (47) in which young Jo dies this way. Kingsley's *Two Years Ago*, published in

February 1857, is similarly explicit about the implications of his story: it was, he writes in the Introduction, a fictionalised attempt to spell out 'the deep lesson' of the cholera epidemic of 1854. We first see the hero, Doctor Tom Thurnall, with his father (a wise and benevolent old physician). His father is poring over a microscope – 'till [he explains to his son] you can take my place at the microscope, Tom: or till we have, as we ought to have, a first-rate analytical chemist settled in every country town, and paid, in part at least, out of the country rates' (ch. 1). There, all too obviously, we have Kingsley plugging a pet idea. Later, young Tom, having studied in London, Glasgow and Paris (it is always worth noticing what medical schools these novelists specify), and having knocked about the world, returns to Britain, foresees the onset of cholera, and makes himself a sort of unofficial, unpaid Medical Officer of Health, striving in vain to persuade the various local vested interests to spend money in advance to prevent or mitigate the epidemic. He subsequently cleans the place up, with a new drainage system, and persuades some prominent landlords to improve housing conditions. Though tempted to marry a local heiress who could settle him into a very comfortable practice ('he would take his MD of course' [ch. 25]), he departs for the Crimea 'to dose [as he says] the Bashi-Bazouks' (ch. 24), and the girl whom he ought to marry (and does) follows him there as a nurse.

Tom Thurnall, like Lydgate and Woodcourt, and like Fitzpiers in Hardy's *The Woodlanders* (1887), is a *young* doctor. Such characters have an obvious double usefulness to a novelist. They can represent new ideas, new professional ideals in conflict with the old. Lydgate uses the stethoscope, and tries to reduce his patients' hydroptic thirst for drugs; Thurnall 'charged his patients as little, instead of as much as possible, and applying to medicine the principles of an enlightened political economy, tried to increase the demand by cheapening the supply' – a doctrine which his elder colleagues saw as revolutionary and ruinous (ch. 8). But also, and predictably, all these young doctors are unmarried when the story begins, so, as reasonably eligible, young professional men of gentlemanly status, they can help to provide the conventional romantic interest – though if, like Lydgate and Fitzpiers, they choose hastily, they can discover how important to a doctor is the character of his wife. Middle-aged fictional doctors like Trollope's Doctor Thorne or Mrs Gaskell's Mr Gibson tend to have nubile daughters or wards – but here again the doctor can be a specially promising figure in his joint role as physician and father or husband. Mr Gibson, a widower, has to protect his daughter Molly from his apprentices' calf-love; then he remarries, to gain her some motherly care, but discovers, like Lydgate after him, that his wife is unsympathetic to the duties and ethics of medicine. She complains to her stepdaughter:

> 'I think your dear papa might have put off his visit to Mr Craven Smith for just this one evening.'
>
> 'Mr Craven Smith couldn't put off dying,' said Molly bluntly.
>
> 'You droll girl,' said Mrs Gibson, with a faint laugh. 'But if this Mr Smith is dying, as you say, what's the use of your father's going off to him in such a hurry? Does he expect a legacy, or anything of that kind? . . . Really, if I had heard all these details of your father's profession, I doubt if I could have brought myself to have him!' (*Wives and Daughters*, ch. 15)

This opinion is echoed by Rosamond Lydgate, a few years later, in conversation with her husband: 'Do you know, Tertius, I often wish you had not been a medical man. . . . I do not think it is a nice profession, dear' (*Middlemarch*, v, ch. 45). Mr Gibson, like Doctor Thorne, finds himself in a moral dilemma, caught between his love for his daughter and his professional knowledge about the health of the man who could affect her future. For Mrs Gibson, of course, there is no dilemma; having overheard the news that an eligible elder son in the neighbourhood has a fatal illness, she promptly transfers her favours, as a hostess and a mother, to his younger brother.

No professional man is so well placed to be the repository of such embarrassing intimate secrets as the doctor, except perhaps the solicitor: but the doctor has the advantage over the solicitor, in popular fiction, that lawyers are traditionally regarded with suspicion, hatred or derision, whereas doctors – unless they are manifestly quacks – are generally respected. Morever the medical profession was changing, in many important respects, during this period, and this gave novelists, many of whom were interested in dramatising processes of social change, special opportunities with their doctors. The concern over public-health issues has already been mentioned – the new awareness of the importance of preventitive measures in housing and sanitation, even if the doctor has in mind only his richer and well-housed patients, since epidemics do not respect class barriers (a point made forcibly by Dickens in *Bleak House*). Also during these decades there were many important developments in medical practice – which inevitably led to professional infighting, with the old hands distrusting and resenting the new methods, and the innovators encountering much resistance too from their patients, who generally had more faith in the old and tried procedures than in the unknown or experimental. *Middlemarch* provides an anthology of such difficulties, from Lydgate's medical colleagues' ruffled feeling that his introducing new practices was 'a libel on their time-honoured procedure', an ungentlemanly breach of professional solidarity, a 'fouling' of the group's nest, to the famous remark of Mrs Mawmsey, the grocer's wife, that 'what keeps me up best is the pink mixture, not the brown', though Lydgate tells her 'that there is no use in taking medicine' (v, ch. 45). Lydgate suffers also from the condemnation of Mrs Dollop, the landlady of the Tankard Inn – an opinion of some importance, because a large Benefit Club holds its meetings in the Tankard, and thus comes to vote down a suggestion that Lydgate be appointed medical officer to the Club in place of old Doctor Gambit: but Mrs Dollop had become

> more and more convinced by her own asseveration, that Doctor Lydgate meant to let the people die in the Hospital, if not to poison them, for the sake of cutting them up without saying by your leave or with your leave; for it was a known 'fac' that he had wanted to cut up Mrs Goby, as respectable a woman as any in Parley Street, who had money in trust before her marriage.

– and so on, to similar effect (v, ch. 45).

Other irrational hazards encountered by a young doctor trying to establish himself may be illustrated from Harriet Martineau's *Deerbrook* (1839) and Thomas Hardy's *The Woodlanders*. In the former, the excellent young apothecary Edmund Hope feels it his duty to vote in a parliamentary election, though warned that inactive neutrality would be more prudent. He votes against the nominee of the local magnate, who thereupon incenses the mob against him, spreads canards about his dissecting bodies from the local graveyard and effectively ruins his practice, until Hope restores his reputation by heroic efforts during – predictably in novels of this period – a cholera epidemic. (Many novels set in country areas make the point that a doctor's practice was much affected by the favour or disfavour of the local Big House.) Hardy's Fitzpiers, though not a very conscientious practitioner, develops a comfortable practice because, coming from a local gentry family, he is more of a gentleman than his rivals: but he spoils this, and loses patients, by marrying a timber-merchant's daughter. As his old housekeeper tells him: 'they won't believe you know such clever doctrines in physic as they once supposed of 'ee, seeing as you could marry into Mr Melbury's family, which is only Hintock-born such as I be meself' (ch. 25).

It is in such ways that, as Sir William Osler said, novels may provide a better register than the *Lancet* does of 'the little everyday struggles and aspirations of the profession'. This may be illustrated further by the indications novels give of the currency of medical practices. Take for instance this passage from Wilkie Collins's *The Woman in White* (1860):

> Beside the medicine, [Doctor Goodricke] brought a bit of hollow mahogany wood with him, shaped like a kind of trumpet; and after waiting a little while, he put one end over the lady's heart and the other to his ear, and listened carefully.

Evidently the stethoscope was not so familiar an object in 1860 that Collins could take it for granted: he describes it and says how it is used. Two minor novelists from the mid-1860s may also be quoted:

> He took his stethoscope out, applied it to the chest of the patient, and for some minutes seemed to be looking with his ear through a sort of telescope.

> in another moment the doctor had his stethoscope at his ear, and was listening to her inspiration as he instructed her to assume different positions, and to draw her breath in various ways.[5]

These two passages surely suggest that if the word 'stethoscope' was now comprehensible to the general reader its use was still enough of a novelty as to merit describing. *Middlemarch* is set in the early 1830s, so Lydgate was much ahead of his time in using the stethoscope (as George Eliot remarks). Invented in 1816, it came into general use very slowly. Indeed, as a medical historian points out, it was uncommon in Lydgate's time for a doctor to examine the patient at all beyond looking at his tongue; instead, he listened to a patient's account of his condition, and observed the appearance of shed blood, urine and faeces.[6] Myron F. Brightfield, to whom I owe these passages about the stethoscope (though the interpretation of their significance is mine), also quotes from minor novels various passages which, taken together, suggest that it was in the 1850s and 1860s that the traditional practices of blood-letting, blistering and physicking eventually became conspicuously old-fashioned. 'There's a prejudice just now against the use of the lancet, I know', remarks one old such practitioner, in a novel of 1868; another 'practitioner of the good old school', in a novel of 1862, is described as 'physicking and phlebotomising, cauterising and torturing, after the manner of his predecessor'. By then only French doctors had the reputation of being reactionary old bleeders, 'very free' (as Mrs Henry Wood says in 1866) 'with the lancet – with leeches – with anything that draws blood'.[7]

Another respect in which medicine was changing during this period was in the social status and professional organisation of its personnel. 'In the mid-century', writes W. J. Reader in his study of nineteenth-century developments in the professions, 'the general practitioners and the attorneys were well in the lead over all other occupations . . . in the march towards full professional status.'[8] For the novelist, doctors were socially in a particularly interesting position, rather as governesses were among their female characters. Doctors were not indubitably gentlemen, but they might be, or be so regarded. Their status was rising, and their profession was becoming better organised and recognised and more qualified; the old tripartite division was giving way to the pattern we now have of physicians and surgeons, specialists and general practitioners. The ramshackle training system of apprenticeship followed by generally nominal examinations by the Apothecaries' Hall and the College of Surgeons was giving way too – to the now-familiar university and teaching hospital education system. Elements of these changes, and of the inevitable conflicts as the new systems and men clashed with the old, could provide useful fictional material. 'Then, indeed, there was war in Barsetshire', concludes Trollope after describing Doctor Thorne's arrival in the area – a change from Barsetshire's usual wars between various Church parties. Doctor Thorne offends his colleagues by compounding medicines as well as prescribing them. His fees are lower than the professional norm (he charges seven-and-sixpence instead of a guinea); but

> The guinea fee, the principle of giving advice and selling no medicine, the great resolve to keep a distinct barrier between the physician and the apothecary, and, above all, the hatred of the contamination of a bill, were strong in the medical mind of Barsetshire. Doctor Thorne had the provincial medical world against him, and so he appealed to the metropolis. The *Lancet* took the matter up in his favour, but the *Journal of Medical Science* was against him. (*Doctor Thorne*, 1858, ch. 3)

Middle-aged Doctor Thorne is a Janus figure: professionally innovatory in flouting some of the shibboleths, but retrograde in selling as well as prescribing medicine (this practice became regarded as unprofessional, since it gave the physician a financial inducement to overprescribe).

Thorne's position is complicated also by his being indubitably a gentleman by birth, and he overtrades on his consciousness of this. The social position of doctors, particularly whose who were not physicians (and thus usually graduates of Oxford or Cambridge), was equivocal. Thus, Trollope's Miss Marrable, a lady of the old school for whom 'Rank . . . was a thing quite assured and ascertained', was sure that letters to attorneys should be addressed 'Mister' because they did not rank as 'Esquires', and that the only professions 'intended for gentlemen' were the clergy, the armed services and the better branch of the law (barristers). Medicine, however, raised problems for her: 'She would not absolutely say that a physician was not a gentleman, or even a surgeon: but she would never allow to physic the same absolute privileges which, in her eyes, belonged to law and the church' (*The Vicar of Bullhampton*, 1870, ch. 9). Here was another good reason for doctors dropping the apothecary side of their operation, since this indeed smacked of trade, particularly as many surgeon-apothecaries (the Medical Practitioners, as they were called)[9] also stocked toiletries.

How a successful career might lead to gentility is described by Thackeray in *Pendennis* (1850). The hero's father is born a gentleman but, his father having died insolvent, he has had to abandon his undergraduate career and become a surgeon-apothecary. 'He always detested the trade' but set up a humble shop in Bath with his name on a board outside and a gilt pestle and mortar over the door, and with tooth-brushes, hair-powder and London perfumery on sale within. Success with an aristocratic patient enlarges and upgrades his practice: 'First his humble little shop became a smart one: then he discarded the selling of tooth-brushes and perfumery: then he shut up the shop altogether, and only had a little surgery attended by a genteel young man: then he had a gig', and ultimately he ran a carriage emblazoned with his family arms. Though now rejoicing in the courtesy title of 'Doctor' he still hankers after being a gentleman, and finally amasses enough money to set up in an estate, discarding his professional 'black breeches and stockings' for the bottle-green coat of a country gentleman. He now never speaks of the old shop: 'It was now his shame, as it formerly was his pride, to be called Doctor, and those who wished to please him always gave him the title of Squire' (ch. 2).

Trollope, an invaluable witness on such matters, makes a useful distinction among the professions in his *Rachel Ray* (1863). For a clergyman, he remarks, it is '*a vital necessity*' to be a gentleman; other professions were less exacting in this respect – good birth is 'the greatest of *aids* to the doctor, the lawyer, the member of Parliament – though in that position a man may perhaps prosper without it' (ch. 6; my italics).[10] So medicine was, to some extent, a career open to talents, but being a doctor was of itself no certificate of gentility. How far below the salt a doctor existed was strikingly demonstrated by a non-fictional countess, who disdained to address her local practitioner directly but conveyed her wishes through her lady's maid, ending with the splendid pronouncement: 'Inform the doctor that he may bleed the Countess of Carlisle.'[11] A fictional grandee, George Eliot's Lady Chettam, is not altogether pleased to hear that Lydgate is 'one of the Lydgates of Northumberland, really well connected'. 'One does not expect it in a practitioner of this kind', she remarks. 'For my own part, I like a medical man more on a footing with the servants; they are often all the cleverer' (*Middlemarch*, I, ch. 8).

The uncertain status of medical men added to their fictional usefulness at a time when social class was a fascinating preoccupation. Another attraction of the medical man was that, in most communities, he was the only discernable man of science, and this was, as everyone reiterated, an age of science. It is interesting to observe the emergence of some stereotypes. Unusually for a novelist in the 1860s, Mrs Gaskell has a scientist for hero in her *Wives and Daughters*, but he is an ostentatiously unromantic one, being ugly and ungainly, though a good, honest, loving fellow, eventually rewarded by becoming a professor; and as for his senior colleagues, 'the leaders of the scientific world', they are 'odd-looking, simple-hearted men, very much in earnest about their own particular subjects, and not having much to say on any other' (ch. 4). The doctor's representing science could take several forms. He could, for instance, speak with the authority of science, thus giving quasi-objective warrant to what otherwise might seem a mere opinion. A simple example occurs near the end of Hardy's *Jude the Obscure* (1895) when Jude's queer little son hangs himself and his siblings, 'because we are too menny', and a doctor is called in. Jude reports on his verdict:

> The doctor says there are such boys springing up amongst us – boys of a sort unknown in the last generation – the outcome of new views of life. . . . He says it is the beginning of the coming universal wish not to live. He's an advanced man, the doctor. (vi, ch. 2)

Hardy is not presenting Jude ironically here, nor regarding him as naïve to talk such baloney; this is a clumsily transparent subterfuge for claiming that 'science' supports the novelist's highly improbable assertion. Doctors do not bring out the best in Hardy, indeed. In *The Woodlanders* (1887) there appears another of the potentialities of the doctor-as-scientist, the assumption that science so truncates the humanity of its professional adherents as to incline them to regard mankind merely as automata explicable in scientific terms, and thus to disregard traditional notions of feeling and morality. Early in the story, young Dr Fitzpiers, noting the charms of Grace Melbury, quotes Shelley on the subject of female beauty (not a good sign) when in conversation with honest Giles Winterborne, her humble local unscientific admirer, though Fitzpiers is unaware of this fact. 'You seem to be mightily in love with her, sir', replies the simple and perturbed Winterborne, but Fitzpiers rejects such old-time terminology:

> O no – I am not that, Winterborne; people living insulated, as I do by the solitude of this place, get charged with emotive fluid

> like a Leyden jar with electric, for want of some conductor at hand to disperse it. Human love is a subjective thing – the essence itself of man, as that great thinker Spinoza says – *ipsa hominis essentia* – it is joy accompanied by an idea which we project against any suitable object in the line of our vision.

And more to similar effect. Giles Winterborne has an apt reply: 'Well, it is what we call being in love in these parts, whether or no' (ch. 16). Fitzpiers, it is here evident, is not destined to prove a good husband nor an exemplary general practitioner. Capable of being, as he declares, 'possessed by five distinct infatuations at the same time (ch. 29), he lacks the steady reliability expected of a country doctor.

After his marriage Fitzpiers continues to indulge the proclivities apparent in his haystack tumbles with the buxom Suke Damson, and his way with patients may strike the layman as verging on the unprofessional. Thus, attending the local *grande dame* and *femme fatale*, Mrs Charmond, he fails to register the danger-signal that, on his first visit to her, she is discovered smoking a cigarette (the first lady I can recall doing that, in Victorian fiction), and that she not only offers him a cigarette but also *throws* him a box of matches. Obdurately unwarnable, he is soon peeling a plaster off a non-existent bruise on her luscious shoulder; and when she exclaims 'O – you hurt me!', he displays an unprofessional ardour in his response. 'Wait a moment then, I'll damp it,' he says: whereupon

> He put his lips to the place and kept them there, without any objecting on her part, till the plaster came off easily. . . . [He] examined her so closely that his breath touched her tenderly, at which their eyes rose to an encounter. (ch. 27)

That would do, in the circumstances: but the British Medical Association expects its members to guard against such circumstances arising. *The Woodlanders*, though containing episodes of such unintentional hilarity, is elsewhere perceptive about the problems of a young doctor – a young intellectual, indeed, of any kind – in a conservative and altogether unintellectual rural community. The heroine reflects, before meeting him, how strange it was to find, in one of the nooks of Little Hintock, 'like a tropical plant in a hedgerow, a nucleus of advanced ideas and practices which had nothing in common with the life around' (ch. 6).

The doctor as experimenter – usually amoral or unscrupulous – is another aspect of the fictional doctor-as-scientist in this period when science fiction was emerging. Dr Jekyll, ahead of his time in 1886 in discovering a mind-transforming drug 'long before pharmacological research showed that one could be compounded',[12] might indeed have been simply dubbed 'scientist', but by making him a doctor, whose proper activity is *ex officio* virtuous, and one moreover displaying 'every mark of capacity and kindness', Robert Louis Stevenson easily established a fuller contrast between the estimable Jekyll and his evil *alter ego* Hyde. His discovery of this wonder-working potion is the product of what is called 'transcendental medicine' (*Dr Jekyll and Mr Hyde*, 1886, ch. 9). Another such fancy term, unknown to the medical schools, was 'metaphysical medicine'. This is the speciality of the 'medical philosopher' Doctor Hesselius, a German (ambiguous sign) in Sheridan le Fanu's famous shocker 'Green Tea' (1872). Doctor Hesselius has achieved command over the mystical. Doctor Moreau, in H. G. Well's parable story (1896) about men made from beasts and men reverting to the beast, is a prominent if eccentric physiologist, not a medical practitioner, but he has in tow a drink-sodden surgeon named Montmorency (a bad sign from a novelist of Wells's outlook). Like the legendary girl with a curl in the middle of her forehead, fictional doctors could easily be horrid once they had chucked their Hippocratic oath to be very very good. Wilkie Collins, the English inventor of the detective story, realised what splendid potentialities the bent physician provided: sinister sanatoria, doctors handy with dope or poison or fatal fumes. As a sardonic character remarks in the Epilogue to *Armadale* (1866), 'We live in an age eminently favourable to the growth of all roguery which is careful enough to keep up appearances. In this enlightened nineteenth century, I look upon the doctor as one of our rising men.' An equivocal note, this, on which to end my discussion of some of the reasons for the novelistic popularity of the medical man.

I end with a final salute to *Middlemarch*. Writing in the 1870s about the inadequate medical practices of the early 1830s, George Eliot registers a sense – well based on her preliminary research – of things now being 'not so ill with you and me as they might have been' (to quote from the novel's final sentence):

> For it must be remembered that this [the 1830s] was a dark period; and in spite of venerable colleges which used great efforts to secure purity of knowledge by making it scarce, and to exclude error by a rigid exclusiveness in relation to fees and appointments, it happened that very ignorant young gentlemen were promoted in town, and many more got a legal right to practise over large areas in the country. Also, the high standard held up to the public mind by the College of Physicians, which gave its peculiar sanction to the expensive and highly-rarified medical instruction obtained by graduates of Oxford and Cambridge, did not hinder quackery from having an excellent time of it. (II, ch. 15)

Her irony here about the College of Physicians, like all the rest of her commentary, is well justified. She aptly entitled her substantial notebooks for this novel 'Quarry for *Middlemarch*', and they provide impressive evidence of the breadth and depth of her reading in medical history. Patrick J. McCarthy, has shown how much relevant scientific and technical knowledge she possessed before she made these special investigations, with this novel in mind, and why a Lydgate can emerge only in the fiction of the 1870s, and from the pen of George Eliot:

> By the sixties, in fact, the early signs of this great breakthrough, the sense that the medical profession was at last benefiting from scientific research, brought at first a slow and then a sharp rise in its public esteem. It would seem from all this that Lydgate appeared just as the change in public opinion was beginning to gather momentum. . . . Lydgate is the 'new' fictional surgeon I have described him to be because of the conjunction of the moment in medical history with an up-to-date, completely aware, happily mated novelist and her desire to write a novel dealing with the expanding world she had come to know.[13]

George Eliot was 'happily mated' in the sense, here, that her common-law husband, G. H. Lewes, was a distinguished populariser and theorist of science, specially interested in biology and medicine, and intelligently aware of the latest research. Besides having this fireside coadjutor, she alone among English novelists of her day possessed the intellectual equipment to comprehend, in detail and in all their bearings, the great range of scientific, professional, political and social material which she had studied and absorbed. Equally important, she had the imaginative capacity to make these factual bones live in the fully imagined context of Middlemarch society.

Lydgate's ambitions are characteristic of the live-minded, forward-looking medical man of his period: to use new techniques such as the stethoscope, to reduce the amount of treatment and drugging, to busy himself in public health matters, to undertake research (institutions and university departments hardly existed for such purposes then) and to make the local hospital a teaching hospital (one could then set up a medical school with less fuss than is now entailed). And the difficulties he encounters, from colleagues and patients, are typical too. George Eliot increases some of these difficulties, of course, in a novelistic way: thus, he *would* find himself in the invidious position of having to give the casting vote in the highly contentious election to the hospital chaplaincy; and *would* of course become implicated in the dubious death for which his patron Mr Bulstrode is arguably responsible. But the points made in these episodes about the medical problems and pressures are just, and are presented with great intelligence. For instance, the obligation to choose between the Reverend Mr Tyke and the Reverend Mr Farebrother as hospital chaplain annoys him: 'he had a vexed sense that he must make up his mind on this trivial Middlemarch business'. But then he realises that it will be very difficult not to vote for Tyke, much as he detests him and prefers Farebrother, because Mr Bulstrode, who holds the key to his access to the Fever Hospital, favours Tyke: 'For the first time Lydgate was feeling the hampering threadlike pressure of small social conditions, and their frustrating complexity. . . . In his student's chambers [in Paris], he had prearranged his social action quite differently' (I, ch. 18). But this is how problems present themselves in the real world, far otherwise than in the idealistic student's imagination. Lydgate's problem here is personal and political, and has nothing to do with his medical and technical expertise; he is not even interested in the ecclesiastical controversies central to this election, but his vote is crucial, and if he is to gain full access to the Fever Hospital, as is essential to his medical ambitions, dare he offend its chief benefactor, Mr Bulstrode? What Lydgate, as a novice in Middlemarch society and in medical reform, did not realise at this time – though 'being seven-and-twenty, he felt himself experienced' (II, ch. 15) – was, as Asa Briggs comments, that

> the problems of running a hospital are not restricted to medical organisation or to smooth administration. Politics and personalities intruded perpetually. Bulstrode did not build the hospital for the same reasons that inspired Lydgate. . . . For the student of history . . . the specific point about medical reform is underlined, the point that half the problem was not medical at all. In the twentieth century, social advance depends to a large extent on technical ability, and administrative competence. In the early nineteenth century . . . personal integrity and unflinching determination were at a premium.[14]

Lydgate, to use a modern locution, hadn't got what it took in such circumstances. As the narrator early warns us, 'that distinction of mind which belonged to his intellectual ardour' co-existed with some 'spots of commonness' (II, ch. 15), which were to betray him into courses fatal to his medical and scientific aspirations. Even his research project, though a plausible and honourable one around 1830, would never have worked out, as George Eliot, knowledgeable about such matters, well knew by the 1870s.[15] He could hardly be blamed for that mistake, but it was his lack of the requisite toughness and integrity – and luck – that caused the failure of his more realisable hopes in Middlemarch, followed by the specious 'success' of what remained of his career before his premature (and self-willed?) death, recounted in terms which must terrify any professional man, for such a fate is not unique to the medical profession:

> Lydgate's hair never became white. He died when he was only fifty. . . . He had gained an excellent practice, alternating, according to the season, between London and a Continental bathing-place; having written a treatise on Gout, a disease which has a good deal of wealth on its side. His skill was relied on by many paying patients, but he always regarded himself as a failure: he had not done what he once meant to do.

After further summary of his downfall, George Eliot – with the ironic pith so evident in this passage – concludes: 'In brief, Lydgate was what is called a successful man' (Finale). The issues dramatised in Lydgate's career receive their final comment in the novel's concluding paragraph, though it is primarily concerned with political and social advance rather than with medical reform. Lydgate had begun with the ambition 'to do good small work for Middlemarch, and great work for the world' (II, ch. 15). Few men could achieve such a double aim, but George Eliot rightly pays tribute to those who never aspired to, or who abandoned the pretensions of, a Jenner or a Bichat or the other historic figures referred to in *Middlemarch*, incidentally but with an impeccable sense of their significance:

> for the growing good of the world is partly dependent on unhistoric acts; and that things are not so ill with you and me as they might have been, is half owing to the number who lived faithfully a hidden life, and rest in unvisited tombs.[16]

Middlemarch dramatises what were the special difficulties, in its period, of remaining faithful to a vision of how medicine should be practised, and of gauging what 'great work for the world' might be accomplished by well-directed research, even by a doctor with so strong a conviction – as he replied to his wife – that his was 'the grandest profession in the world' (V, ch. 45)

NOTES

1. Sir William Osler, *Aequanimitas* (1905) p. 49, and manuscript notes, quoted by Jessie Dobson, 'Doctors in Literature', *Library Association Record*, 71 (1969) 272.
2. Asa Briggs, 'Middlemarch and the Doctors', *Cambridge Journal*, 1 (1948) 754, 760; cf. Patrick J. McCarthy, 'Lydgate, "the New Young Surgeon" of *Middlemarch*', *Studies in English Literature*, 10 (1970) 805–16. Briggs's essay is reprinted, in revised form, in his *Collected Essays* (Brighton, 1985) II, 49–67.
3. *Little Dorrit* (1857) II, ch. 25; cf. F. R. and Q. D. Leavis, *Dickens the Novelist* (London, 1970) pp. 183, 240 and 267–8.
4. F. R. and Q. D. Leavis, *Dickens the Novelist*, pp. 179–83.
5. Wilkie Collins, *The Woman in White* (1860) pp. 391–2; Percy Fitzgerald, *Bella Donna* (1864) II, p. 107; Edward Bradley, *Mattins and Muttons* (1866) I, p. 124, all cited by Myron F. Brightfield, *Victorian England in its Novels (1860 – 1870)*, 4 vols (Los Angeles, 1968) II, 216. Brightfield's chapter here, which contains much valuable material, was originally published as 'The Medical Profession in Early Victorian England, as

depicted in the Novels of that Period (1840–1870)', in the *Bulletin of the History of Medicine*, 35 (1961).

6. Charles Newman, *The Evolution of Medical Education in the Nineteenth Century* (London, 1957) pp. 86–7, quoted in the Penguin Edition of *Middlemarch* (1965) p. 904.
7. Edmund Yates, *The Rock Ahead* (1868) I, p. 38; Matilda Charlotte Houston, *Recommended to Mercy* (1862) I, p. 43; Mrs Henry Wood, *Saint Martin's Eve* (1866) p. 335, cited by Brightfield, *Victorian England*, II, pp. 215, 210.
8. W. J. Reader, *Professional Men: The Rise of the Professional Classes in Nineteenth-Century England* (London, 1966) p. 68.
9. 'This term [medical practitioner] is of comparatively modern date', writes a novelist in 1848, 'and is applied to the Pariahs of the medical profession. Men who are compelled to unite the acquirements of a physician with those of a surgeon.' The medical practitioner's remuneration and social position were 'far from enviable. He . . . may possibly be admitted to the tables of the higher classes in the neighbourhood; but his family holds an uncertain and slippery position. . . . No gentleman ought to enter this profession' (Ellen Wallace, *Mr Warrenne, the Medical Practitioner*, 1848, I, pp. 11–12, cited by Brightfield, *Victorian England*, II, p. 207).
10. Cited by Richard Faber, *Proper Stations: Class in Victorian Fiction* (London, 1971) p. 133. Faber's book contains many useful references to doctors in this respect.
11. Cited by Mrs C. S. Peel, 'Homes and Habits', in *Early Victorian England 1830–1865*, ed. G. M. Young (London, 1934) I, 97.
12. Dobson, 'Doctors in Literature', p. 272.
13. McCarthy, 'Lydgate', pp. 810, 815.
14. Briggs, 'Middlemarch and the Doctors', pp. 758–9.
15. See W. J. Harvey, 'The Intellectual Background of the Novel: Casaubon and Lydgate', in *Middlemarch: Critical Approaches to the Novel*, ed. Barbara Hardy (London, 1967) pp. 25–37.
16. *Middlemarch*, Finale. The wording of this passage had originally been even more emphatic: see Jerome Beaty, 'The Text of the Novel', in Hardy, *Middlemarch: Critical Approaches*, pp. 61–2.

9

Trollope's Love-stories: From *Framley Parsonage* to *The Belton Estate*

JULIET McMASTER

'There must be love in a novel', Trollope declared uncategorically in the *Autobiography*.[1] Sometimes he seems to have felt somewhat constrained by the rule. He tried in *Miss Mackenzie* to write a novel without love, and found it could not be done. And in *Phineas Finn*, he said, he had included the love interest only 'for the sake of [his] readers' (*Autobiography*, p. 272). Nevertheless, since it was his principle that 'very much of a novelist's work must pertain to the intercourse between young men and women' (p. 192), he set about the work zealously, devoting many plots to the choice of the right mate, and countless scenes to tender courtships. He considered that a proposal scene should be the focus of dramatic intensity in a novel. He even took Jane Austen to task for skimping her duty in this respect. 'In the final scene between Emma and her lover', he wrote in his copy of *Emma*, '– when the conversation has become almost pathetic, – [Miss Austen] breaks away from the spoken dialogue, and simply tells us of her hero's success. This is a cowardice which robs the reader of much of the charm which he has promised himself.'[2] Trollope had a stronge sense of what the romantically inclined reader had a right to expect. And he clearly intended to satisfy the taste of such a reader.

And yet we would hardly call many of Trollope's novels 'love-stories' without serious qualification. If we want to be moved by the dramatisation of strong passion, as in *Troylus and Criseyde* or *Antony and Cleopatra*, or if we are looking for the joyous sense of comic fulfilment afforded by romantic comedy like *As You Like It*, it is hardly to Trollope's novels that we would turn. The novel *can* evoke comparable responses: I think of *Pride and Prejudice*, *Jane Eyre*, *Wuthering Heights*, *Anna Karenina*. Here we are made to feel that love is a fit subject for great art; and its consummation, whether achieved or not, is at least devoutly to be wished. But can we call *The Three Clerks*, or *Can You Forgive Her?*, or *He Knew He Was Right*, love-stories in this sense? Hardly, though undoubtedly they contain a prominent love interest. (They may be fine novels, but my present concern is limited to a particular kind of achievement.) And yet by his own account Trollope worked so hard at 'the fabrication of love-stories' (*Autobiography*, p. 294), and by his own estimation so successfully. What goes wrong?

For one thing, Trollope's loves do not engage the whole character as, say, Jane Austen's do – so that we come to feel that morally, psychologically and aesthetically these two and no others are fit for each other. Who for Elizabeth but Darcy? Or who for Jane but Rochester? 'Jane suits me: do I suit her?', asks Rochester. 'To the finest fibre of my nature, sir', responds Jane; and the novel has fully dramatised that this is so. How many of Trollope's heroines could convincingly answer in the same way? Eleanor Harding to John Bold? – or should it be Eleanor Bold to Arabin? Ayala to Jonathan Stubbs? Norah Rowley to (what's his name?) Hugh Stanbury? No. For Trollope, in fact, makes a point about the fortuitousness of love. He insists on the chancy mechanism that attracts men and women to one another, the random circumstance that anchors love in one place and not another. The women are often irrecoverably smitten by the 'first half-joking word of love' (*Doctor Thorne*, p. 352), and the men in uttering the half-joking word are usually moved by external conditions, such as contiguity, the beauty of the night or the quality of the wine.[3] This may be the way things happen in life, but it does not make for the most compelling love-story in art.

And then of course Trollope distrusts romance, and his avoidance of passionate engagement between his men and women is part and parcel of his avoidance of high rhetoric, heroes, heroines and villains. It is to be expected that he should take the sensible and down-to-earth view of love, the sceptical view of Rosalind when she tells her lover, 'Men have died from time to time and worms have eaten them, but not for love.' But this is less a limitation on the satisfying dramatisation of love than it might be. Jane Austen works within the same limitations, rejecting the high-flown rhetoric of the high mimetic mode, and yet achieves her own intensity in love-scenes which – for all Trollope's reservations about Mr Knightley's proposal – to my ear beat most of his own proposal scenes hollow.

It is fair, I think, to take *Framley Parsonage* as an example of Trollope's kind of love-story. The situation is typical, at least of the Barset novels, and Trollope was particularly proud of his management of the love between Lucy Robarts and Lord Lufton. 'It was downright honest love', he claimed in the *Autobiography*, '– in which there was no pretence on the part of the lady that she was too ethereal to be fond of a man, and no half-and-half inclination on the part of the man to pay a certain price and no more for a pretty toy. Each of them longed for the other, and they were not ashamed to say so' (*Autobiography*, pp. 123–4). But the novel does not quite live up to this claim.

Of course Trollope makes the most of the class situation. He doesn't disdain the romance plot of the low-born maiden and the prince, and our sympathy is enlisted for Lucy as it is for Pamela, and Jane Eyre and Cinderella, and all the other lowly girls who are sought out in marriage by their social superiors. But as we would expect, once he has made this initial concession to romance, he fills in the social and psychological detail thoroughly, and with an eye to all the nuances and qualifications that belong in realistic fiction. Lucy, though she cannot but be moved that a lord proposes to her, is proud of her own autonomy as an individual, and resists being swept off her feet. She refuses the lord; but nevertheless falls irreversibly in love with him as she does so (a familiar situation in Trollope's novels). At his proposal, when with a surge of power she recognises 'the game was at her feet', she is remarkably self-possessed in the midst of her contrary responses of pride and awakening love:

> She did feel her triumph; but there was nothing in her face to tell him that she did so. As to what she would now do she did not for a moment doubt. He had been precipitated into the declaration he had made not by his love, but by his embarrassment. She had thrown in his teeth the injury which he had done her [in making it appear that she had set her cap at him], and he had then been moved by his generosity to repair that injury by the noblest sacrifice which he could make. But Lucy Robarts was not the girl to accept a sacrifice. (p. 179)

So she sturdily refuses him; she even swears, with her hand on her heart, that she does not love him; and then she goes upstairs to throw herself on her bed, reproaching herself bitterly, 'Why, – oh! why had she told such a falsehood?' (p. 180). This is classic Trollope, and deservedly remembered as a great as well as a typical crisis in his works.

The conflict of passion and duty is the stuff of great love-stories – of Antony's, of Catherine Earnshaw's, of Maggie Tulliver's. And Lucy's own little agony (it does seem little in comparison with the tragic struggles of the others) is memorably dramatised. But one wishes that in Trollope's works duty would not so inevitably triumph: 'Strong as her love was', the narrator tells us of Lucy, 'yet her pride was . . . stronger' (p. 181). And so it is with all the good girls: Mary Thorne, Lucy, Grace Crawley, Isabel Boncassen all love the men who propose to them, but because the men's families disapprove, they all refuse on principle, suppressing their passion, and clinging to their determination to be right, until the families recognise that their moral rectitude makes up for their lack of social standing, and back up the young men's proposal.[4] The passion is to be allowed only when duty has been observed to the last letter. In the face of the frequent repetitions of this situation, it is difficult to suppose that the passion can have much force, if it is to be so invariably subordinated.

Then in this particular case Lucy makes her moral stand on what one can only call finicky moral grounds. At first she believes that Lufton does not really love her, so she refuses him because she will not accept his 'sacrifice'. When he proves, by a second proposal, that he means it, she shifts her ground. Because his mother, Lady Lufton, has let it be known that she would disapprove of such a match, nothing will satisfy Lucy but that Lady Lufton should climb down and actually plead for the match herself. It is surely a scruple of abnormal delicacy to insist on being proposed to by one's mother-in-law elect. One might as well expect Elizabeth Bennet to hold out for an invitation from Lady Catherine to hold the wedding at Rosings. A comparison of Lucy's behaviour with Elizabeth's, in fact, is instructive. Elizabeth, who is faced with Lady Catherine's disapproval of the proposed match with Darcy, as Lucy is faced with Lady Lufton's, is strong enough to see when she is being unwarrantably bullied by relations, and to state her own position bravely. She refuses to renounce Darcy, thus bringing down on herself Lady Catherine's accusation that she is neglecting 'the claims of duty, honour, and gratitude'. But

Elizabeth rejects this moral pressure: 'Neither duty, nor honour, nor gratitude . . . have any possible claim on me, in the present instance. No principle of either, would be violated by my marriage with Mr Darcy' (*Pride and Prejudice*, III, ch. 14). Why doesn't Lucy say that? The same is true of the proposed match between her and Lord Lufton, but with a scrupulosity that looks like moral snobbery, Lucy insists that *everybody* must approve. (It is true that Lady Lufton is a far more sympathetic character than Lady Catherine, and that Lucy owes her some allegiance; but both ladies require the heroine to subordinate her own feelings and her lover's to their authority.) Jane Austen is rejecting a tradition of sensibility according to which a heroine must be as perfectly irreproachable as Lucy. Emma, too, wryly discovers she has not 'that heroism of sentiment' to refuse Mr Knightley for Harriet's sake, 'or even the more simple sublimity of resolving to refuse him at once and forever without vouchsafing any motive' (*Emma*, III, ch. 13). In claiming that Lucy is not 'too ethereal to be fond of a man', Trollope would seem to be rejecting the same tradition. But Lucy has just that perverse heroism of sentiment and simple sublimity of unaccountable behaviour that Jane Austen mocks in the heroines of fiction. Even though Elizabeth and Emma do not discover their feelings until late in their novels, their readiness to snatch at happiness when they recognise it, and to brave a little censure, makes them more satisfying as the principals in their love-stories than Lucy with her scruples.

Nevertheless Trollope dramatises Lucy's love with great tenderness and precision. His best touches are his light ones, where instead of making assertions about the state of her feelings, he registers them indirectly. Here she feels her first stab of jealousy, but the emotion is displaced, and rendered through her conduct of the pony carriage:

> 'Do you know, I have an idea,' [Fanny Robarts] said in the pony carriage that day, 'that Lord Lufton will marry Griselda Grantly.' Lucy could not refrain from giving a little check at the reins which she was holding, and she felt that the blood rushed quickly to her heart. But she did not betray herself. 'Perhaps he may,' she said, and then gave the pony a little touch with her whip. (p. 230)

That unwarrantable treatment of Puck the pony is Trollope's

means of bringing home Lucy's emotion, of making it local and familiar. Lucy has the same instinct of attaching the concrete to the abstract, and in recollecting Lufton's proposal, the moment that for her is touched with a wonder that makes it seem unbelievable, she associates his words of love with the spot in the room where he stood, so that she will have something solid and apprehensible to keep in hand.

> 'Well, it was not a dream [she tells Fanny of his proposal]. Here, standing here, on this very spot – on that flower of the carpet – he begged me a dozen times to be his wife. I wonder whether you and Mark would let me cut it out and keep it.' (p. 288)

The proposal to cut up the carpet as a souvenir is characteristic of Lucy's most engaging characteristic, her lively faculty for self-mockery in the midst of her sorrows. She is quite a Rosalind, able to joke about her love even as it makes her wince. And in her cheerful admission of her susceptibility to Lufton's physical attractions[5] she lives up to Trollope's claim about the downright honest love.

> 'I'll tell you what he has: he has fine straight legs, and a smooth forehead, and a good-humoured eye, and white teeth. Was it possible to see such a catalogue of perfections, and not fall down, stricken to the very bone? But it was not that that did it all, Fanny. . . . It was his title that killed me. I had never spoken to a lord before. Oh, me! what a fool, what a beast I have been!' And then she burst out into tears. (p. 283)

Apart from the burst of tears, Lucy is here as piquant as Elizabeth Bennet, who confesses when pressed that her love for Darcy began when she first saw his beautiful grounds at Pemberley.

But when we turn to the other principal in this love-story we are hardly apt to be as moved or as delighted. Though Lufton is a lord ready to stoop to ask the resident clergyman's dependent sister to marry him, Trollope has emphasised his undistinguished ordinariness. And in other ways Trollope defeats and disappoints the expectations of the romantically inclined reader. We get no fierce struggles of a Darcy or a Rochester before they decide to set aside the social sanctions that make their courtships improper.

Lufton, balked of Lucy's company for a while, goes to seek her out, but without any further intention. He simply drifts towards his proposal:

> He hardly knew what it was for the saying of which he had so resolutely come thither. He had by no means made up his mind that he loved Lucy Robarts; nor had he made up his mind that, loving her, he would, or that, loving her, he would not, make her his wife. (p. 175)

He might almost be plucking the petals off a daisy to discover if he loves her, or he loves her not. Then because of certain almost accidental turns in the conversation, and also because Lucy gives him no encouragement, he improvises a fine proposal speech. She prudently tells him not to address her by her first name, and in a spirit of contentiousness he bursts out, 'By heavens! but it shall be Lucy – Lucy before all the world. My Lucy, my own Lucy – my heart's best friend, and chosen love. Lucy, there is my hand. How long you may have had my heart it matters not to say now' (p. 179). How long? Well, now, should we say five minutes? Or, since Lufton seems to make things up as he goes along, would thirty seconds be more accurate? 'It matters not', he says. The poetic inversion suggests that Lucy at least, probably Lufton himself, and possibly even the reader, are meant to be moved by his declaration. But in view of the information we have been given on Lufton's perfectly uncommitted state, his implied claim of a lasting devotion is utterly discredited. Are we supposed to laugh, just 'when the conversation has become almost pathetic'?

Lufton's downright honest love does not preclude his dangling in the same uncommitted way after an alternative wife. Despite Trollope's claim that 'there was no half-and-half inclination on the part of the man', a half-and-half inclination is exactly what he has presented. Trollope is careful to let us know that Lufton feels nothing at all for his mother's candidate for his hand, Griselda Grantly, except a distant admiration for her beauty. And yet but for chance he might have made her Lady Lufton instead of Lucy.

> Had she been one whit more animated, or had his mother's tactics been but a thought better concealed, Griselda might have been asked that night to share the vacant throne at Lufton, in

> spite of all that had been said and sworn in the drawing-room of Framley parsonage. (p. 220)

It is only by such featherweight influences that Lufton is moved to marry Lucy rather than the marble-hearted Griselda. It is hardly satisfactory for the reader of a love-story to have to do with a lover who plays eeny-meeny-miny-mo with his girls in this way.

But there is another qualification in the Lucy–Lord Lufton match that is also typical of Trollope, and it has to do with the consummation of their love. In the final chapter occurs this rather unpleasant passage:

> But it was October before Lord Lufton was made a happy man; – that is, if the fruition of his happiness was a greater joy than the anticipation of it. I will not say that the happiness of marriage is like the Dead Sea fruit – an apple which, when eaten, turns to bitter ashes in the mouth. Such pretended sarcasm would be very false. Nevertheless, is it not the fact that the sweetest morsel of love's feast has been eaten, that the freshest, fairest blush of the flower has been snatched and has passed away, when the ceremony at the altar has been performed, and legal possession has been given? There is an aroma of love, an undefinable delicacy of flavour, which escapes and is gone before the church portal is left, vanishing with the maiden name, and incompatible with the solid comfort appertaining to the rank of wife. To love one's own spouse, and to be loved by her, is the ordinary lot of man, and is a duty exacted under penalties. . . . No; when the husband walks back from the altar, he has already swallowed the choicest dainties of his banquet. (pp. 522–3)

In a way this resembles the ending to *Vanity Fair* ('Which of us has his desire? or, having it, is satisfied?'), and Trollope may have been influenced by Thackeray here.[6] But the love of Amelia and Dobbin has been treated ironically throughout, and Thackeray's ending is of a piece with that treatment, as well as with the theme and tone of the rest of his novel; whereas Trollope has offered us Lucy and Lufton as romantic comedy, and this passage, with its distasteful imagery of consumption and nausea and defloration, jars with the story he has tried to sustain of a downright honest love.

Similar imagery is frequently attached to an achieved love in his novels. Women may be casually seen as desirable dishes,

> whom men, with tastes that way given, feel inclined to take up and devour on the spur of the moment. . . . They are like water when one is athirst, like plovers' eggs in March, like cigars when one is out in the autumn. No one ever dreams of denying himself when such temptation comes in his way. (*Phineas Finn*, I, pp. 22–3)

But once the male has devoured them he is apt to be sickened, or to find some fault with the dainties that have now ceased to be dainties. The flower imagery recurs too. Of Carry Brattle in *The Vicar of Bullhampton*, the vicar reflects,

> There is a bloom on the flower which may rest there until the flower has utterly perished, if the handling of it be sufficiently delicate; – but no care, nothing that can be done by friends on earth, or even by better friendship from above, can replace that when once displaced. (p. 195)

Carry Brattle is a fallen women, and although Trollope is trying to be liberal on this issue it is perhaps to be expected that he will talk about lost bloom in this context. But apparently an innocent girl like Lucy loses her bloom at marriage too, for at the very altar 'the freshest, fairest blush of the flower has been snatched and has passed away'. And it does not take the loss of virginity to lose this bloom. Lady Mabel Grex in *The Duke's Children*, who has merely refused to marry a man she loves and *considered* marrying someone else, is also blighted, despoiled, deflowered.

> The sweet bloom of her maiden shame . . . of which she quite understood the sweetness, the charm, the value – was gone when she had brought herself to such a state that any human being should know that, loving one man, she should be willing to marry another. (II, p. 181)

Hence the rule that pertains with astonishing consistency in Trollope's works that a woman must be allowed to love only once and for all.[7] A second love would be rather disgusting, as coming from damaged goods. But even a first love when consummated can seem disgusting in some of Trollope's moods.

One can only call this degree of concern about purity fanatic. It is an attitude that Meredith memorably exposed when he attached it to his egoist, Sir Willoughby Patterne. Sir Willoughly successfully courts the beautiful and vivacious Constantia Durham, to whom one Captain Oxford has also paid court. In spite of his success, Sir Willoughby is offended.

> She had been nibbled at, all but eaten up, while he hung dubitative. . . . She had not come to him out of cloistral purity, out of perfect radiancy. . . . He wished for her to have come to him out of an egg-shell, somewhat more astonished at things than a chicken, but as completely enclosed before he tapped the shell, and seeing him with her sex's eyes first of all men. (*The Egoist*, ch. 3)

This attitude is of course part of Willoughby's egoism, his need to be first and foremost, to fill the entire vision of his chick from the egg, like a god. But it is also a rather repellent sensuality in him to like his women to be so pure that they resist even *his* caresses. When his next fiancée, Clara Middleton, shrinks from his sexual advances, he is delighted. 'Sir Willoughby was enraptured with her. Even so purely, coldly, statue-like, Dian-like, would he have prescribed his bride's reception of his caress' (ch. 7). How far Trollope shared these rather perverse tastes of Sir Willoughby we cannot know. But more than he would admit, I suspect.

If the woman is not pure, she is dangerous. And just as we get imagery of defloration and poison attached to the women who have ceased to be fresh from the egg, so we get the familiar imagery of entrapment and castration that goes with the engaged man.[8] Crosbie, newly engaged to Lily Dale, feels that he is being 'presented . . . as a victim caught for the sacrifice, bound with ribbon for the altar' (*The Small House at Allington*, I, p. 116). The wild and peremptory Lord Chiltern, once he has been accepted by Violet Effingham, kneels at her feet, and she tells him, 'You are like Samson with his locks shorn, or Hercules with a distaff' (*Phineas Finn*, II, p. 152). Paul Montague, in *The Way We Live Now*, notices a triumphant exchange of smiles among the women when he is admitted as an accepted lover, and the narrator sympathises with such males: 'We have felt that something of ridicule was intended, because we have been regarded as cocks with their spurs cut away' (I, p. 258). The engaged man, we hear in *Ayala's Angel*, feels as though he has been 'brought at length into a cage and tamed' (p. 628). In *The American Senator* there is a whole sub-plot concerned with hunting which is designed to emphasise Arabella Trefoil's ruthless pursuit of Lord Rufford, for she actually performs the manoeuvres of her manhunt while fox-hunting, by riding with him, borrowing his horses and fainting in his arms after a fatiguing day in the field. Lord Rufford recognises 'he was being hunted and run down' (p. 307). And though he successfully evades this danger, he finally succumbs to a patient fisherwoman, the quiet but cunning Miss Penge, and finds himself 'hooked' (p. 513).

Whenever a love is successful, that is, it seems likely to turn nasty, and the happy ending is apt to be qualified by some twinge of nausea or horror. This vision of love bears some relation to that in Shakespeare's bitterest sonnet:

> Enjoyed no sooner but despisèd straight,
> Past reason hunted, and no sooner had,
> Past reason hated, as a swallowed bait.

Of course this is not Trollope's total vision of love, for it remains lurking in his imagery and in half-buried local comments, rather than in the main structure of his fables. But it is certainly an aspect of his vision, and one that tends to make his novels less than satisfactory as love-stories.

Because of Trollope's involuntary distrust of love fulfilled, it is perhaps to be expected that he should be best able to move us by the depiction of love denied. Lady Laura's long and bitter passion for Phineas Finn, an adulterous love that she at first does not recognise, and then suppresses, and then goes on to express and even to parade, is a triumph in the delineation of irrepressible passion. 'It was not my engagement or my marriage that had made the world a blank for me', she tells him, when she is separated from her husband. 'It was, and has been, and still will be my strong, unalterable, unquenchable love for you' (*Phineas Redux*, I, pp. 123–4). And that love is movingly and successfully dramatised – partly, one suspects, because it is unreciprocated.

It sometimes seems in Trollope's novels that the most irresistibly endearing action a girl can take is to reject her suitor. By that means she enormously increases her desirability, and her suitor is almost bound to ask her again and again (thus giving Trollope renewed opportunities for the proposal scenes on which he prided himself); for 'the flight of the quarry ever adds eagerness to the pursuit of the huntsman' (*Doctor Thorne*, p. 348). Another long-term unconsummated love that is successfully dramatised is Johnny Eames's persistent and occasionally rather ludicrous courtship of Lily Dale. Johnny is ruefully aware that he has become a byword among all his acquaintances and Lily's as the perpetual lover endlessly dangling after a perpetually reluctant lady. But Trollope marvellously captures the tone of mournful tenderness that characterises Johnny's meditations on his love. After one of his many unsuccessful proposals he constructs a long-term fantasy of his own love-story:

> He thought that he would write to her every year, on the same day of the year, year after year, it might be for the next twenty years. And his letters should be very simple. Sitting there on the gate he planned the wording of his letters; – of his first letter, and of his second, and of his third. They should be very like to each other, – should hardly be more than a repetition of the same words. 'If now you are ready for me, then, Lily, am I, as ever, still ready for you.' And then 'if now' again, and again 'if now'; – and still 'if now.' When his hair should be grey, and the wrinkles on his cheeks, – ay, though they should be on hers, he would still continue to tell her from year to year that he was ready to take her. . . .
>
> Such letters as those she would surely keep. Then he looked forward, down into the valley of coming years, and fancied her as she might sit reading them in the twilight of some long evening, – letters which had been written all in vain. He thought that he could look forward with some satisfaction towards the close of his own career, in having been the hero of such a love-story. . . . And then as he remembered that he was only twenty-seven and that she was twenty-four, he began to marvel at the feeling of grey old age which had come upon him. (*The Last Chronicle of Barset*, I, pp. 372–3)

Such a passage achieves the pathos that Trollope considered to be a necessary constituent of the novel, and none the less for the gentle irony at Johnny's expense, as he sees himself as the hero of this melancholy tale. Trollope can move us with the pain of a disappointed lover as he can seldom stir us with the joy of an accepted one.

Does Trollope ever successfully dramatise a great love that is joyfully consummated, in the manner of romantic comedy? It seems to me that his best love-story, and one that is almost free of the uncomfortable qualifications of the *Framley Parsonage* class of novels, is *The Belton Estate*, which he wrote in 1865, after all the Barset novels except *The Last Chronicle of Barset*, and after the first of the Palliser series. This has never been a novel much admired, either by the original reviewers or by subsequent critics,[9] and Trollope himself spoke slightingly of it. Nevertheless in a consideration of Trollope as a writer of love-stories it has a special place, for it almost symmetrically reverses the pattern of the love relationships in *Framley Parsonage*, and is a fervent endorsement of a passionate and ultimately fulfilled love. One might call it Trollope's *Wuthering Heights*: Clara Amedroz, like Catherine Earnshaw with Edgar Linton and Heathcliffe, is to choose between the refined and passionless Captain Aylmer, MP, and her turbulent, headstrong, passionate cousin, the farmer Will Belton. And whereas in such novels as *Can You Forgive Her?* Trollope had been prudently on the side of the tame man against the wild man, here with a fervour almost reminiscent of D. H. Lawrence he champions the physical earthy force represented by Will.

Clara is no innocent brown girl of Barsetshire like Lucy, but a woman of twenty-six who takes some of her colouring from the time-worn and depleted estate she lives on. Like Lucy and the other nice girls, she holds the familiar Trollopian belief about woman's constancy; but she is shown to be mistaken. 'Clara knew, or thought that she knew, that men and women differed in their appreciation of love. She, having once loved, could not change. Of that she was sure' (p. 76). And so, having been once attracted to Captain Aylmer, she assumes that she must accept him when he offers, and reject all other comers. She has 'taught herself' this doctrine, as she has 'taught herself' that she loves Will Belton only as a brother (p. 296);[10] but these are the maxims she has to abandon in order to follow the more reliable dictates of instinct. When she has broken her engagement she does indeed feel 'feminine shame' (p. 373), and the need to be punished for her inconstancy (p. 403). But she does not remain long in this condition – not nearly so long as the fanatically self-condemnatory Emily Lopez in *The Prime*

Minister, for instance – and at the last she joyfully accepts Will Belton.

In that moral crux of reconciling herself with her suitor's family, in which every good Barset heroine triumphs through submitting, Clara is fiercely recalcitrant. In this case, as in Lucy's, the suitor's mother is hostile to the match and inclined to bully her son's proposed bride. But we have none of Lucy's readiness to sacrifice her love to a disapproving relative. And after a stormy stay at her fiancé's home, she turns the tables utterly on Lady Aylmer by delivering her own ultimatum: 'I shall let Captain Alymer know that our engagement must be at an end, unless he will promise that I shall never in future be subjected to the unwarrantable insolence of his mother' (p. 347). Clara strikes out her own moral course and is ready to bear some disapproval.

We find again the usual doctrine about the flight of the quarry adding eagerness to the pursuit of the huntsman, but this time it is presented not just as a piece of general wisdom from the narrator, but as a doctrine dramatically located in a faulty character. When Clara accepts Captain Aylmer without hesitation and at the first asking, he is immediately contemptuous of her.

> What is there that any man desires . . . that does not lose half its value when it is found to be easy of access and easy of possession? Wine is valued by its price, not its flavour. . . . Captain Aylmer, when he heard the hearty tone of the girl's answer, already began almost to doubt whether it was wise on his part to devote the innermost bin of his cellar to wine that was so cheap. (p. 126)

The familiar image of woman as consumable, and as likely to leave a nasty taste in the mouth like Dead Sea fruit or cheap wine, is less a part of the author's vision than Captain Aylmer's, who is seen as despicable for it. Likewise it is Aylmer who, once he is engaged, considers that he is being made a 'sacrifice' (p. 133).

Neither of Clara's men goes dangling after other women as Lufton does. Here it is the woman who hesitates between two men. But Lufton's indecisiveness is a matter of casual non-commitment, and so destroys the reader's belief in his downright honest love (if he does not care, why should we?); whereas Clara's hesitation is an absorbing crisis that fully engages her (and therefore us). Of course she does not have Lucy's charm and vitality. But she is grown up and responsible, and ready to shoulder her share of blame in a fallen world. She breaks her mistaken engagement to Aylmer, and finally commits herself joyfully to Will, whom she has loved all along.

The two suitors are effectively contrasted to represent the conflict of reason and passion, duty and instinct, mind and body – the familiar opposition of Linton and Heathcliff, St John Rivers and Rochester, Angel Clare and Alec D'Urberville, Clifford Chatterley and Mellors. And this time all Trollope's sympathies are on the passional, instinctual, physical side. Aylmer is characterised as effetely civilised, a stickler for equity without generosity, an observer of forms without conviction, a suitor without desire: 'A cold-blooded fish of a man, who thinks of nothing in the world but being respectable', as Will describes him (p. 264). It is appropriate that in his half-hearted courtship he should need the stimulus of the lady's playing hard to get.

Will Belton, on the other hand, is one of the most outspokenly passionate lovers among Trollope's males. When the two suitors have dinner together with Clara, Aylmer behaves impeccably, whereas Will in his extremity breaks a wine glass, spills the coffee and inappropriately bursts out with a declaration of his love. And 'There were symptoms throughout the dinner that the untamed man was longing to fly at the throat of the man that was tamed' (pp. 315–16).

For all the exaggerated scruples of many of his women, Trollope shows them to be highly susceptible to masculine beauty. And like many of Trollope's men – Phineas, Burgo Fitzgerald, Sir Felix Carbury – Will is handsome. But more than the others he is seen in strongly physical terms. He is usually vigorously active – busy at farm work, loading dung, walking sixteen miles in three hours, driving his dog-cart sharply round corners. He is precipitate in action and forceful in language. He is connected with images of fertility: we early hear of him as throwing 'his seed corn into the earth' (p. 46), and of his ploughing the fields; his love is strongly associated with the land, with the two estates of Belton and Plaistow that he tills and tends, and it appropriately follows the cycle of the seasons,[11] culminating in marriage at harvest time (p. 429). The vigorous force of his passion is of a piece with his intense physicality. He is very different from the long array of feeble, vacillating males like Lord Lufton, Frank Greystock, Ralph Newton and so on, who are like moths fluttering from one candle to another. Will is a whole-hearted, unwavering lover who proposes to Clara two days after he has met her, keeps blurting out his love in season and out, and once, Heathcliff-like, snatches her in his arms and kisses her fiercely although she is by law committed to another man. (And Catherine-like, Clara enjoys it.) Trollope has succeeded here in suggesting something elemental in Will's love. There is a force in the rendering that exceeds the gentle tenderness of the delineation of Johnny Eames's long-drawn-out courtship.

> He loved her. He could not get over it. The passion . . . was with him when he was hunting. He was ever thinking of it when the bird rose before his gun. As he watched the furrow, as his men and horses would drive it straight and deep through the ground, he was thinking of her. (p. 253)

Trollope does not often venture on so outright and unqualified a representation of love in a man. And it is a love that is mutual, joyfully consummated and almost without the disenchanting suggestion that the dainties of the feast are now consumed or the male's proud masculinity quelled.[12] For once passion triumphs. *The Belton Estate* is a remarkably concentrated novel for Trollope, too, having no sub-plot, and with a high proportion of dramatised scene to narration summary. And the concentration and consequent intensity of effect are undoubtedly an advantage in a novel that is primarily a love-story.

And yet Trollope treated *The Belton Estate* as something of an outcast among his numerous literary offspring. Although he claimed in the *Autobiography* to remember the hundreds of characters in his fiction with the fondness of a parent, he said of this novel,

> It has no peculiar merits, and will add nothing to my reputation as a novelist. I have not looked at it since it was published; and now turning back to it in my memory, I seem to remember almost less of it than of any book that I have written. (p. 168)

He evidently preferred that his reputation as a fabricator of love-stories should rest on the *Framley Parsonage* kind of novel. And inasmuch as *The Belton Estate* constitutes a kind of recantation of the attitudes embodied in Lucy and Lord Lufton, in the *Autobiography* he recants his recantation.

Of course we do not want Trollope to be constantly writing Trollopian versions of *Wuthering Heights*; we go to his novels for other things, and we find them in abundance. But inside Trollope the realist, who eschewed romance and distrusted passion, was another Trollope who might have written another kind of novel, and who occasionally did so. (It is interesting that when he wrote the anonymous novels *Nina Balatka* and *Linda Tressel*, with the aim of 'obtaining a second identity', he permitted himself, he said, 'more of romance proper than has been usual with me' (*Autobiography*, pp. 175–7). But this other Trollope was kept on a tight rein. The more official Trollope was anxious about sex, and sceptical of the joyful consummation that is an essential part of romantic comedy. And when he turned his hand to the love part of the business, he generally wrote stories which, however charming, however moral, however true to life, fall short of success as essays in the genre of the love-story.

NOTES

1. I use the Oxford World's Classics Editions of Trollope's novels, where possible. The present quotation from the *Autobiography* is from the revised edition (London, 1953) p. 123. Subsequent page references will be given in the text. A version of this paper was delivered at the Trollope Centenary Conference at London University in June 1982.
2. See Trollope's annotated copy of *Emma* in the Robert H. Taylor collection at Princeton.
3. I have discussed this aspect of the relation of men and women in Trollope's work in *Trollope's Palliser Novels: Theme and Pattern* (London, 1978) pp. 155ff.
4. Hugh Walpole points out with exasperation that many of Trollope's heroines, including Mary Thorne, Lily Dale and Grace Crawley, 'do nothing else for hundreds and hundreds of pages but refuse their patient and persistent lovers' (*Anthony Trollope*, London, 1928, p. 53). See also E. L. Skinner, in a similarly impatient consideration of 'Mr Trollope's Young Ladies', *Nineteenth-Century Fiction*, 6 (1949) 197–207.
5. In 'Trollope's "Most Natural English Girl" ', *Nineteenth-Century Fiction*, 28 (1974) 477–485, John Glavin has shown how Lucy's vitality and her love are connected with the seasonal cycle, and with motifs of death, birth and fertility.
6. James Kincaid sees this passage as part of Trollope's strategy to 'open the closed form' of the novel by qualifying the conventional happy ending; see *The Novels of Anthony Trollope* (Oxford, 1977) pp. 40–2.

7. See David Aitken in 'Anthony Trollope and "The Genus Girl" ', *Nineteenth-Century Fiction*, 28 (1974) 425: 'It is Trollope's idea that woman, unlike man, can love but once, and that indeed she will love her first lover forever even if she does not wish to.' There are notable exceptions, like Glencora, Alice Vavasor, and also Clara Amedroz, whom I consider below.
8. See ibid., pp. 431–2.
9. See, for instance, Kincaid, *The Novels of Anthony Trollope*, p. 88: 'Despite its complexity, the novel has always seemed to be among Trollope's most forgettable.' Henry James's review in *The Nation* (4 January 1866) is memorably hostile: 'To be involved in one of [Trollope's] love stories is very like sinking into a gentle slumber. . . . "The Belton Estate" is a *stupid* book.' See *Anthony Trollope: The Critical Heritage*, ed. Donald Smalley (London, 1969) pp. 255, 257.
10. As Walter M. Kendrick has pointed out in *The Novel Machine: The Theory and Fiction of Anthony Trollope* (Baltimore, 1980), p. 88, 'Trollope's . . . characters are never more wrong than when they teach themselves something.'
11. See Kincaid, *The Novels of Anthony Trollope*, p. 90.
12. Trollope is still Trollope, and does not entirely avoid his customary imagery. Clara jokingly tells Will once she has accepted him that he 'has fallen into a trap' (p. 422), and Mrs Askerton tells her, 'it's always as well to catch your fish when you can' (p. 429). But there is no indication that Will himself considers his position as successful suitor in these terms.

10

Under the Greenwood Tree and the Victorian Pastoral

LAWRENCE JONES

In his correspondence with Macmillan & Co. in 1871 concerning the possible publication of *Under the Greenwood Tree*, Thomas Hardy made clear that he considered the story to be of a given genre, a 'pastoral', 'entirely a story of rural life', and that he had undertaken this genre because reviews of his first novel, *Desperate Remedies*, convinced him that 'a story wholly of this tone' would be 'the *safest* venture'.[1] Writing in 1872 to William Tinsley, the book's eventual publisher, he confirmed that he had attempted 'this class of writing' with its given 'manner & subject' because critics had been 'unanimous' in saying that he was 'strongest' in that area.[2] This correspondence, then, indicates both that *Under the Greenwood Tree* was written in response to the criticism of Hardy's earlier work and that it was conceived of as an example of a recognised genre, the Victorian pastoral. This essay will briefly review the first point and then focus on the second.

I

When in 1868 Hardy had taken the advice of Chapman and Hall's reader, George Meredith, not to ' "nail his colours to the mast" so definitely in a first book', and had withdrawn *The Poor Man and the Lady* from consideration for publication,[3] he seemed to distinguish two commercially viable options before him. On the one hand, he could take Meredith's advice and attempt a novel with 'a purely artistic purpose', focusing on 'a more complicated plot', which he interpreted as meaning a sensation novel;[4] or, he could follow up the implicit suggestions of Alexander and Malcolm

Macmillan, and of John Morley, Macmillan's reader, to develop further the pictures of country life from the opening sections of *The Poor Man and the Lady*, which they had found 'strong and fresh' and 'admirable'.[5] Hardy seemed first to take up the second option, for he wrote to Alexander Macmillan in September 1868 that he was going to begin 'hunting up matter for another tale, which would consist entirely of rural scenes and humble life', and in an interview years later he said that he had actually completed 'about half' of this new work (which was to become *Under the Greenwood Tree*) before he put it aside.[6] However, he then decided to go ahead with Meredith's suggestion, and the result was *Desperate Remedies*, which he completed early in 1870, and which Tinsley Brothers published in March 1871 (but only when Hardy advanced a guarantee against loss). Hardy seems to have planned to follow this up with another sensation novel which he outlined,[7] but the cutting review of *Desperate Remedies* in the *Spectator* by John Hutton sent him back to the idea of a pastoral novel.[8] The only part of the novel that Hutton had liked were the scenes of country life which, although 'few and slight', none the less 'indicated powers that might and ought to be extended largely in this direction'.[9] The *Athenaeum* had also praised those scenes as being 'almost worthy of George Eliot',[10] and, taking up these hints, Hardy returned to his half-finished pastoral, completed it in four months and submitted it to Macmillan.

Even then the sailing was not smooth, for Macmillan put off any definite acceptance of the book. Morley in his reader's report praised the story as 'natural and delicate', but found it 'wanting in the fine poetic breath which gives such charm to George Sand's work in the same kind' and too lengthy and detailed in its opening scenes, while Malcolm Macmillan found that despite the 'charming writing' it contained, it would be felt 'very slight and rather unexciting by the reading public'.[11] Taking their reservations as a refusal, Hardy put the manuscript aside, but then resuscitated it five months later for submission to Tinsley, who accepted it. In the interim, he may have attempted to add a bit of 'excitement' by emphasising more the threat to the love-affair of Dick Dewey and Fancy Day posed by Parson Maybold, for the manuscript indicates that four of the five passages in the first part of the book that deal with Parson Maybold's interest in Fancy are probably later additions.[12] The novel, then, was conceived and perhaps revised to comply with the comments of reviewers and editors, and, as we shall see, was consciously written as much to the generic prescription of the Victorian 'prose idyll' as *Desperate Remedies* had been to the prescription of the Victorian sensation novel.[13]

II

If Hardy saw *Under the Greenwood Tree* as a 'pastoral', 'a little rural story', 'this class of writing', or, later, an 'idyll',[14] it is clear that his contemporaries similarly assumed a recognised generic identity. From Morley's contrast of the book in 1871 to 'George Sand's work in the same kind' to W. P. Trent's description of it in 1892 as an 'idyll' distinctly better than 'most genre sketches of the modern school',[15] Victorian critics and publishers clearly saw it in terms of a conventional genre. Thus Tinsley called it 'the best little prose idyll [he] had ever read'; Hardy's friend Horace Moule reviewed it as 'the best prose idyll we have seen for a long while past'; Leon Boucher used it as a prime exhibit in an 1875 article on 'Le Roman Pastoral en Angleterre' in 1875; Charles Kegan Paul in 1881 called it 'a most delightful idyll, in the true sense of that much-suffering word'; Coventry Patmore in 1887 praised it as 'a prose-idyll which deserves to rank with the *Vicar of Wakefield*'; and J. M. Barrie wrote in 1889 that 'perhaps since Goldsmith's death there has been no such idyll of country life'.[16]

Hardy's contemporaries, then, agreed that the novel was an example of a recognised although perhaps relatively rarely practised genre. The models that they had in mind seemed to be Goldsmith, the George Eliot of *Adam Bede* and the Rainbow scenes of *Silas Marner* and George Sand. George Eliot was perhaps the primary model. The *Athenaeum* had mentioned George Eliot in relation to Clerk Crickett in *Desperate Remedies*, and Moule had localised the comparison to Mr Macy in *Silas Marner*.[17] In reviewing *Under the Greenwood Tree*, Moule again pointed to *Silas Marner*, this time Mr Snell (in relation to Reuben Dewy), and Patmore and Barrie also referred to the same book, as did the *Saturday Review* in 1875 when it called *Under the Greenwood Tree* 'a series of rustic sketches – Dutch paintings of English country scenes after the manner of *Silas Marner*'.[18] More generally, the *Pall Mall Gazette* commented in 1873 that 'there are chapters in "Under the Greenwood Tree" which rival the most admirable rustic pieces of George

Eliot herself'.[19] Similarly, the London *Standard*, in a review quoted by Tinsley in an advertisement for the book, stated that 'for light, happy touches of life and humour we know of no rustic dialogues to be compared with these but in the earlier and best pages of George Eliot'.[20] Boucher similarly noted that in viewing Hardy's rustics 'one is involuntarily reminded of the farmers of George Eliot', for 'the principal characters of *Under the Greenwood Tree* are of the same race'.[21] The *Spectator* was less generous, stating that 'if it had not been for George Eliot's works, we should not, we are inclined to think, have had *Under the Greenwood Tree*'. George Eliot was referred to in that review as 'the author of "Adam Bede" ', but it is clear from a reference to 'taprooms' that it was the Rainbow sequence in *Silas Marner* that the reviewer had in mind.[22]

George Sand was almost as significant a generic model. Patricia Thomson has demonstrated her status to the Victorians as a contemporary model for the pastoral,[23] and Hardy's readers certainly had her in mind. As we have seen, Morley saw Hardy's work as in the 'same kind' and recommended that Hardy 'study' her best work. In 1876 Leslie Stephen made a similar suggestion, noting that her work had 'a certain affinity' to his, and commenting that although Hardy could not hope to 'equal her in her own line', he could aim at a similar 'harmony and grace'.[2 Among reviewers, Andrew Lang in 1875 compared *Far from the Madding Crowd* unfavourably with her work, while in 1883 Havelock Ellis was more positive, finding *Under the Greenwood Tree* 'a sketch of the freshest and most delightful order, only comparable if at all, with the best of George Sand's rural studies, with *La Mar au Diable*'.[25]

Underlying the generic attribution of *Under the Greenwood Tre* is an understood definition of the genre of 'prose idyll', a definition that implied a reconciliation of the traditional pastoral idyll and the realistic novel. The *locus classicus* for such a definition is, of course, Chapter 17 of *Adam Bede*, with its insistence on 'faithful pictures of a monotonous homely existence'. However, while George Eliot prescribed the general area of the subject matter some of her critics seemed to think that she was too inclusive in her treatment of it, too unsparing in her realism. Thus the *Saturda Review* had complained of *Adam Bede* that 'The degree of horro and painfulness is . . . out of keeping with the calm simplicity o rural life', for although such incidents as Hetty Sorrel's seductio and consequent child-murder might be 'within the bounds of fact', these 'startling horrors of rustic reality' should be kept out of a 'picture of village character and village humour'.[26] That is, as Michael Squires has noted, the realism of the pastoral novel should be selective, stripping country life of 'its coarsest features' to make it acceptable to urban readers.[27] Hardy indicated his awareness of the need for such selective realism in the pastoral in writing of William Barnes's work. He noted in 1879 that Barnes's subject matter was the common reality called for by George Eliot, 'incidents . . . of everyday life, cottagers' sorrows and cottagers' joys', but idealised in that they were 'tinged throughout with that golden glow . . . which art can project upon the commonest things'.[28] In 1918 he noted the selection involved in such art, contrasting Barnes, who 'held himself artistically aloof from the ugly side of things', with George Crabbe, who revealed 'sordid miseries . . . often to the destruction of charm'.[29]

'Charm' relates to another aspect of the pastoral as understood by the Victorians – its tone. In the contemporary reviews of George Eliot's early works, repeatedly the operative words are 'charming' and 'quaint', both implying the traditional pastoral tone of a sophisticated writer speaking to a sophisticated audience about simple people, usually with an element of condescension in the attitude towards the subject. Leslie Stephen's obituary essay on George Eliot is perhaps the definitive Victorian statement, with its preference for the early works because of their 'charm' and 'idyllic effects' based on an awareness of 'those quaint aspects of the little world . . . which only show their quaintness to the cultivated intellect'.[30] Hardy was quite aware that he had adopted this tone in relation to country life and characters. Thus in his letter to Macmillan accompanying the manuscript, he stated that 'the attempt has been to draw the characters humorously, without caricature', and went on to speak of reasons for attempting 'a story wholly of this *tone*' (my italics).[31] In later years he several times apologised for the tone and the resultant failure to 'probe life so deeply' (as he said of Barnes in relation to Crabbe).[32] Thus he was reported in the *Life* as having implied that he had condescended to the choir, making them too humorous, and blamed 'never having seen or heard the choir as such, they ending their office when he was about a year old':

He was accustomed to say that on this account he had rather

burlesqued them, the story not so adequately reflecting as he could have wished in later years the poetry and romance that coloured their time-honoured observances.[33]

In his 1912 Preface, he implied that the limitations of the genre and the audience were to blame for the tone:

> In rereading the narrative after a long interval there occurs the inevitable reflection that the realities out of which it was spun were material for another kind of study of this little group of church musicians than is found in the chapters here penned so lightly, even so farcically and flippantly at times. But circumstances would have rendered any aim at a deeper, more essential, more transcendent handling unadvisable at the date of writing.[34]

Those 'circumstances' almost certainly included the reviews and the responses from publishers' readers that had made Hardy decide in mid-1871 that 'a pastoral story would be the *safest* venture'. The tone of apology and the sense of writing within a circumscribed genre also appeared in his speech given at a performance of the dramatisation of the novel in 1910, when he called it a 'comedy', made his usual remark about comedy being superficial compared to tragedy, and ended by saying that 'to-night, at any rate, we will all be young and not look too deeply'.[35]

If Hardy and his contemporaries had a clear idea of the tone and subject matter appropriate to the pastoral, so also they had a concept of appropriate structure. Hardy's subtitle, *A Rural Painting of the Dutch School*, picks up George Eliot's comparisons in *Adam Bede* and makes explicit the generic expectation of a series of relatively static pictures or sketches. At least from the time of *Daphnis and Chloe* such pictures were held together by the narrative string of a love-story in the mode of New Comedy, and, as we shall see, Hardy's readers expected this of him and he was aware of the expectation.

Thus, although the pastoral was not as clear cut or popular a genre as the sensation novel, Hardy and his readers would have had an adequate sense of what was meant by 'a pastoral story' or a 'prose idyll' – a novel about everyday rural life, presented with a kind of understanding sympathetic realism as charming and quaintly humorous, seen from the outside in a series of typical genre pictures, held together by an uncomplicated love-story. And this, of course, is exactly what Hardy presented his readers with in *Under the Greenwood Tree*, as the reviewers were quick to point out.

Humble rural life of the sort that was praised in *The Poor Man and the Lady* and *Desperate Remedies* is the almost exclusive concern of the story. The ordinary quality of the characters is clear from the first, emphasised in the four uses of 'ordinary' in the opening description of Dick Dewy (I, ch. 1). The events are likewise the typical happenings of the sort that Barnes deals with in his poetry: the quire's Christmas Eve rounds and party (see Barnes's 'Hallowed Plëaces', 'Keepen' up o' Chris'mas' and 'Chris'mas Invitation'); the courting during honey-taking, nutting and the drive from town (see Barnes's 'Out A-Nutten', 'Meaken up a Miff', and 'A Bit o' Sly Coorten'); the wedding day (see 'Jeane's Wedden Day in Mornen').

This everyday rural life of the quire and the courtship is presented with an appropriate sympathetic realism, as W. P. Trent noted in 1892, stating that Hardy is 'realistic, but at the same time idealistic'.[36] The realism is more inclusive, the idealisation less than in Barnes, as one can see by putting the descriptions of the church services next to Barnes's 'Church on Happy Zunday' or the character of Fancy next to the subject of 'The Maid for My Bride'.[37] But the element of idealisation is still there in both the selection and the treatment. It is there partly in the choice of a remembered past, fulfilling Squires's dictum that the modern pastoral should make a 'retreat' to 'a life of harmony existing in an actual past'.[38] The harmony is maintained by a further selection, the omission of the less positive aspects of rural life dealt with in Hardy's later novels – poverty, hard labour, illegitimacy, drink, family friction. Tess's Marlott and Flintcombe-Ash may be only a few miles and two generations from Dick's Mellstock, but the distance in the conventions of treatment is much greater.

Hardy accomplishes this avoidance of the ugly partly by social selection; as Moule stated, the book is made up of 'studies of the better class of rustics'.[39] The characters are drawn from what Hardy in 1927 distinguished as the higher of the 'two distinct Castes' of village life in the nineteenth century, the 'artisans, traders, "liviers" ' rather than the ' "work-folk" '.[40] Mrs Dewy, for example, prides herself on never saying 'taties' in 'a work-folk way', but rather always saying ' "taters", and very often "pertatoes'' outright' (I, ch. 8). More seriously, the main obstacle to Dick's and Fanny's romance is the further class distinction made by the Days, who consider themselves above the villagers, on the brink of the middle class, so that their daughter might marry a gentleman (and she almost does, although Parson Maybold considers her below him). Geoffrey Day's concern with money (and a first wife who was a governess) is matched by the second Mrs Day's humorous sense of being more respectable than the rest of the parish (similar to the prejudice of George Eliot's Dodsons in *The Mill on the Floss*). The two families upon which Hardy concentrates, then, come from the middle and upper strata of village society.

Hardy has avoided 'the ugly side of things' not only in his selection of the 'better class of rustics' but also in his treatment of them. For a 'deeper, more transcendent, more essential handling' of them might have uncovered painful areas of their lives. Mrs Day, for example, might have been presented as painfully difficult for her family to live with, as George Eliot had shown what difficulties the Dodsons caused Maggie Tulliver. However, she is treated almost entirely humorously. There is only a hint of the cost for others of her behaviour, when Fancy is shown thinking 'of how weary she was of living alone; how unbearable it would be to return to Yalbury under the rule of her strange-tempered step-mother; that it was far better to be married to anybody than do that' (IV, ch. 6). The dominant tone concerning Mrs Day is humour, as in the scene in which Dick has lunch with the Days. Moule even praised that scene as being 'very amusingly done'.[41] Again, with Thomas Leaf Hardy scarcely plays the role for which Chesterton cast him, as the 'village atheist brooding and blaspheming over the village idiot'.[42] The Spirit of the Pities in Hardy does not even whisper 'Why?', but rather Leaf is treated with humorous sympathy as part of the local colour. The *Pall Mall Gazette* could even quote Leaf's remarks concerning his late brother Jim and find him quite humorous, 'little less sharp than his companions'.[43]

Thus Hardy restricted his tone to that appropriate to the pastoral as he and his audience understood it. He did this primarily by remaining outside even his main characters most of the time, describing them from a social and psychological distance and emphasising what could be seen as charming, quaint or humorous, or at least different from the mores of the middle-class audience. The procedure is very much like that of George Eliot, tellingly described by Raymond Williams as a 'complacently powerful' formula offering the rural characters to the urban readers as ' "knowable", in a deeply inauthentic but socially successful way'.[44]

The social position behind this procedure – that of one who has been part of the rural culture but who has moved out of it into the middle-class world of his audience – is evident in the descriptions of Mellstock customs. The somewhat anomalous social position is revealed in the shifting tone. Sometimes the tone is explanatory and disinterested, almost anthropological, as in the careful explanation for the custom of discussing important business in the garden (IV, ch. 2). Even when the descriptions are evidently based on personal experience, the social distance is maintained, as in the description of the dance at the Christmas party, with its exactly remembered physical detail concerning the dancers and the musicians. The generalising parenthesis about 'country parties of the thorough sort' (I, ch. 7) shows that the narrator is standing outside the experience, noting its quaint and colourful aspects for the urban reader. Moule captured the tone of the book well when he said 'It is a book that might well lie on the table of any well-ordered country house, and that might also be borne in mind by the readers during kindly rounds undertaken among the cottages.'[45]

The external approach and condescending tone carry over into Hardy's treatment of the characters as individuals. They are often described in terms of visible idiosyncrasies, as when Michael Mail, Robert Penny, Elias Spinks, Joseph Bowman and Thomas Leaf are distinguished by their posture and walk in the opening description, or as with the repeated association of Robert Penny with his spectacles, from the glint of 'moons of light' in his first appearance to his final appearance, cleaning his spectacles.

Related to this approach to character through externals is Hardy's use of reductive visible images for them; as in the description of William Dewy's face as like 'the sunny side of a ripe ribstone pippin' (I, ch. 3). This is similar to George Eliot's handling of such a character as Mr Casson in *Adam Bede*; equally similar to her practice is Hardy's use of the device of punctuating rustic dialogue with humorous descriptions of the quaint gestures, tone or mannerisms of the speaker, so that Elias Spinks, for example, is interrupted in his discussion of watered cider by the narrator's description of how 'his eyes seemed to be looking at the case in an abstract form rather than at the scene before him' (I, ch. 2), and again in his unfinished discussion of music by a description of his 'shaking his head at some idea he seemed to see floating before him, and smiling as if he were attending a funeral at the time' (I, ch. 6).

The dialogue that is modified by these narrative interruptions likewise follows the pattern set by George Eliot. Her Rainbow *habitués* boast of professional knowledge (the butcher and the farrier), argue about church music (Mr Macey and Bob Tookey) and tell anecdotes about the past (Mr Macey, primed by Mr Snell). Hardy's rustics talk in a very similar manner, as we hear Mr Penny on shoes and feet, Reuben and William Dewy on music, and almost everyone on the past, whether of the antics of that 'husbird of a feller Sam Lawson', or the peculiarities of the Penny courtship, or the respectability of Susan Dewy's family, or the sad fate of poor Thomas Leaf's brother Jim.

Characterised by visible idiosyncrasies, quaint mannerisms and the observed tone and content of their dialogue, the quire members and other rustics are treated almost entirely externally, viewed from a social and psychological distance with a condescending appreciation of their quaintness. Williams captures the tone and method almost perfectly when he says that in the book there is an 'external observation of customs and quaintness, modulated by a distinctly patronizing affection'.[46] The affection is there (Hardy wrote to Florence Henniker in 1896 that the quire were 'the characters that I like best in my novels'[47]), but the narrative tone leaves no doubt that the characters are on the other side of a social divide from the narrator and the reader. Even Dick Dewy, the hero, comes in for similar treatment. His dialogue and action are often as humorous as those of other rustics, as when he is caught by his father mooning below the dark window where Fancy had appeared (I, ch. 5), or when he is attempting to express 'the dignity of the writer's mind' in his incoherent letter to Fancy (II, ch. 7), or when he naïvely wonders how it is that all middle-aged people seem 'so blind to romance' (I, ch. 8). The narrative distance is maintained; there is almost never the sympathetic identification of the Spirit of the Pities in Hardy with his character as there had been with Cytherea Graye in *Desperate Remedies*, much less what there was to be with characters such as Henchard or Tess.

Thus in his handling of his characters in these pages 'penned so lightly, even so farcically and flippantly', Hardy kept to an external approach that emphasised humour, quaintness, charm. And it was for just this that some of his reviewers were most lavish in their praise. 'Remarkable for quaintness and originality', a 'charming little tale' that is 'told with a delicious humour', 'one of the brightest, freshest little stories that we have come across in many a day; full of sparkling bits of description, vivacious conversation, quaint sketches of character, and amusing incident'; 'a most picturesque portraiture of village life'; 'full of humour and keen observation' – most of the reviewers indicate that Hardy had established just the desired tone for a pastoral.[48]

The references to 'observation' and 'description' point to another aspect of Hardy's basically external approach – the pictorialism of genre scenes such as the cider-making scene in *Desperate Remedies*, which had been compared to the paintings of Wilkie, Teniers and Hobbema. Moule chose this aspect of the book for his primary praise, calling it 'a series of rural pictures full of life and genuine colouring . . . drawn with a distinct minuteness'.[49]

Some of the pictures are of landscapes, often to open a chapter and indicate the season. There is, for example, the brief description of the spring morning when Dick is going to help Fancy move her belongings into the schoolhouse, a morning described in terms of a painting:

> the damp slopes of the hill-sides . . . steamed in the warmth of the sun. . . . The distant view was darkly shaded with clouds; but the nearer parts of the landscape were whitely illumined by the visible rays of the sun streaming down across the heavy grey shade behind. (II, ch. 6)

Horace Moule's brother, Charles, in a letter to Hardy in 1873, asked for more of that sort of landscape (with figures):

> In your next 'Dutch' work, describe a woody slope blue with hyacinths, & happy children eager to pick them and careless to keep. It is what I can't paint, and Teniers neither could nor wished to do it![50]

Most of the pictures are not simple landscapes, but genre pictures of buildings and/or people, as noted in the unidentified review in Hardy's Scrapbook:

> The book is interesting to those who love glimpses of village interiors, and the descriptions are so graphic that you can see each detail as in a Dutch picture.

Such pictures include those of both the exterior and interior of the Dewy cottage (based on Hardy's own birthplace), seen lighted at night (I, ch. 2), and the exterior and the interior of the Day cottage, seen in bright daylight, with striking painterly effects of light and colour:

> the sun shone obliquely upon the patch of grass in front, which reflected its brightness through the open doorway and up the staircase opposite, lighting up each riser with a shiny green radiance and leaving the top of each step in shade. (II, ch. 6)

The description of the interior of the keeper's cottage includes an especially detailed picture of the chimney corner, with its special window with the sill marked with the circles left by cups that had been heated in the fire, a picture reminiscent of Barnes's nostalgic 'The Settle an' the Girt Wood Vire'. Moule commented that the parts of the sequence 'combine to make up the picture of an interior entirely justifying the author's mention of the Dutch school upon his title-page'.[51] Later there is a picture of the Day storehouse that is clearly imagined as a Dutch still-life (with the touch of motion in the bubbling cider being like the smoke from the burning fuse in Jans Olis's *Still-life with Crab and Smoker's Requisites*):

> Geoffrey Day's storehouse at the back of his dwelling was hung with bunches of dried horehound, mint, and sage; brown-paper bags of thyme and lavender; and long ropes of clean onions. On shelves were spread large red and yellow apples, and choice selections of early potatoes for seed next year; – vulgar crowds of commoner kind lying beneath in heaps. A few empty beehives were clustered around a nail in one corner, under which stand two or three barrels of new cider of the first crop, each bubbling and squirting forth from the yet open bunghole. (IV, ch. 2)

Another genre picture is explicitly related to a Bergamese rather than a Dutch painting – the description of Mr Penny at work in his shop, seen from the road 'working inside like a framed portrait of a shoemaker by some modern Moroni', with Mr Penny with awl in hand forming the foreground, while 'rows of lasts, small and large, stout and slender, covered the wall which formed the background' (II, ch. 2). Outside the shop is another picture, that of the choir, 'brightly illuminated' in the evening sunshine, each 'backed up by a shadow as long as a steeple'. Such pictures are perhaps what Havelock Ellis was referring to when he said that Jan Steen is the only Dutch painter whose work Hardy approaches.[52] Other such pictures include the 'well-illuminated picture' of Grandfather James in his fustian coat and mason's apron (I, ch. 3), and, more like Rembrandt or Caravaggio in the use of chiaroscuro, the portrait of Fancy with the candle at her window, 'framed as a picture by the window architrave' (I, ch. 5). More extreme in its use of bright colour is the picture of Fancy at Budmouth, standing against the 'brilliant sheet of liquid colour' on a street corner when 'the white angle of the last house in the row cut perpendicularly an embayed and nearly motionless expanse of salt water projected from the ocean – to-day lit in bright tones of green and opal' (III, ch. 1). More extreme in the use of shadow is the opening picture of the quire against the night sky 'like some processional design on Greek or Etruscan pottery' (I, ch. 1).

The genre pictures and accounts of typical happenings are arranged, like Barnes's first volume of *Poems of Rural Life in the Dorset Dialect*, by the seasons, but they are held together by the pastoral romance of Dick and Fancy, nicely integrated into it, as Moule noted when he said that the 'subsidiary scenes . . . are worked in with as much care as if the writer had been constructing a sensation plot of the received model', so that 'each of these scenes contributes its share to a really pleasant and entertaining whole'.[53] The romance follows the conventional pattern: lovers meet, there is love at first sight (for Dick, at least), a courtship, with rivals, the lovers kept apart by the heavy father, the father defeated by a stratagem (with the 'witch' playing the New Comedy part of the clever slave who aids the heroine), and finally the wedding with its communal celebration. Moule approvingly quoted 'the course of true love' (as Hardy himself referred to it when he wrote of Dick's 'first day of smooth experience in a hitherto obstructed love-course' – IV, ch. 5): and praised 'the unpretending thread of the story' in which, 'needless to say . . . all ends happily'.[54] The *Athenaeum* similarly praised the story as one that showed that 'there is just as much romance, together with just as keen an interest in the loves of two young persons of this humble station' as in the courtship of wealthier characters, so that Hardy was able to 'produce out of such simple materials a story that shall induce us to give up valuable time in order to see the marriage fairly accomplished' (a passage Florence Hardy quoted in the *Life*).[55] However, the more Hardyan note of the Parson Maybold episode did not please the reviewers so much, perhaps because it involved a little too much realism for an idyll. Moule indicated his disapproval gently, referring in passing to the 'curious episode' and later brushing it away:

> Serious mischief threatens for a moment, just towards the close, on the side of the Vicar; but this episode, whether wisely introduced or not, is too brief to signify much in the working out of the story.[56]

The *Pall Mall Gazette* was more unequivocal, saying that the love-story 'is considerably marred by an episode regarding the vicar which destroys the simple character of the tale, otherwise well maintained throughout'.[57]

Aside from that one possible lapse into the complex and the serious, Hardy kept to the tone and simplicity considered appropriate to the idyll. He clearly had the generic conventions in mind and held to them, and, although the book did not sell so well as Hardy and Tinsley hoped, the reviews show that his attempts to remain within those limits were recognised and appreciated.

III

Of course *Under the Greenwood Tree* is more than merely conventional; Hardy himself indicated as much when he placed the book among his 'Novels of Character and Environment', those of his books which he considered to 'approach most nearly to uninfluenced works'[58] (that is, those in which his 'idiosyncratic mode of regard' was expressed with the least limitation from the conditions of serialisation and publication). However, it is the slightest and least idiosyncratic of the novels in that group, in many ways having more in common with *The Trumpet-Major* (placed by Hardy among the 'Romances and Fantasies') than with the major novels.

None the less it does have hints of the major Hardy, in the occasional naturalistic detail of setting, in the naturalistic undertone of the handling of Fancy Day, that 'sexual magnet', as Merryn Williams calls her.[59] Havelock Ellis, looking back on the book from the perspective of *Jude the Obscure* in 1896, nicely caught the implications of the tone, pointing out that by confining himself to early courtship, that field in which 'human love and human caprice can have free play without too obviously conflicting with established moral codes', Hardy could present a character (Fancy) whose actions were 'very immoral, as Nature is', but without any 'collision with the rigid constitution of Society'.[60] And of course there is the muted irony of the ending, where Dick's naïve romanticism is placed from the perspective of a sceptical naturalism.[61]

Even in the handling of the rustic society, selective and superficial as it is, there are hints of the mature Hardy in the implicit appreciation of the rustics' unthinking acceptance of the nature of Nature, their ability to live in tune with it, unburdened by the 'ache of modernism'. The Mellstock rustics at least imply what Hardy was to make explicit in his 1883 essay on 'The Dorsetshire Labourer':

> it is among such communities as these that happiness will find her last refuge on earth, since it is among them that a perfect insight into the conditions of existence will be longest postponed.[62]

Further, he implies that modernity and its discontents will not be forever shut out of such rural retreats. Rather, their advent is only 'postponed'. *Under the Greenwood Tree* is a nostalgic look at the rural society of twenty-five years before, but even in that society the germs of social change can be discerned in Fancy and Parson Maybold. The defeat of the quire is offset by the marriage of Dick and Fancy, celebrated by the traditional community, but the modern world is beginning to impinge. In succeeding novels that process of change becomes more explicit as it advances further, and Hardy the naturalist is forced to acknowledge its inevitability, while Hardy the humanist mourns the loss (and recognises the gains). But this theme, like those concerning external nature and sexual love, remains muted, implicit, kept within the 'safe' bounds of the pastoral. As Jeanne Howard states, 'Accurate "history" strains against a wistful "pastoral", evincing in embryonic form the concerns and tensions of Hardy's later, more uncompromising recognition of social change and alienation.'[63]

Whatever hints of the mature Hardy we can see with the wisdom of hindsight, the dominant note of *Under the Greenwood Tree* is that of the 'wistful pastoral', and Hardy's conscious intention to stay within the limits of that 'class of writing' is the formative force making the book what it is. A 'deeper, more essential, more transcendent' (and more idiosyncratic) handling of his rural materials would not come until he stepped outside those generic limits.

NOTES

1. *The Collected Letters of Thomas Hardy*, ed. Richard Little Purdy and Michael Millgate (Oxford, 1978) I, pp. 11, 12.
2. *Letters*, I, p. 16.
3. Florence Emily Hardy, *The Life of Thomas Hardy, 1840–1928* (reprinted London, 1962) pp. 61–2.
4. Ibid., pp. 61–2.
5. Charles Morgan, *The House of Macmillan (1843–1943)* (London, 1942) pp. 87–8.
6. *Letters*, I, p. 8; interview in *Cassell's Saturday Journal*, 25 June 1892, p. 944, quoted in Michael Millgate, *Thomas Hardy: A Biography* (Oxford, 1982) p. 135.
7. For the outline, see Thomas Hardy, *Old Mrs Chundle and Other Stories*, ed. F. B. Pinion (London, 1977) pp. 117–18; for a discussion of it as a prospective sensation novel, see my 'Thomas Hardy's Unwritten Second Sensation Novel', *Thomas Hardy Annual*, 2 (London, 1984) ed. Norman Page, pp. 30–40.
8. For a discussion of Hardy's relation to Hutton, see my '*The Spectator* and Thomas Hardy's Early Fiction', *Thomas Hardy Year Book*, 6 (1977) pp. 49–61.
9. *Spectator*, 22 April 1871; reprinted in *Thomas Hardy: The Critical Heritage*, ed. C. B. Cox (London, 1970) pp. 3–4.
10. *Athenaeum*, 1 April 1871; in *Thomas Hardy: The Critical Heritage*, p. 2; 'Callzer', to whom C. B. Cox attributes the *Athenaeum's* review (*Thomas Hardy: The Critical Heritage*, p. 1), when he came to review *Under the Greenwood Tree* in the same journal stated more strongly his preference for the pastoral over the sensation novel (and perhaps implied that he deserved some credit for guiding Hardy in the right direction):

    > we are glad to meet again with the author of *Desperate Remedies*, and to find that in his new novel he has worked principally that vein of his genius which yields the best produce, and wherein his

> labours result in more satisfaction to his readers than did his explorations into the dark ways of human crime and folly. Our readers may possibly remember, that while praising *Desperate Remedies* for many marks of ability, we especially commended it for its graphic pictures of rustic life somewhere in the West Country. Here the author is clearly on his own ground, and to this he has confined himself in the book before us. (15 June 1872; in *Thomas Hardy: The Critical Heritage*, p. 9)

11. Morgan, *The House of Macmillan*, pp. 96–7, 99.
12. See Michael Millgate, *Thomas Hardy: His Career as a Novelist* (London, 1971) p. 43. The manuscript additions are on pp. 43, 73, 87 and 95 of the original MS in the Dorset Country Museum, appearing in the book in I, ch. 6; II, chs 2, 4 and 5. References are to the New Wessex Edition (London, 1974).
13. *For Desperate Remedies*, see my '*Desperate Remedies* and the Victorian Sensation Novel', *Nineteenth-Century Fiction*, 20 (1965) 35–50.
14. See ibid., and *Letters*, I, p. 13; *Life*, p. 86.
15. W. P. Trent, 'The Novels of Thomas Hardy', *Sewanee Review*, 1 (1892); in *Thomas Hardy: The Critical Heritage*, p. 223.
16. William Tinsley, *Random Recollections of an Old Publisher* (London, 1900) I, p. 127; Horace Moule, *Saturday Review*, 28 September 1872, in *Thomas Hardy: The Critical Heritage*, p. 11; Leon Boucher, 'Le Roman Pastorel en Angleterre', *Revue de deux mondes*, 18 December 1875, pp. 839–42; Charles Kegan Paul, *British Quarterly Review*, in *Thomas Hardy: The Critical Heritage*, p. 83 (for Paul's authorship, see Millgate, *Thomas Hardy: His Career as a Novelist*, p. 121); Conventry Patmore, *St James Gazette*, 2 April 1887, in *Thomas Hardy: The Critical Heritage*, p. 187; J. M. Barrie, 'Thomas Hardy: the Historian of Wessex', *Contemporary Review*, 56 (1889), in *Thomas Hardy: The Critical Heritage*, p. 160.
17. *Thomas Hardy: The Critical Heritage*, p. 9; *Saturday Review*, 34 (28 September 1872), in *Thomas Hardy: The Critical Heritage*, p. 12.
18. Moule, in *Thomas Hardy: The Critical Heritage*, p. 12; Patmore, in *Thomas Hardy: The Critical Heritage*, p. 148; Barrie, in *Thomas Hardy: The Critical Heritage*, p. 160; *Saturday Review*, review of *Far from the Madding Crowd*, 39 (9 January 1875), in *Thomas Hardy: The Critical Heritage*, p. 39.
19. *Pall Mall Gazette*, review of *A Pair of Blue Eyes*, 25 October 1873, p. 12.
20. Quoted in Carl Weber, *Hardy in America: A Study of Thomas Hardy and His American Readers* (1946; reprinted New York, 1966) p. 14.
21. Boucher, 'Le Roman Pastoral', pp. 840–1.
22. *Spectator*, 2 November 1872, p. 1403.
23. *George Sand and the Victorians: Her Influence and Reputation in Nineteenth Century England* (London, 1977) pp. 185–99.
24. Frederic William Maitland, *The Life and Letters of Leslie Stephen* (London, 1906) p. 276.
25. Andrew Lang, review of *Far from the Madding Crowd*, *Academy*, 8 (January 1875), in *Thomas Hardy: The Critical Heritage*, p. 26; Havelock

Ellis, 'Thomas Hardy's Novels', *Westminster Review*, 119 (April 1883), in *Thomas Hardy: The Critical Heritage*, p. 109. Hardy himself may not have been acquainted with George Sand's work when he wrote *Under the Greenwood Tree*. The first evidence of any contact with her work is a letter from Henry Holt, his American publisher, in December 1873 stating that copies of three Sand novels in translation had been sent to Hardy as requested, evidently on behalf of Horace Moule (Weber, *Hardy in America*, p. 20). Notes on one of these translations appear in Hardy's literary notes in 1876 (*The Literary Notes of Thomas Hardy*, ed. Lennart A. Bjork (Göteburg, 1974) I, 50).

26. *Saturday Review*, 7 (26 February 1859), in *George Eliot: The Critical Heritage*, ed. David Carroll (London, 1971) p. 75.
27. Michael Squires, *The Pastoral Novel: Studies in George Eliot, Thomas Hardy, and D. H. Lawrence* (Charlottesville, Va., 1974).
28. *The Personal Writings of Thomas Hardy*, ed. Harold Orel (London, 1967) p. 96.
29. *Personal Writings*, p. 84.
30. *Cornhill*, 43 (February 1881), in *George Eliot: The Critical Heritage*, pp. 469–71.
31. *Letters*, I, p. 11.
32. *Personal Writings*, p. 84.
33. *Life*, p. 12.
34. *Personal Writings*, p. 6.
35. *Life*, p. 353.
36. *Thomas Hardy: The Critical Heritage*, p. 223.
37. It is probably significant that, as W. J. Keith has shown, Hardy made cuts in 54 of the 138 poems he included in his 1918 selection, most of them of didactic or optimistic passages ('Thomas Hardy's Edition of William Barnes', *Victorian Poetry*, 15 (1977) 121–31). In a letter to Florence Henniker, Hardy complained that Barnes's clerical position 'compelled him to write parsonically' (*Letters*, II, p. 270). Of the poems mentioned in this essay, Hardy included the following in his selection: 'Hallowed Plëaces', 'Chris'mas Invitation', Meaken up a Miff', 'A Bit o' Sly Coorten' and 'The Settle an' the Girt Wood Vire'.
38. Squires, *The Pastoral Novel*, pp. 13, 18.
39. *Thomas Hardy: The Critical Heritage*, p. 11; see also Andrew Enstice, *Thomas Hardy: Landscapes of the Mind* (London, 1979) pp. 37–47.
40. *English Folk Dance Society Journal*, 2nd series, 1 (1927); in *Under the Greenwood Tree*, New Wessex Edition, pp. 217–18.
41. *Thomas Hardy: The Critical Heritage*, p. 13.
42. G. K. Chesterton, *The Victorian Age in Literature* (London, 1913) p. 143.
43. *Pall Mall Gazette*, 5 July 1872, p. 11.
44. Raymond Williams, *The Country and the City* (London, 1973) p. 170.
45. *Thomas Hardy: The Critical Heritage*, p. 13.
46. Williams, *The Country and the City*, p. 203; see also Robert A. Draffan, 'Hardy's *Under the Greenwood Tree*', *English*, 22 (1973) 58. For an account of Hardy's use of George Eliot's pastoral devices in *Far from the Madding Crowd*, see my 'George Eliot and Pastoral Tragicomedy

in Hardy's *Far from the Madding Crowd*', *Studies in Philology*, 77 (1980) 406–15.
47. *One Rare Fair Woman: Thomas Hardy's Letters to Florence Henniker 1893–1922*, ed. Evelyn Hardy and F. B. Pinion (London, 1977) p. 59.
48. Unidentified review in Hardy's scrapbook, Dorset County Museum; *Nation*, 16 July 1873, p. 27; W. H. Browne, review of *A Pair of Blue Eyes*, *Southern Magazine*, 3 (1873) 365; John Hutton, review of *A Pair of Blue Eyes*, *Spectator*, 28 June 1873, p. 831; Moule, in *Thomas Hardy: The Critical Heritage*, p. 14.
49. *Thomas Hardy: The Critical Heritage*, p. 11.
50. Letter of 11 May 1873, in Dorset County Museum.
51. *Thomas Hardy: The Critical Heritage*, p. 14; for an account of Hardy's use of 'Dutch' verbal pictures in *Far from the Madding Crowd*, see my ' "Infected by a Vein of Mimeticism": George Eliot and the Technique of *Far from the Madding Crowd*', *Journal of Narrative Technique*, 8 (1978) 57–64.
52. *Thomas Hardy: The Critical Heritage*, p. 127.
53. Ibid., p. 12.
54. Ibid., p. 14.
55. *Athenaeum* 59 (15 June 1872), in ibid., pp. 9–10; quoted in *Life*, p. 89.
56. *Thomas Hardy: The Critical Heritage*, p. 14.
57. *Pall Mall Gazette*, 5 July 1872, p. 11.
58. *Personal Writings*, p. 44.
59. Merryn Williams, *Thomas Hardy and Rural England* (London, 1972) p. 184.
60. Havelock Ellis, 'Concerning Jude the Obscure', *Savoy Magazine*, October 1896, in *Thomas Hardy: The Critical Heritage*, p. 304.
61. See John F. Danby, 'Under the Greenwood Tree', *Critical Quarterly*, 1 (1959) 5–13.
62. *Personal Writings*, p. 169.
63. Jeanne Howard, 'Thomas Hardy's "Mellstock" and the Registrar General's Stinsford', *Literature and History*, 6 (1977) 200.

11

The Complex Simplicity of *The Ambassadors*

D. W. HARDING

The Ambassadors, to Henry James in the considered retrospect of his Prefaces, 'the best, "all round", of all my productions', seemed to F. R. Leavis in the 1940s 'so feeble a piece of word-spinning that I should have been inclined to dismiss it as merely senile if James hadn't himself provided an explanation in telling us that it had been conceived as a short story'.[1] F. O. Matthiessen filled out the story by supposing that Strether himself was deeply in love with Mme de Vionnet and claiming that it was the development of her character that gave the novel 'the stamina to survive the dated flavour of Strether's liberation'.[2] Quentin Anderson still more gratuitously elaborated the novel into part of a symbolic treatment of the religion that James's father had constructed.[3] Even a generation later, Leon Edel, in the introduction to his edition, was still stressing the supposed simplicity of the tale: 'Strether has come to bring Chad home: now he believes Chad should stay. And Chad on his side – to compound the irony – is quite prepared to leave. This is almost all the "plot" to be found in the novel.' Leavis, judging so differently, was yet reacting to the same supposed simplicity: '*The Ambassadors* I judge to be an utter failure; it hasn't a theme capable of sustaining treatment at novel length.'[4]

For James himself it was precisely the hidden complexities of the theme that were stimulating and rewarding. In his Preface the initiating anecdote (of Howells seeing late in life that he had somehow never 'lived' and admonishing a young man not to make the same mistake) is compared to a packet of treasure – 'sealed up values infinitely precious'. He could remember no occasion when, 'confronted with the initial hint for a story, I had found it of a livelier interest to take stock, in this fashion, of suggested wealth'.

The unfolding of implications becomes the mode of construction that shapes the novel. The opening scene in Chester is not a mere preamble. It states attitudes and preferences by which Strether unwittingly commits himself to much else: when he walks on the walls with Miss Gostrey it is, says James, 'the bearing of the occasion itself on matters still remote' that concerns us.[5] It shows him as a person who, beneath a lifetime's deposit of New England categories and preconceptions, could still renew a natural openness to experiences that the New England outlook resisted. He rediscovers not just 'Europe' but the relaxed acceptance of it that his first youthful visit had permitted. In Chester his decisive choice was to enjoy, in spite of a slightly guilty conscience, a walk on the city walls with Miss Gostrey instead of going with Waymarsh, who, as they returned to the hotel (having by then luckily unlinked their arms), was waiting; Strether saw 'even at this distance, that Mr Waymarsh was, for his part, joyless' (p. 44). It is this ending of Chapter 1 that is made to mark Strether's renewal of loyalty to an earlier possible self that he has allowed himself to fail. The novel proceeds by unfolding what that means for his mission and his identity.

A central part of the process is his discovery of the sort of people he likes and the sort who like him. What begins when he and Maria Gostrey find each other congenial continues when Bilham quickly likes him and having introduced him to Miss Barrrace, who also likes him, notifies the lovers that this emissary from Woollett is someone they can work with. Finally Chad and Mme de Vionnet, if they begin by seeing him simply as a potential ally in weakening Woollett's antagonism, rapidly move to the respect and affection for him that give the novel much of its pervasive flavour. Henry James apologised in the preliminary Project[6] for the fact that everyone is to be made to like Strether (overlooking Sarah Pocock); but he made no concession, and it is an essential part of his concept that after a lifetime of occupational non-success in a career-oriented culture, followed by the small distinction of editing the Review that Mrs Newsome subsidises, Strether comes by accident into a society of people who value him for the person he is. By the end of the Chester episode 'Miss Gostrey was convinced that she did not want to be better than Strether' (p. 62). And when he has poured out, in Gloriani's garden, his sense of not having lived, 'holding little Bilham, from step to step, deeply and gravely attentive' and warning him 'don't make my mistake. For it was a mistake. Live!', the young man replies 'Oh, but I don't know that I want to be, at your age, too different from you!' (p. 184). This welcome given him by his natural allies helps to define an identity that Woollett has not perceived and would not know what to do with.

At this point the misconception might arise that James is simply aligning Strether with the Europeans and uprooted Europeanised Americans against the New Englanders. This is the easiest misreading of the book, since of course James did make full use of the simpler transatlantic contrasts for his tone of ironic amusement. But from the beginning, in his earliest note on Howells's exclamation in Whistler's studio, he saw the theme as something wider or more general than a topic for one more of his 'international' stories: the 'elderly man who hasn't "lived" ', James muses, 'may be an American – he might be an Englishman'. If he had been, James could still have told his central story of a man who renounces his allegiance to a code that has ruled his life from youth to late middle-age; an Englishman would not have needed to renounce his national identity any more than Strether who, in spite of his affection for the Europeans and expatriates, and in spite of opportunities of remaining in Europe cared for and comfortable, still insists on returning to America.

The use that James finally made of Mamie Pocock is specially interesting for its denial that any simple transatlantic contrast forms the basis for the social conflicts and alliances that provide the connective tissue of the novel. In his long Project, or synopsis, she appears briefly, chiefly to exemplify Woollett's conception of a charming girl who may be offered as a bait (in addition to the money bribe) to lure Chad home; and Chad 'really lets fly at' his sister 'for the folly of her supposing him amenable to her view of the little Pocock', and this has revealed to her, in a manner that she feels to be quite lurid and that makes her shudder off across the sea, the intimate difference now existing in their standards of value. She is *proud* of 'the little Pocock'.[7]

In the novel itself, however, Mamie is handled very differently. In the scene of the Pococks' arrival in Paris James employs unobtrusive skill in giving Strether (and us) no reason to distinguish Mamie from the other two in her impression of Chad. The emphasis falls on Strether's almost incredulous astonishment that the transformation is totally unnoticed by Sarah and Jim. Strether sees how attractive Mamie is in person and manner but she is then left to merge with the other impercipient Pococks. By the time of his talk with Mme de Vionnet two days later he has decided she does at least see that Chad is changed, but what she thinks of him is still obscure; 'Strether gave it up. "How can one tell how a deep little girl sees a deep young man?" ' (p. 322). By the end of the week, after depicting the developing relations and pairings among all the actors before the crescendo of the drama, he can startle Maria Gostrey with the revelation that of all the New Englanders Mamie is the one 'who really does know' that Jim Pocock is 'impossible' (p. 336).

That disclosure is immediately followed by the chapter devoted to Strether's long talk with Mamie when by accident he finds her alone, an episode more arbitrarily contrived than his exchanges with the central characters. And in the very next chapter he is urging Bilham to marry her, having subtly detected their mutual attraction. The ruthless foreshortening suggests belated development of this sub-plot (of which there was no hint in the Project).

The sub-plot, however, is vitally important as a denial that this is just another 'international' tale. Through it Strether is made to realise that what he has been wrestling with is not the conflict of outlook between Europe and New England but a contrast between types of people; he has to recognise that people who take their own perceptions directly and sensitively, not reaching them through a prefabricated framework, may just as well be American as European. During their conversation (in which James pushes to the limit the technique of postulating unspoken communications between two people who are 'in relation') Strether finds that Mamie is on his side, not Sarah's, and that her subtle insight embraces his own difficult position and the delicate web of feelings that enwraps Chad, Mme de Vionnet and her daughter. Finding himself so unexpectedly appreciating Mamie, despite the marks she bears of Woollett, Strether realises how American he himself remains:

> The hour took on for Strether, little by little, an odd, sad sweetness of savour; he had such a revulsion in Mamie's favour and on behalf of her social values as might have come from remorse at some early injustice. She made him, as under the breath of

> some vague western whiff, homesick and freshly restless. (p. 343)

The essentially American quality of Bilham too, for whom Mamie is waiting, had been proclaimed earlier, again in the form of a realisation that comes as a surprise to Strether, who sees with a sudden shift of vision that Bilham's amazing serenity is not the result of European corruption but one way 'of being more American than anybody' (p. 118). Having discovered that he has no talent for painting and must give up the aim that had brought him to Paris he yet has none of the distress that Woollett's prejudgements would have led Strether to expect. He

> looked on, as it had first struck Strether, at a world in respect to which he hadn't a prejudice. The one our friend most instantly missed was the usual one in favour of an occupation accepted. Little Bilham had an occupation, but it was only an occupation declined; and it was by his general exemption from alarm, anxiety, remorse on this score that the impression of his serenity was made. (p. 118)

This is the kind of American that Strether wants Mamie to marry, and he promises to leave Bilham what money he has, to be added to Mamie's own:

> 'I want', Strether went on, 'to have been to that extent constructive – even expiatory. I've been sacrificing so to strange gods that I feel I want to put on record, somehow, my fidelity – fundamentally unchanged, after all – to our own.' (p. 353)

It is because Mamie and Bilham are still American that Strether wants to reinforce their quiet disregard of what Woollett stands for. At the end of the novel Bilham has joined Mamie for the Pococks' holiday in Switzerland and they are on their way home to America. They remain one kind of American – as Mrs Newsome, Sarah and Waymarsh remain another. The sub-plot carries James's recognition that people who share Strether's way of meeting new experiences must do so independently, not expecting to find in reality a ready-made society of congenial people in a fictive 'Paris' or 'Europe'.

Throughout his progress Strether has to deal with the conflict between his direct perception of Chad's startling improvement and the system of standard concepts and codified appraisals that comprise the morality of Woollett. Unlike Woollett's the alternative morality cannot be specified in advance; it has to be derived gradually from seeing and appreciating the valuable qualities of individual people who are met directly face to face without being framed within a preconceived category. Speaking of Mrs Newsome, Strether tells Maria Gostrey that 'she doesn't admit surprises. . . . She had, to her own mind, worked the whole thing out in advance, and worked it out for me as well as for herself' (p. 406). He, by contrast, finds himself sensitive to excellence in people as a primary thing; it is disturbing if they prove to be in the wrong category but the perceived excellence is not to be denied on that account.

In remaining true to their perceptions the 'sensitive' have to resist pressures from the 'sensible' majority, as James makes explicit through Strether's baffled reflections on realising that Sarah and Jim Pocock see nothing of the transformation in Chad. He wonders whether he has been deceiving himself about Chad's improvement and is now feeling his vain delusion to be 'menaced by the touch of the real': had the Pococks come to be sane where Strether was destined to feel that he himself had only been silly?

> He glanced at at such a contingency, but it failed to hold him long when once he had reflected that he would have been silly, in this case, with Maria Gostrey and little Bilham, with Mme de Vionnet and little Jeanne, with Lambert Strether, in fine, and, above all, with Chad Newsome himself. Wouldn't it be found to have made more for reality to be silly with these persons than sane with Sarah and Jim? (p. 291)

The circularity of the 'argument', brought out by making 'Lambert Strether, in fine' one of the people whose judgement supported Lambert Strether, simply states the fact that the 'sensitive' person has to trust to the validity of his own perceptions and judgements and to the rightness of the allies he values.

In the novel the test that identifies the sensitive people is their ability to gauge the change in Chad and see it as excellent. He represents a confident development of the outlook and attitudes that Strether had begun to feel in Chester as a possibility once his own. Nothing 'passed more distinctly for Strether than that striking truth about Chad of which he had been so often moved to take note: the truth that everything came happily back with him to his knowing how to live' (p. 385). His being able to 'live' was a moral condition, essentially different from what Strether had acquiesced in at Woollett. Chad is enviably exempt from that 'terror of the other' which haunts Strether, as he tells Maria, the guilty glance over the shoulder at something else that he perhaps ought to be doing. The relaxed welcome that Strether finds himself giving to minor pleasures, whether the stroll in Chester or the theatre dinner with Maria Gostrey in Paris, expresses an attitude to pleasant opportunity which he might once have allowed himself to take and now sees developed in Chad's new life.

But if this and the accompanying manners had been all he saw in Chad, some of the current misreadings of the novel would be valid and we could agree with Edel (in the Introduction to his edition) that Strether will return to Woollett 'with a feeling that if Europe is amoral, it also offers him greater emotional and aesthetic freedom'. On the contrary, Chad's urbanity and knowledge of the world are the surface of something much more important: referring to the way Mme de Vionnet has 'saved' him, Strether says he is speaking 'of his manners and morals, his character and life. I'm speaking of him as a person to deal with and talk with and live with – speaking of him as a social animal' (p. 231).

His morals, his character and life are precisely what Sarah Newsome, applying the Woollett standards, finds 'hideous'. But it would not do to suppose that she is referring to his sexual immorality (or 'amorality' in Edel's cooling term). A young man's fornication and adultery could be known of and perfectly well accommodated to the Woollett outlook. Just as Mrs Newsome can pursue her high-minded course undisturbed by her late husband's questionable business practices in amassing the wealth that supports her, so sexual lapses could be ignored as the discreditable but apologetically concealed features of otherwise acceptable men. The ladies of Woollett would not have been inquisitorial about Chad's private life if he had come back in reasonable time to his advertising post; James makes it clear in the brief retrospect of Chad's Parisian progress, given as Strether's musings in the Luxembourg Gardens, that Mme de Vionnet had not seduced him from Woollett chastity, but had withdrawn him from a commonplace sequence of mistresses in the Latin Quarter, an aspect of life which, however much deplored ('scarce permissably to be mentioned') in Woollett, was classed among the lamentable proclivities of men that a morally matriarchal culture held in check. What was intolerable to Mrs Newsome was to be asked to view Chad's adulterous mistress and the change she has worked in him as a continuing part of a new, good Chad instead of the usual lapse.

The crux of Strether's conflict lay in his own lifelong loyalty to this code in which 'an adulterous woman' fell into a category to be condemned and socially excluded without question, while yet his direct perception of Mme de Vionnet was of a fine individual person whose influence on Chad was admirable. To accept Chad's continuing attachment to her was not to condone a commonplace lapse or to accept promiscuity as a regrettable part of Chad's character; it meant totally overturning a principle that he himself, equally with Mrs Newsome, had woven into the social fabric of everyday life. It meant affirming that the quality of an individual person should count for more than the category 'adulterous woman' into which she fell. At least this is what it would mean if in fact Chad's relation with Mme de Vionnet were adulterous. Hence his desperate search for any conceivable way that might let him believe in the 'innocence' of the liaison – is it certain that M. de Vionnet is still alive? – is a divorce quite out of the question? – is Chad perhaps tied to Mme de Vionnet by his love for her daughter? – and he lets himself be lulled by Bilham's 'gentlemanly' and ambiguous assurance that it is a 'virtuous relation'. In effect he shelves the problem, adopting the stance with which he meets Sarah in their concluding confrontation when they both stand firm, she in seeing 'an adulterous woman', he a woman of fine quality who has transformed Chad: challenged to say what he thinks of her life with him he replies 'I think tremendously well of her, at the same time that I seem to feel her "life" to be really none of my business.' The ironic quotation marks of 'life' make his comment on Sarah's reduction of everything to the question of their sexual relation.

To complain that James overdoes Strether's improbable naïvety in clinging to uncertainty until his riverside meeting with the lovers is to forget how curiously ambiguous the close attachments between nineteenth-century men and women sometimes were. An example with which James had been closely acquainted at first hand was the devotion of Turgenev to Mme Viardot. As late as 1980 Patrick Waddington was obliged to say of this 'marvellous, exceptional personality' that 'Although she was never a wife to him and conceivably never his mistress, for forty years she meant as much as either of these things.'[8] The puzzling uncertainty could hardly have been less to Henry James when as a young man he attended her musical gatherings and parties *en famille* (with Turgenev very much one of the family) and described them to his father (11 April 1876), calling her 'a most fascinating and interesting woman'. He may not have had the name 'Mme Viardot' clearly in mind as he created 'Mme de Vionnet', but it looks as if there was some nudging from a latent memory of this other fascinating woman for whose sake a man chose to live as an expatriate in Paris. It is at all events certain that a woman whose devoted friendship, of supreme importance to a man, might include adulterous sexual partnership, but also might not, was among the possibilities of the milieu in which James chose to set Strether. In telling Sarah that the question was none of his business, Strether was, as she knew, in effect at the point of saying that it did not matter, the point he reached after the question had been conclusively answered by the riverside encounter.

The change in his outlook – to the Newsomes his sinister transformation – has come about gradually as he finds himself made welcome among people whose code differs from Mrs Newsome's in the moral status and responsibility it gives to men. For Mrs Newsome, men are to be morally managed; at a distance she carries on the management through her second embassy with 'daily cables, questions, answers, signals' (p. 371). Strether himself had been an uncritical tool of the Woollett code in undertaking the first embassy to fetch Chad back and rearrange his life. Miss Gostrey faces him with it from the first: 'What you *really* want to get him home for is to marry him' (p. 80). The form of words is repeated with a more emphatic hint at possessiveness when Mme de Vionnet challenges Strether about the outcome if Mrs Newsome gets Chad to come home even temporarily:

> 'Do you give me your word of honour that if she once has him there she won't do her best to marry him?'
>
> It made her companion, this inquiry, look again a while out at the view; after which he spoke without sharpness. 'When she herself sees what he is –'
>
> But she had already broken in. 'It's when she sees for herself what he is that she'll want to marry him most.' (pp. 248–9)

Woollett marriage is a means of bringing men under control within the women's moral and cultural network. James puts it explicitly through his caricatural sketch of Jim Pocock, who is determined to have a good time on this unexpected trip to Paris and passes no judgement on Chad's behaviour or Strether's procrastination:

> Jim, in fact, he presently made up his mind, was individually out of it; Jim didn't care; Jim hadn't come out either for Chad or for him; Jim, in short, left the moral side to Sally. . . . Pocock was normally and consentingly, though not quite wittingly, out of the question. (pp. 291–2)

In this, Strether realises, he plays the accepted part of 'a leading Woollett business man': 'He seemed to say that there was a whole side of life on which the perfectly usual *was* for leading Woollett business men to be out of the question' (p. 292). And Strether wonders if this would become his own fate if he married Mrs Newsome. He offers himself a partial reassurance:

> He was different from Pocock; he had affirmed himself differently; and he was held, after all, in higher esteem. What none the less came home to him, however, at this hour, was that the society over there, of which Sarah and Mamie – and, in a more eminent way, Mrs Newsome herself – were specimens, was essentially a society of women, and that poor Jim wasn't in it. He himself, Lambert Strether, *was*, as yet, in some degree – which was an odd situation for a man; but it kept coming back to him in a whimsical way that he should perhaps find his marriage had cost him his place. (p. 292)

Marriage in that society of women completes the moral subjugation of men.

In James's Paris men's responsibilities are emphasised. Chad explores his social milieu with enterprise and judgement to arrange the marriage that Mme de Vionnet is glad to accept for her daughter. And instead of Mrs Newsome's receptions we have the great party in which he displays his formidable social resources to Sarah. More casually the same note is sounded in Strether's interpretation of the encounter he watches between Gloriani and the Duchess: 'He was sure she was prompt and fine, but also that she had met her match, and he liked – in the light of what he was quite sure was the Duchess's latent insolence – the good humour with which the great artist asserted equal resources' (p. 184). But of course the sharpest contrast to the Woollett women's relation with men is Mme de Vionnet's helpless love for Chad, which, as Bilham reveals, has become greater than his for her. 'How indeed then she must care!' Strether exclaims to Miss Barrace, who in reply 'dropped a comprehensive "Ah!" which perhaps expressed a slight impatience at the time he took to get used to it' (pp. 364–5). And when Strether has spoken of all the contrasts of background that divided Chad from her, Maria Gostrey replies 'Those things are nothing when a woman is hit. . . . She was hit' (p. 450). The implicit contrast is with Mrs Newsome's firm discarding of Strether when it is clear that he has become a dissident in her moral regime.

In the imaginary society that James calls 'Paris' Strether finds himself among people to whom he is not just a useful ally, as he had been to Mrs Newsome, but morally important, himself a centre of judgement. The sensitive people – Chad and Bilham as well as the women – discern a quality that not only makes them fond of him but leads them to treat him as a judge whose good opinion they want to secure and keep. James adopts the device of stating that fact about Strether's role quite explicitly but at a point where it emerges from a particular context, its more general significance appears only in the light of later events (and may not be noticed without a re-reading). It occurs when Mme de Vionnet tries to allay Strether's shock on finding that she is disposing of her daughter in an arranged marriage and to persuade him that he must accept her plan:

> Thus she could talk to him of what, of her innermost life – for that was what it came to – he must 'accept': thus she could extraordinarily speak as if, in such an affair, his being satisfied had importance. (p. 327)

Then, as he leaves her and says that he will not as yet speak to Chad about Jeanne's marriage, Mme de Vionnet replies

> 'Ah, that's as you'll think best. You must judge.' She had finally given him her hand, which he held a moment. 'How much I have to judge!'
>
> 'Everything', said Mme de Vionnet: a remark that was indeed

> – with the refined, disguised, suppressed passion of her face – what he most carried away. (p. 328)

He has to judge everything; lodged in the local context the statement in reality describes his role throughout the book. Both Mme de Vionnet and Miss Gostrey in their different ways show from point to point as the novel develops that they need to vindicate themselves in his eyes. Even after the danger of Chad's return to America has been averted, Mme de Vionnet is greatly concerned with what Strether thinks of her: 'You don't care what I think of you; but I happen to care what you think of me' (p. 440). It is the possibility that she has lost his good opinion that, according to Maria Gostrey in the concluding retrospect, most troubles Mme de Vionnet; 'She thinks just the contrary of what you say. That you distinctly judge her' (p. 450).

His judgements are accepted because his companions feel that he will judge for himself instead of applying a ready-made code. 'Do I strike you as improved?' (p. 134) is Chad's prompt question at their first meeting, and Strether at once feels guilty when he resorts to an evasion instead of honest assent. Chad continues to treat him as a valid guide who is not a mere cat's-paw of the exigent mother, and whose advice he will accept once Strether has agreed to see and judge the whole situation. James, of course, makes Strether's role far more complicated than that of a legal judge. True, as Strether says at the end, he must gain no personal advantage from his decisions. But he has none of the legal judge's secure detachment; his judgements are given at high personal cost. Moreover he backs them with advocacy and, if necessary, practical help. And yet, finally, he does remain detached from the outcome of the developing events once his judgement has been conveyed.

This complex balancing appears in Strether's dealings with Bilham and Mamie. Seeing their mutual attraction and their common detachment from Woollett values, he advocates their marriage and promises financial help. After that he leaves it to them. When Maria asks if they will in fact marry, he can put that aside as none of his business: 'it won't matter a grain if they don't – I shan't have in the least to worry' (p. 397). It is enough that he has fulfilled the role proper to him in committing himself openly and practically to his judgement that the alliance of these two young Americans would be good; having done that, he will interfere no further.

With more painful effort he eventually achieves the same stance in his anxious concern about Chad's fidelity, a concern that forms a vital part of the novel's moral implications. Strether is imagined as showing a civilised composure, outdoing Mme de Vionnet's, when the adultery has to be openly recognised between them. He can accept the lovers' putting aside the institutional bond of marriage, as between two members of society, but, as between two persons, he will not relinquish the high value he sets on fidelity and mutual trust. James gave himself the difficult task of making Chad unquestionably admirable in his transformation, but by no means the 'hero' of the novel and certainly not someone in favour of whom Strether could morally abdicate. He conveys the mixed feelings with which Strether observes how Chad leaves placidly to others the emotional stresses set up by his own situation. The excitement with which Strether waits to tell him of the final encounter with Sarah corresponds, he realises, with nothing Chad felt himself:

> That was exactly this friend's happy case; he 'put out' his excitement, or whatever other emotion the matter involved, as he put out his washing; than which no arrangement could make more for domestic order. It was quite for Strether himself, in short, to feel a personal analogy with the laundress, bringing home the triumphs of the mangle. (p. 386)

The choice of simile is not just in line with the ruefully humorous tone Strether's reflections often have; it adds a shade of the questionable – the irresponsible or the selfish – to Chad's admirable facility for living without undue moral strenuousness. And Strether sees that, while this was one side of 'the truth that everything came happily back with him to his knowing how to live', it left him in danger. Strether is perturbed at his failure to meet him at the depth of his own feeling about fidelity to Mme de Vionnet. He has told him that it would be an infamy to desert her, and Chad repeatedly seems to agree but repeatedly turns his agreement into the assurance that he is not tired of her:

> Strether, at this, only gave him a stare: the way youth could express itself was again and again a wonder. He meant no harm,

> though he might after all be capable of much; yet he spoke of being 'tired' of her almost as he might have spoken of being tired of roast mutton for dinner. (p. 458)

Summing it all up with Maria,

> 'I've done', said Strether, 'what I could – one can't do more. He protests his devotion and his horror. But I'm not sure I've saved him. He protests too much. He asks how one can dream of his being tired. But he has all life before him.' (p. 467)

Deeply as Strether feels the precarious situation of Mme de Vionnet, ten years older than her lover ('the only certainty is that I shall be the loser in the end'), it is Chad himself who, James implies, may be heading for disaster: 'I'm not sure I've saved him.' Maria focuses his uneasiness about Chad's recent absence:

> 'And is your idea', Miss Gostrey asked, 'that there was some other woman in London?'
>
> 'Yes. No. That is, I *have* no ideas. I'm afraid of them. I've done with them.' (p. 467)

This is his last word on Chad's relation with Mme de Vionnet. To have attempted further investigation would have been like Sarah's 'visit of inquisition' (p. 282). Once more, he has done his part by showing he understands the situation, defining his own values and making his judgement unmistakably plain to Chad.

The novel has proceeded through Strether's progressively revised perception of the facts to his final judgement – his choice between the moral personalities of Mrs Newsome and Mme de Vionnet. On Mrs Newsome he pronounces judgement in his last talk with Maria; it is not, he says, that she is now different for him:

> 'She's the same. She's more than ever the same. But I do what I didn't before – I *see* her.'
>
> He spoke gravely and as if responsibly – since he had to pronounce; and the effect of it was slightly solemn, so that she simply exclaimed 'Oh!' (p. 466)

Pronouncing against Mrs Newsome and in favour of Chad's life was his act of reparation for the injury he had done to the young man he might himself have been. Chad and Mme de Vionnet gave him the sense of youth in spite of their actual age:

> 'I don't say they're, in the freshest way, their *own* absolutely prime adolescence, for that has nothing to do with it. The point is that they're mine. Yes, they're my youth, since somehow, at the right time, nothing else ever was.' (p. 271)

This implies that nothing like the glib pseudo-psychological idea of 'vicarious satisfaction' is involved. It emerges from the complex treatment which James has given to the germinal anecdote of Howells in Whistler's studio. Strether's outpouring in Gloriani's garden balances two facts: one, that it is too late for him to undo the fatal mistake of not having 'lived'; the other, that 'the right time' for making one's free choice (even if the 'freedom' is an illusion) 'is any time that one is still so lucky as to have' (p. 183). Although he envies Bilham's having plenty, that cannot cancel the other fact, and the story gives Strether time enough to confront the opportunity – equally the appalling challenge – to make his free choice. It is here that the novel differs decisively from the anecdote: Howells could return to his life of smooth output in America unchanged; but Strether must totally renounce the niche he had worn in Mrs Newsome's world, with all its offers of social esteem, domestic comfort and money. This is the free choice which he has been 'lucky enough' still to have time to make.

But that, much as it is, is all he can do; he cannot cancel his past error: 'It's too late. . . . What one loses one loses; make no mistake about that' (p. 183). So he had told Bilham in Gloriani's garden. And again, almost at the end of the novel, as he waits late at night in Chad's apartment,

> He felt, strangely, as sad as if he had come for some wrong, and yet as excited as if he had come for some freedom. But the freedom was what was most in the place and the hour; it was the freedom that most brought him round again to the youth of his own that he had long ago missed. He could have explained little enough today either why he had missed it or why, after years and years, he should care that he had; the main truth of the actual appeal of everything was none the less that everything represented the substance of his loss, put it within

> reach, within touch, made it, to a degree it had never been, an affair of the senses. That was what it became for him at this singular time, the youth he had long ago missed. (p. 384)

After the living experience of the three months in Paris, during which he can feel that for once in his life he has been 'magnificent', he comes back to the past mistake that can never be undone.

Biographically there are ample reasons why James could not have accepted a late-life consolatory marriage for a hero who had so much in common with himself at the age when he was writing. But within the logic of the novel Strether's refusal of Maria's offer is intrinsic to his act of atonement with his own true values. That has meant stripping himself of the compensating advantages that his fundamental mistake had brought in prospect; it would have been alloyed by any effort of small salvage in grasping consolations and minor restitutions as an expatriate ('I'm not', he tells Maria during their last talk, 'in real harmony with what surrounds me. You are.'). The allies he had found (most of them Americans) were not representative of 'Europe'. They were people who had learnt, or were learning in time, to expose themselves to what they saw and felt regardless of the way it had been socially precoded; they would be a small minority in any society. Strether, transformed by coming to accept his own perceptions and judgements, could give the younger of them vital support. But because he has previously submitted to those who know in advance of experience what is right, he remains a man who lost the chance of living his own youth; what he can do is to recognise what has happened: 'What's lost is lost. Make no mistake about that.'

NOTES

1. F. R. Leavis, 'Henry James and the Function of Criticism', *Scrutiny*, 15 (1948) 100.
2. F. O. Matthiessen, *Henry James: The Major Phase* (London, 1946).
3. Quentin Anderson, 'Henry James, his Symbolism and his Critics', *Scrutiny*, 15 (1947) 12ff.
4. F. R. Leavis, 'The Appreciation of Henry James', *Scrutiny*, 14 (1947) 233.
5. *The Ambassadors*, ed. Leon Edel (London, 1970) p. 40. All subsequent references to the novel are to this edition.
6. Published in full in *The Notebooks of Henry James*, ed. F. O. Matthiessen and Kenneth B. Murdock (Oxford, 1947) pp. 372–415.

7. 'Project of Novel by Henry James', ibid., p. 403.
8. Patrick Waddington, *Turgenev and England* (London, 1980) p. 3.

12

'When 'Omer smote 'is bloomin' lyre'

SYDNEY MUSGROVE

et haec olim meminisse iuvabit
(Virgil, *Aeneid*, I, 203)

Kipling, born in 1865, was one of 'Missis Victorier's sons' (p. 413),[1] and wrote about half his stories in her reign. He belongs to the same popular tradition as Dickens. The general public, who knew what it liked, admired and bought them both. M'Turk recalled the bewildering speed with which Kipling 'devoured' book after book, eyes 'jiggering' across the pages, then bolted back to the library for more.[2] Here I wish to trace out, in the complex weave of his writings, a few strands – taken mainly but not solely from Victorian writers – which will show how he used what he read. He was a romantic, an evoker of wonder and terror, but always, he insisted, a craftsman. Craftsmanship is innocent, an Edenic survivor in a dark world. In fear 'lest all thought of Eden fade', God brings 'Eden to the craftsman's brain' (p. 512).

In 'The Propagation of Knowledge' (*Debits and Credits*, 1926), Beetle is let loose amid the treasures of the head's library, as happened to Kipling in 1882. There he stumbles upon Isaac D'Israeli's *Curiosities of Literature*. He ranges up and down:

> Then, at the foot of a left-hand page, leaped out on him a verse – of incommunicable splendour, opening doors into inexplicable worlds – from a song which Tom-a-Bedlams were supposed to sing. It ran:
>
> With a heart of furious fancies
> Whereof I am commander,

With a burning spear and a horse of air,
  To the wilderness I wander.
With a knight of ghosts and shadows
  I summoned am to tourney,
Ten leagues beyond the wide world's end –
  Methinks it is no journey.

He sat, mouthing and staring before him, till the prep-bell rang. . . . He carried his dreams on to Number Five. They knew the symptoms of old. (XIV, pp. 284–5)

Here indeed is romance: here is Xanadu, and Childe Roland, and an outlawed beggar world like Kim's, and the fear of madness which always haunted Kipling's mind, 'leaping' out of the last stanza of a poem first published in 1660, which is mainly of antiquarian interest. (D'Israeli himself noted, in the next line: 'the last stanza of this Bedlam song contains the seeds of exquisite romance; a stanza worthy many an admired poem'.) But this fantasy is nailed down hard to the reality of the boy in the library by its placing 'at the foot of a left-hand page'. In my own battered copy of the *Curiosities*, an undated 'close-printed, thickish volume' of about 1850 which may well be the same edition as Beetle used, there the stanza is – at the bottom of the left-hand page 294. Kipling has seen it, and held it in his mind, and used it to give his vision a local habitation and almost a page reference, thereby helping to ensure its credibility.

This is true craft; but, to succeed, it must await its proper hour. Kipling had already used the song, to no good purpose, as the epigraph to the last chapter of *The Light That Failed* (1890). In a general way the song is relevant to Dick Heldar's quixotic journey to death in the desert, but there is no imaginative link, no 'leap' from the page. *The Light That Failed*, so strained and false, stirs neither heart nor mind. Whether the illumination that bewitched Beetle was experienced by the boy Kipling is largely immaterial. At the proper time, he knew how to use what was given.

In the opening chapter of *Something of Myself*, writing of his earliest memories of books, Kipling considers tentatively the possibility of unconscious memory – 'unless it be that the brain holds everything that passes within reach of the senses, and it is only ourselves who do not know this' (XXIV, p. 360) – and mentions lines and details from sources beyond recall. But in general he speaks from conscious memory of books read and of what he got from each, even tracing Corbet's 'Farewell Rewards and Fairies' to a 'little purple book' called *The Hope of the Katzekopfs*. In following his tracks we shall not usually have to do with the unconscious associative processes popularised in *The Road to Xanadu*, but with the art of a conscious writer with an extensive memory and a formidable eye for detail. As between fellow craftsmen, property is communal:

> When 'Omer smote 'is bloomin' lyre,
> He'd 'eard men sing by land an' sea;
> An' what he thought 'e might require,
> 'E went an' took – the same as me!
> (p. 351)

Yet we must not forget that Kipling was often evasive, and sometimes downright deceptive in what he told his readers.

The memory can, of course, throw up things outside normal comprehension – indeed, Kipling built several of his 'supernatural' stories on such experiences. But these uncovenanted gifts also serve the purposes of conscious craft. In *Something of Myself* Kipling remembers that the schoolmaster Crofts (in part, the prototype of King) 'in form once literally threw *Men and Women* at my head', which proved a profitable introduction to Browning (XXIV, p. 378). In 'Slaves of the Lamp, Part I' (*Stalky and Co.*, 1899) this event takes on a different shape. The boys are searching through a 'book' – apparently a volume of Browning for ammunition to use against King: peculiarly apt, since 'He gave me that book', says Beetle. Beetle runs his finger down the page, and begins to read 'at random'. The eleven obscure and inapposite lines with which he begins are not from *Men and Women* (1855), but from 'Waring' (ll. 109–19), published in *Dramatic Lyrics* (1842). Then, 'licking his lips', and still apparently working from the same book, he follows with stanza seven of 'Soliloquy of the Spanish Cloister', also published in *Dramatic Lyrics*. This is the famous 'There's a great text in Galatians', with its promise of 'twenty-nine distinct damnations', which would seem to be just the job. But nothing is made of it, and immediately at the end of the stanza, Kipling, with characteristic discontinuity and evasiveness, lets the text continue thus:

Then irrelevantly:

> 'Setebos! Setebos! and Setebos!
> Thinketh he liveth in the cold of the moon.'
> (XIV, pp. 72–3)

These two lines are from 'Caliban Upon Setebos' (ll. 24–5) published in *Dramatic Personae* (1864), which could hardly have appeared on the page contiguously with the poems of 1842. The lines seem to burst out of Beetle's memory, unexpected and unbidden, as is obscurely suggested by the word 'irrelevantly'. Plucked thus out of context, they have something of the magical force, the haunted quality of the Bedlam song. They are almost an automatism, and they are not used again in the story. What is more curious is that the second line is misquoted. It should run:

> 'Thinketh, He dwelleth i' the cold o' the moon.

'He' is Setebos, and the subject of ''Thinketh' (indicated by the apostrophe, as throughout the poem) is Caliban. Either Kipling has misunderstood the line, or deliberately distorted it, or it has come welling up out of memory and he has not checked what he thought he knew. The quotations from the other Browning poems, both intricate and far less memorable, are (punctuation aside) word-perfect. The example is not isolated: we shall find many other instances where his memory lets him down, especially in insignificant details of passages long remembered. Even as a boy, Beresford (p. 244) recalls, 'he relied on his memory to store up all that was needful'.

We are to deal, then, with a writer of great virtuosity and wide reading, who employs literary reference as part of his legitimate material, sometimes using it to tap deep memories. We may slip unobtrusively into the subject with a phrase from 'An Habitation Enforced' (1905), collected in *Actions and Reactions* (1909). Here the Chapins, incoming Americans, are befriended by the presiding local deity, Lady Conant. She presents them with a family christening mug, and then, says the text, 'She marched off amid her guard of grave Airedales' (VIII, p. 344). That sentence has stayed in my mind, fixing scene and event, since I first read it some forty years ago. It is memorable, not so much for the military irony of 'marched' and 'guard', as for the precision, and the implications, of one detail – the 'grave Airedales'. The breed, more popular then than now, is exactly right; slightly forbidding stiff-legged dogs, soberly coloured in disciplined black and brown, reliable and self-possessed: above all, 'grave' by nature. These dogs, like Lady Conant, recognise and perform their social duty – with pleasure, perhaps; with conviction, certainly. Their quality, as proper for grown-up women as for responsible dogs, is a Roman one: *gravitas*.

Kipling's knowledge of Latin was banged into him by 'King', who is based in part on F. W. Haslam, appointed Professor of Classics at Canterbury University College in 1879.[3] Kipling visited him briefly when he came to New Zealand in 1891, and affected to 'pity' him because the girls in his mixed classes, when rebuked for false quantities, only 'made eyes' at him (XXIV, p. 380). Kipling's main passion was for Horace, as the 'translations' from the supposed fifth book of *Odes* testify; but Virgil too has his place. The *locus classicus* for his Horatian devotion is the story 'Regulus' (1908), which astonishingly consists for more than half its length of a word-by-word construe, in class, of *Odes*, III, 5. The moral and social implications emerge later in intricate action and reaction. But it is of Virgil that Kipling speaks when he makes King (who 'could read Latin as though it were alive') 'pay out the glorious hexameters' for forty minutes without book as the defaulter Winton writes them out, 'pausing now and then to translate some specially loved line or to dwell on the treble-shot texture of the ancient fabric' (XIV, p. 210). That, indeed, is the right way to read Kipling himself: his fabric too may be turned many ways as the light falls, revealing a shifting complexity.

From 'Regulus' we may learn how to read the commonly underrated quatrain on Auckland in 'The Song of the Cities' (1893). In the story King asks 'Howell, what do you make of that doubled "Vidi ego – ego vidi"? It wasn't put in to fill up the metre, you know' (XIV, p. 200). Howell correctly explains that the repetition is 'intensive', and analyses the details. This is precisely the device used in the stanza:

> . . . On us, on us the unswerving season smiles,
> Who wonder 'mid our fern why men depart
> To seek the Happy Isles!
>
> (p. 177)

The emphatic repetition of 'on us' is 'intensive', and also a directional hint pointing forward to the double sense of the ending. The 'Happy Isles' are not merely those of New Zealand, but the *Insulae Fortunatae*, the fabled Isles of the Blessed, lost at the world's end amid eternal summer. Kipling notes, so early and with polite astonishment, the habit by which New Zealanders leave their blessed land almost as soon as they have found it. The poem is a courteous compliment, its smile covering irony and sad wonder.

The first line ('Last, loneliest, loveliest, exquisite, apart'), too thoughtlessly parodied, in fact shares the same exact and subtle control as the rest of the stanza. Each liquid *–l–*, with its danger of luxuriance, is balanced and disciplined by a firm dental *–t–*, in the manner of Horace's *'silvae laborantes, geluque / flumina constiterint acuto'* (*Odes*, I, 9).[4] The epithets are accurate, since Auckland in 1891 was the most remote, the final port of call. The concluding 'apart' points forward to the double meaning of the end; and the whole line is beautifully balanced on the Latin sense of *exquisitus* – that which is especially 'sought out'. Kipling's feeling for the place is remembered in *Something of Myself*: Auckland, lying 'soft and lovely in the sunshine', is for him a 'magic town' (XXIV, p. 425). Perhaps this is why the stanza is the best in the poem.[5]

The ironic tact with which Kipling uses Horace appears in the popular 'My Son's Wife' (1913). Midmore, in danger of being swallowed by the unhealthy miasma of 'permissive' London, inherits a house from an aunt in the country. His first appearance there is described in a devastating sentence packed with the hard-edged, sometimes animistic detail which Kipling learned in part from Dickens:

> There he faced the bracing ritual of the British funeral, and was wept at across the raw grave by an elderly coffin-shaped female with a long nose, who called him 'Master Frankie'; and there he was congratulated behind an echoing top-hat by a man he mistook for a mute, who turned out to be his aunt's lawyer. (IX, p. 296)

When Midmore appears likely to fail in his duty – moral, not legal – towards his inherited servant, the lawyer Sperrit, by no means a mute, rebukes him quietly, winding up with *'Ne sit ancillae,* you know' (IX, p. 300). The phrase is the opening of *Odes*, II, 4 – *'Ne sit ancillae tibi amor pudori'* – which urges a friend not to be ashamed of loving a servant. Horace had in mind such youthful beauties as Briseis and Tecmessa, but Midmore's love is owed to Rhoda, the 'coffin-shaped female' of the funeral, who reminds him later, when he is prudish about changing his clothes in her presence, 'Suit yourself. I bathed you when you wasn't larger than a leg o' lamb' (IX, p. 317). Yet these verbal indirections are no more complex than the history under the surface of the story, for Rhoda has had her hour, and borne her son out of wedlock. Ancient passions and jealousies writhe through the story like serpents.

There are finer details. Sperrit had cited Horace in his first conversation with Midmore: 'I call it [i.e. the brook] Liris – out of Horace, you know' (IX, p. 297) – apt enough for the *'taciturnus amnis'* of *Odes*, I, 31. But Midmore, for all his metropolitan gloss, misses the point, as he misses the planted clue of Charlie's inherited 'long' nose, which seems merely 'annoying'. The other occasion where Sperrit resorts to Horace is an event in the hunting field (a setting to which we shall return). As a horseman thrusts past, he says testily, 'Go on, sir! *Injecto ter pulvere* – you've kicked half the ditch into my eye already' (IX, p. 313). This is neat enough as a joke, but the full text from *Odes*, I, 38 – *'licebit / Injecto ter pulvere curras'* – reminds us that even 'Go on, sir!' is from Horace, and that the original words were spoken of one about to die, the dust being thrice sprinkled in funerary ritual. Death, as well as love, each familiar, awkward and inescapable, lies behind the whole story.

But Horace is only a secondary ingredient in 'My Son's Wife'. The main matter of memory comes from one of the best loved of Victorian parlour pieces, Jean Ingelow's 'High Tide on the Coast of Lincolnshire' (1863), from which Kipling takes his title. This, the only truly memorable poem written by its author, shares with Kipling's own best verse the power to touch the subliminal seats of emotion so strongly that it can hardly be read without a spring of tears. It forms a choric background: the village choir is rehearsing it, and Connie Sperrit, whom Midmore eventually marries, hums its melody constantly. The little local flood which empties a flower-bed, ruins carpets and strands a squealing piglet, also rearranges lives and brings primal terror to some. It is a type of the universal Lincolnshire deluge, when 'all the world was in the sea', and death overwhelmed 'my son's wife, Elizabeth':

> But each will mourn his own, she saith,
> And sweeter woman ne'er drew breath

Than my son's wife, Elizabeth. . . .
(IX, p. 300)

It is noteworthy that all Kipling's quotations from this poem are inaccurate, in the way of memorial reconstruction.[6] The poem must have lain in his memory from early days. It was certainly in his memory – again, inaccurately – as early as 1888, when 'Under the Deodars' was published. The epigraph to the macabre story 'At the Pit's Mouth' is a stanza conflated, with minor errors, from the second and sixteenth stanzas of the poem. The flood here is minuscule, but horribly frightening. The guilty lovers habitually meet in a hidden corner of Simla cemetery, near the half-dozen graves which a prudent government keeps ready for instant use. The lover looks at the foot of water lying in a grave, and shudders: 'Jove! That looks beastly . . . fancy being boarded up and dropped into that well!' He dies when the rains undermine the shoulder of a hill road, causing it to collapse beneath his horse's feet. The rains go on for three days, and at the end he is 'lowered into eighteen inches of water, instead of the twelve to which he had first objected' (III, pp. 38, 40). The flood again conjoins death and love.

Jean Ingelow reappears in the oddest of Kipling's stories, 'The Dog Hervey' (1914), published with 'My Son's Wife'. The disastrous heroine, Moira Sichliffe, is overheard singing 'to the piano an almost forgotten song of Jean Ingelow's' (IX, p. 125). This is 'Sailing beyond Seas', published in 1867, and is again quoted inaccurately and from memory.[7] (The sharp rebuke made by Miss Sichliffe to the narrator – 'You ought always to verify your quotations' (IX, p. 119) – is thus doubly ironical.) The matter is more than trifling, for it is not until the narrator realises that the dog is called 'Hervey' and not 'Harvey' that he recalls Dr Johnson's remark on which the story turns: 'If you call a dog Hervey, I shall love him' (IX, p. 138). The song is simply the cry of a deserted heart for the lover who has sailed 'to the other side of the world'. In the song he is dead, but in the story she wins him back by the strange ministrations of the troubled spirit of the dog. In her own time Jean Ingelow's poems were freely set to music, and presumably they remained in Kipling's memory for their simple, sweeping emotions and their evocation of loss. He may have heard them in the Kensington house, filled with books and peace, belonging to the 'three dear ladies' to whom his mother entrusted him in 1878. Various literary notables called, and 'somewhere in the background were people called Jean Ingelow and Christina Rossetti, but I was never lucky enough to see these good spirits' (XXIV, p. 369).

There is a curious implanted connection in 'The Dog Hervey', linking it with yet another story in the same volume, *A Diversity of Creatures*. The alcoholic hero Shend, as part of his own cure, helps to nurse two Englishwomen in Madeira, and asks, 'You'll let me come home with you – in the same boat, I mean?' (IX, p. 131). 'In the Same Boat' (1911) is another 'supernatural' story in which two haunted people, a man and a woman, are enabled to help each other to identify the childhood origins of the terrors which are destroying them. In both stories the sea is an element of peril and of healing; acting, in its own more complex way, like the cleansing brook of 'My Son's Wife'. The poem attached to that story makes all clear:

> The floods shall sweep corruption clean –
> By the hills, the blessing of the hills. . . .
> (p. 499)

The cleansing brook appears also in 'In Flood Time' (1888), in 'The Bridge Builders' (1898), in 'Below the Mill Dam' (1904), and of course as part of the grand design of *Kim*. In the superb 'Friendly Brook' (1914) it is both intimate ally and benevolent murderer. Clearly, the figure is one of complex power, combining terror and blessing. The early pages of *Something of Myself* speak rather of the borders of a coloured sea, and then of a steamer which carried him off to separation and torment in a cold new land. India was the sea's edge; England the land of brooks. The incantatory rhythms of Jean Ingelow's poem helped to give verbal form to this complex inheritance.

We are not yet quite done with 'My Son's Wife'. Looking for something to read in his dead uncle's mildewed library, Midmore lights by chance on *Handley Cross* (1843), and asks Rhoda if she has heard of characters called 'James Pigg – and Batsey'.[8] She has, of course, since the Colonel had read the stories aloud to the kitchen staff. Midmore now plunges, a 'lonelier Columbus', into the world of Surtees. The passage is famous:

It was a foul world into which he peeped for the first time –

> a heavy-eating, hard-drinking hell of horse-copers, swindlers, matchmaking mothers, economically dependent virgins selling themselves blushingly for cash and lands: Jews, tradesmen, and an ill-considered spawn of Dickens-and-horsedung characters. (IX, p. 306)

Surtees is used to introduce Midmore to the world of rural fox-hunters among whom he is to find his rightful place. By contrast with the steamy London ambience of the Immoderate Left, which he has just abandoned, this is to be the real, and presumably the right-thinking world. Kipling is obviously aware of the ironic contradiction which conjoins this 'foul world' with the wholesomeness of the village choir. Indeed, Midmore sees the point at once: reading of a landlord facing the onslaught of a 'red-eyed' tenant, he recognises not only the truculent and promiscuous Sidney, but himself in 'that very animal'.

Like Kipling, Surtees is a complicated writer. He is not merely a celebrant of hearty fox-hunting, but a savage social satirist with a cold eye and a burning pen. He appears earlier in a bravura passage (involving Cicero, Horace and Browning's dying bishop at St Praxed's) in 'The Last Term', the penultimate story of *Stalky & Co.* This story of mingled schoolboy cunning and hysteria lists a dozen books or so, devoured by Beetle in the library and later regurgitated. Surtees is not among them, but it is obvious that the boys are steeped in him to the point of possession, as the United Idolaters were in *Uncle Remus*. 'Oh, rot! Don't Jorrock', snaps M'Turk to Stalky. They have read more than *Handley Cross*, for 'Stalky knew the Puffington run by heart', and that comes from *Mr Sponge's Sporting Tour* (1853). We are asked to recall 'what the Considerate Bloomer did to Spraggon's account of the Puffin'ton Hounds', an event from Chapter 40 of the *Tour* (XIV, pp. 339–40). The Considerate Bloomer is Miss Lucy Grimes, typesetter, sub-editor and proprietor's daughter of the *Swillingford Patriot*, who is drawn by Leech in all the glory of Mrs Bloomer's original semi-oriental costume, involving harem trousers to astonish the world. Miss Grimes's literary sensibilities compel her to edit Jack Spraggon's plain tale of the famous run so daintily that the 'welkin' rang and the hounds followed an 'exquisite perfume'. This is all relevant, since Study Five has got its hands on the forme of type for King's Latin paper, and are joyously engaged in muddling up Cicero's first *Verrine* with Horace's *Quis multa gracilis*. The schoolboy hysteria, Kipling implies, is controlled and justified by the sheer craftsmanship involved.

Kipling's use of Surtees may be illustrated by the case of Pomponius Ego. Pomponius comes from Horace (*Satires*, I, 4, l. 52), and is obviously God's gift to boys in search of a nickname. It is therefore properly applied, with the addition of Ego, to Carson, 'the head of the school, a simple, straightminded soul' (XIV, p. 342). But Pomponius Ego in full comes from Surtees, appearing in Chapters 51 and 52 of *Handley Cross*. He is a fashionable hunting journalist who will, for a consideration, write up any hunting event with due acknowledgement of hospitality conferred. He too knows his classics, and can quote Horace accurately. Four passages from the *Ars Poetica* with other tags and a dash of Shakespeare, illuminate the pages he contributes. Surtees too has been drilled through his classics, Latin and English. Like Sperrit, Pomponius derives from his time, not from the literary imagination.

Kipling learnt more from Surtees than is apparent. The savagery which often breaks out in single epithet or condensed comparison is characteristic of both. Much of Surtees's satire is aimed at the hypocrisy of the marriage-market and the murderous struggle for status. Such pieces strikingly recall Kipling's early sketches of life in Simla, with its internecine warfare. A prime example is Chapter 62 of *Handley Cross*, which has to do with the impact upon the spa of a gentleman whose correspondence (inscribed 'Upon Her Majesty's Service') is addressed to 'William Heveland, Esq., A.D.C., &c., &c., &c.' The 'A.D.C.' sets all feminine hearts a-flutter, provoking much unseemly shoving and back-stabbing from the Miss D'Oyleys, the Miss Bowerbanks, the formidable Mrs Flummocks (known locally as 'The Crusher', for all the world as though she lived in Simla) and above all from the lovely Constantia Mendlove, known as 'The Bloomer' for her modish costume, enchantingly displayed on a rose-coloured sofa. All dreams come crashing down when it is revealed that 'A.D.C.' here stands, not for 'Aide de Camp', but only for 'Assistant Drainage Commissioner', arrived to survey a local farm. But, in the end, The Bloomer sensibly marries him, amid six bridesmaids all bloomerishly attired.

This could well have been the stuff – Commissioners and all – of a sketch in *Plain Tales from the Hills*, but the connection is stronger. The title of the Surtees chapter is 'William the Conqueror;

or, the A.D.C.'. The nickname was given by the local ladies, who thought him 'very, very handsome'. Kipling gave the title 'William the Conqueror' to a two-part story of an Indian famine, in *The Day's Work* (1898). William is the heroine, who dresses without feminine fuss and cuts her hair scandalously short. Moreover the hero Scott, with whom she works and whom she is to marry, is a highly efficient officer, not indeed of the Drainage Commission, but of the Irrigation Department, much praised for his work on the 'great Moshul Canal' (VI, p. 171). (There is indeed speculation in Handley Cross that Mr Heveland may have been a servant of the Honourable East India Company, for the Crusher 'had had one or two of that breed of suitors through her hands'.) Kipling's story is a tribute to the sacrificial demands made on men and women in service to duty, and is not at all satirical; but the mischievous inversion which sets off this heartbreaking toil against the self-serving malice of social ambition heightens its effect. The title thus has substantive meaning.

Examples examined so far are typical of much of Kipling's work: the older literary material is pervasive and often inconspicuous, enriching by indirect means. Other stories, like 'The Janeites' and the late 'Proofs of Holy Writ', use such material quite openly, and many do not use it at all. Even so, Muller in his Indian forests can happily mangle Swinburne, and, among marine engineers, McPhee 'knows whole pages' of Reade's *Hard Cash* by heart (VI, p. 260). The scandalous McRimmon, making Plymouth Hoe ring with the cry of 'Judeeas Apella' hurled at the head of Steiner (VI, p. 287), draws on Horace, whether he knows it or not. By contrast, I wish to look at two examples of a different kind, one a debt apparently unacknowledged, and one openly owned.

Kim includes a very vivid (and, as I have found, very memorable) 'vision', based on a garbled memory of the rambling words of the boy's dead father. In Chapter 2 he tells the priest at Umballa, 'I shall be made great by means of a Red Bull on a green field, but first there will enter two men making all things ready' (XVI, p. 227). The priest replies that 'at the opening of a vision' it is always thus: after the 'darkness' clears, one or two men enter 'with a broom making ready the place'. All this comes true in Chapter 5, when the advanced guard of his father's regiment enter the 'cool dark' of a mango grove to pitch camp. Two men come forward to mark out the place, with due attention to the siting of the officers' tents. They carry flags on five-foot poles, which are planted as markers. The flags bear the regimental crest, a 'great Red Bull on a background of Irish green'. The regiment marches in, under the light of the setting sun. Then:

> 'But this is sorcery!' said the lama. The plain dotted itself with tents that seemed to rise, all spread, from the carts. Another rush of men invaded the grove, pitched a huge tent in silence, ran up yet eight or nine more by the side of it . . . and behold the mango-tope turned into an orderly town as they watched! (XVI, p. 277)

These details appear to be taken directly from a piece of Egyptian 'sorcery' described by E. W. Lane in Chapter 12 of his *Account of the Manners and Customs of the Modern Egyptians,* first published in 1836 and in definitive form in 1860. The book had a deservedly high reputation, and was republished as an Everyman as late as 1954. The chapter is entitled 'Magic, Astrology, and Alchymy' and includes a detailed description of a vision induced in a magician's boy by gazing into a pool of ink. We must abbreviate the long account. The trembling boy sees first 'a man sweeping the ground'. This man is then made to bring in a red flag, then six others, including a green one. The boy then gives the order 'Bring the Sultan's tent; and pitch it.' This is done by 'some men'. The soldiers are then ordered to 'come, and pitch their camp around the tent of the Sultan'. The boy says, 'I see a great many soldiers, with their tents.' The soldiers are then drawn up in ranks, and a bull is brought in. 'It is red.' Next, the bull is killed and eaten, and the further details divagate from those in *Kim*. The two accounts are very close; I think Kipling simply borrowed what he wanted, using the passage again, perhaps, for magic wrought by Huneefa and Lurgan. As far as I know, he never mentions Lane's book.[9]

The next case is quite different, and hard to assess. In *Something of Myself* Kipling recalls that he borrowed from the ladies of Kensington James Thomson's recent *The City of Dreadful Night* (1880). This, he says, 'shook me to my unformed core' (XXIV, p. 377). Indeed he was apparently so impressed that he used the title twice for writings of his own; yet it is curiously difficult to pin down its effects. The poem is such a shadowy mish-mash of stock romantic terrors and obsessions that one can understand how an adolescent, still seeking his own precarious balance, might stagger drunkenly through it without permanent enrichment. An unsympathetic reader might think that Shelley's single line 'Hell is a city much like London' says it all, but even T. S. Eliot's 'unreal city' owed something to Thomson (as well as to Baudelaire).[10] No doubt the poem offered exciting possibilities of handling that sense of all-pervading depression, thickening to utter horror, which appears so often in Kipling.

In 1888 Kipling wrote a series of sketches, published in book form in 1890, describing the horrors of Calcutta, and called it *The City of Dreadful Night*. He noted that 'Dickens would have loved' the 'mysterious, conspiring tenements', the 'great wilderness of packed houses' (XVIII, p. 204). The general impression of an unclean place – the 'reek' of Calcutta, its steaming drains and foully drenched soil – and the pullulating filth of brothel and grog-shop is strong stuff, but it is a vision of dirt rather than of Hell. He places epigraphs from Thomson at the head of two chapters, misquoting both. Chapter 5 (XVIII, p. 198) is headed by two lines so well known that they appear in Bartlett:

> The City is of Night; perchance of Death,
> But certainly of Night.
> (I, l. 1)

(Kipling gives 'was' for 'is'.) Chapter 6 is headed by a stanza from section XIII (ll. 22–8) with seven variations from the original. These, however, are clearly deliberate and almost shameless: the stanza has been made to refer to the inhabitants of Calcutta and therefore changed throughout from singular to plural. Consequent metrical needs compel him to alter two verbs, 'lavish' for 'wasteth' and 'clamour' for 'claimeth'. Yet another version is prefaced to 'Under the Deodars' in *Wee Willie Winkie*. He seems to have little respect for Thomson's poetical integrity, and I doubt if anything from him mattered deeply to Kipling.

Kipling used Thomson's title again for a much more effective and compact sketch in *Life's Handicap* (1891). This is a finely managed description – almost a vision – of Lahore under the 'dense wet heat' of an intolerable August night. There is no story, merely an evocation of a city gasping under a clear moon. Its inhabitants are 'sheeted ghosts' (IV, p. 378): living and dead can hardly be told apart. It is, he says, a scene for Doré or Zola; but Thomson was certainly in his mind, for the final sentence – 'So the city was of death as well as night after all' (IV, p. 382) – repeats the epigraph used earlier. But another more powerful spirit is at work. Almost at the beginning, the narrator's stick falls to the ground:

> The sound of its fall disturbed a hare. She limped from her form and ran across to a disused Mahomedan burial-ground. . . . The heated air and the heavy earth had driven the very dead upward for coolness' sake. The hare limped on; snuffed curiously at a fragment of a smoke-stained lamp-shard, and died out, in the shadow. (IV, p. 375)

Here, I think, is the genesis of the haunting story 'Wireless'. Like that story, these details from Lahore come from Keats's 'Eve of St Agnes': the limping hare appears in l. 3 – 'The hare limped trembling through the frozen grass' – the lamp at l. 11, and at l. 200 the 'little smoke, in pallid moonshine, died'. Most of all, the dead are omnipresent: freezing, aching, in 'icy hoods and mails' in Keats, and driven upwards from rest by the unbearable heat in Kipling. The 'witchery of the moonlight' (IV, p. 376) falling across the 'long line of the naked dead' is everywhere in Kipling's sketch, as in Keats's poem; and the chief colour is silver in both. Here, it seems, deep memories of Keats coalesced with shallower memories of Thomson and with knowledge of actual nights in Lahore to produce a powerful impression of life and death in bewitched suspension.

Thomson reappears in *The Light That Failed* (1890), in connection with Maisie's hopeless attempt to paint a portrait of Melancolia. She and her unnamed red-haired friend have been reading the poem, and Dick Heldar knows it well enough to quote. The four passages used come from the last section (XXI), where Thomson is describing Dürer's painting, and are quoted almost accurately. They make the goddess into something melodramatic, and even the friend can see through it – 'there was no attempt to conceal the scorn of the lazy voice' (XV, p. 125). Dick (who, as a good craftsman, has vainly advised Maisie to work on her 'line' instead of playing with blobs of colour) also knows that she is on the wrong track. She wants to make a picture out of a book, and 'that's bad, to begin with'. In any case, Dürer had done it already: 'you might as well try to rewrite *Hamlet*' (XV, p. 126). But nothing will turn her; she must go wrong, in art as in life.

In *The Light That Failed* Kipling's imagination is unsteady, but he seems to be aware that Thomson is a false guide through the noisome city. The same point seems to be made in a short story published not long before – 'My Own True Ghost Story', in *Wee Willie Winkie* (1888). The epigraph

> As I came through the Desert thus it was –
> As I came through the Desert.

is from section IV of the poem, where the lines, hypnotically repeated over eleven consecutive stanzas, describe a desert hell, complete with visions. But the point about 'My Own True Ghost Story' is that it is not 'true'. The narrator lies through a sleepless night in a dak-bungalow, hearing in the next dark room the night-long sound of dead men playing billiards on a non-existent table which had once been there. Morning reveals the truth: the sound had been caused by a loose window-sash in the wind, and a 'restless little rat . . . running to and fro' inside the ceiling cloth (III, p. 157). Thomson's ghost is a chimera: the mind is its own creator of terrors, whether we call them real or unreal. This is to be Kipling's true line.

In other stories about this date Kipling's mind is much occupied with hauntings and night terrors caused, or enhanced, by the Indian heat and overwork. None shows any trace of Thomson, unless 'The Strange Ride of Morrowbie Jukes', with its horrible picture of the cannibalistic village of the undead, might be thought to show a general resemblance. Indeed, a sentence in the Allahabad edition of 'My Own True Ghost Story', removed from the standard edition, suggests a more immediate source – Walter Besant, who appears in *Something of Myself*.[11]

Finally, I return to 'Wireless'. The story was published in *Traffics and Discoveries* (1904), and is of a kind with 'The Finest Story in the World' (1893). Kipling plays with the fantasy of getting in touch with the mysterious power of poetic creativity through a fluke of contemporary technology, of the home-grown Marconi era. The 'medium' is a consumptive pharmacist's assistant near to death and preyed on by a girl called Fanny Brand. On a bitter winter night he is unconsciously compelled to recreate the composition of parts of 'The Eve of St Agnes', and then somehow drifts into the 'Ode to a Nightingale'. The hare, which had appeared in the Lahore sketch and in the third line of 'St Agnes', is hanging up outside a game-shop next door, its fur ruffled by the 'brutal' wind (VII, p. 198). There are exotic odours and coloured bottles in the chemist's shop to stir the imagination. The young chemist struggles painfully to reach imperfect versions of various lines. Finally he manages to get the last six lines of stanza thirty exactly right: 'it came away under his hand as it is written in the book – as it is written in the book' (VII, p. 212). Only it did not, unhappily. Kipling gives the first two lines finally achieved as

> Candied apple, quince and plum and gourd,
> And jellies soother than the creamy curd. . .

The true text has an 'Of' before 'Candied', and 'With', not 'And', in the second line. Worse is to follow. The dreamer is striving, and failing to reach the perfection of

> Charmed magic casements, opening on the foam
> Of perilous seas in fairy lands forlorn.

The hearer is entranced, spellbound.

> My throat dried, but I dared not gulp to moisten it lest I should break the spell that was drawing him nearer and nearer to the high-water mark but two of the sons of Adam have reached. Remember that in all the millions permitted there are no more than five – five little lines – of which one can say: 'These are the pure Magic. These are the clear Vision. The rest is only poetry'. And Mr Shaynor was playing hot and cold with two of them!
>
> I vowed no unconscious thought of mine should influence the blindfold soul, and pinned myself desperately to the other three, repeating and re-repeating: –
>
> A savage spot as holy and enchanted
> As e'er beneath a waning moon was haunted
> By a woman wailing for her demon lover.

In fact, Coleridge wrote, not 'A savage spot' but 'A savage place!', and the line as Kipling gives it bears all the signs of memorial transference from the nearby line 'Enfolding sunny spots of greenery'. No textual variants are recorded. The reader would feel less embarrassment had Kipling not built up the passage with such enormous, apocalyptic hyperbole.

I have to add that somebody has covered Kipling's tracks. The text as I have quoted it is that which appears in the 1904 edition of *Traffics and Discoveries*, and was still printed in the anthology *A Second Kipling Reader*, published by Macmillan in 1940. But in the Macmillan edition of *Traffics and Discoveries* published in 1949, Coleridge's opening line is given correctly, and 'With' has been restored in the second line from Keats (though nobody has restored the 'Of'). The Burwash edition follows this corrected version. I do not know whether we owe the corrections to Kipling or to an editor.

In *Something of Myself* Kipling writes of the scrupulous care he took to get both word and matter exactly right, even consulting experts like Saintsbury to ensure that he did not blunder; but he also wrote of his masterful and possessive Daemon, 'When your Daemon is in charge, do not try to think consciously. Drift, wait, and obey' (XXIV, p. 503). His qualities as a writer come from this double allegiance. In tracing a few examples of what his complicated and conscious art made of opportunities offered by some older writers, I have also had to chronicle the waywardness of his poetic memory in passages lying deep. To set the balance right, I conclude with a case in which he proves word-perfect, though he might be suspected of error. It is from the story with which we began, 'The Propagation of Knowledge' (XIV, p. 295). Stalky has turned up the passage from *King Lear* (II. ii. 116ff.) set for parsing in next day's class. He is appalled. This is Shakespeare at his most opaque, presenting the wretched steward Oswald throwing up a cloud of elaborate self-exculpation so dense that Beetle can only suppose he is drunk. The first half-line, read aloud by Stalky from 'the school *Lear*', is brutally terse: 'Never any:'. Most texts give the true reading, 'I never gave him any' – that is, any offence. But this is not a misquotation: the briefer form is an emendation made unnecessarily by Hanmer on metrical grounds, and allowed into the text by Steevens in his classic edition of 1773. The 'school *Lear*', whatever it was, obviously followed this bad tradition, as it did again in printing the Quarto reading 'conjunct' three lines below.

Kipling has looked the passage up, and got it right. Like a good craftsman he has gone to the true source. Moira Sichliffe could not have faulted him here. But Memory is the mother of the Muses, and, as we have seen, she deals with her daughters in unexpected and sometimes subtle ways. What Kipling wrote about learning Horace at school is much more than the standard justification for a classical education.

> C – taught me to loathe Horace for two years; to forget him for twenty, and then to love him for the rest of my days and through many sleepless nights. (XIV, p. 377)

NOTES

1. References to Kipling's verse are to the Definitive Edition (London, 1973), in the form p. 123. References to the prose are to the Burwash Edition of the *Collected Works*, 28 vols (New York, 1970), in the form III, p. 178.
2. G. C. Beresford, *Schooldays with Kipling* (London, 1936) pp. 130–1.
3. Beresford (*Schooldays*, p. 272) remembered Haslam as embodying 'all the repellant traditions of the eighteenth-century academies'; but his memoirs are often oddly wrong-headed.
4. Compare the detail in 'The Eye of Allah' (VIII, p. 269) where the 'liquid' quality of the choir's *'ille supremus'* is balanced by the 'shifting' of 'tone-colours' in the following *'Imminet, imminet'*.
5. But his feeling did not prevent him from blundering when he had ships anchoring in 'Auckland Bay', and his heroine living at 'Hauraki – near Auckland' ('Mrs Bathurst', VII, pp. 316, 314).
6. At IX, p. 326 he writes 'That flood strewed wrecks upon the grass' for 'That flow strewed wrecks about the grass'; and 'An awesome ebb and flow it was,' for 'A fatal ebbe and flow, alas!', transferring 'awesome' from the earlier line 'And awsome bells they were to mee'. The passage quoted from IX, p. 300 errs in spelling and punctuation. Such slips and transferences are typical of memorial reconstruction. There are similar errors in passages from Arnold's 'To Marguerite' ('The Hill of Illusion', epigraph), Browning's 'Any Wife to Any Husband' ('The Tents of Kedar', epigraph), and Blake's 'Tyger' (*The Naulahka*, XV, p. 360).
7. The errors are very minor: an added 'that' and 'when', 'on' for 'at' and 'by', and 'Oh' for 'Ah', though 'apart' for 'in part' is more serious. The passage said to be 'the end' of the poem in fact is not; I think Kipling deliberately omitted the very sentimental concluding refrain.
8. Kipling's memory has again slipped a small cog. The maidservant's proper name is 'Betsey', but she is 'Batsay' in Jorrocks's strident Cockney.
9. I suspect it was the mysterious 'work on Indian magic' which he went to the India Office to read, and so coveted (XXIV, p. 453).
10. Anne Ridler, Introduction to Thomson, *Poems and Some Letters* (London, 1963) p. xliii.

11. *The Phantom Rickshaw and other Tales* (Allabad, n.d.) pp. 332–3: 'Up till that hour I had sympathised with Mr Besant's method of handling them [i.e. ghosts], as shown in *The Strange Case of Mr Lucraft and Other Stories*. I am now in the Opposition.' The title is incorrectly given.

13

Ernest Alan Horsman

A Checklist of Publications and Reviews, 1948–88

1. 'The Language of *The Dynasts*', *Durham University Journal*, 41 (1948–9) 11–16.
2. 'Some Aspects of New Zealand Literature', *Durham University Journal*, 42 (1949–50) 27–34.
3. *Specimens of English Prose*, ed. E. A. Horsman, vol. 1: *Wycliffe to Browne* (Durham, 1951) pp. viii + 84.
4. 'Dryden's French Borrowings', *Review of English Studies*, n.s. 1 (1950) 346–51.
5. *Specimens of English Prose*, ed. E. A. Horsman, vol. 2: *Dryden to Stevenson* (Durham, 1952) pp. viii + 82.
6. Review of Kenneth Sisam, *Studies in the History of Old English Literature* (Oxford, 1953), in *Durham University Journal*, 45 (1952–3) 122–3.
7. Review of *Selected Poems of John Clare*, ed. Geoffrey Grigson (London, 1950), in *Review of English Studies*, n.s. 4 (1953) 93.
8. *The Diary of Alfred Domett 1872–85*, ed. E. A. Horsman (London, 1953) pp. 312.
9. Review of *Pearl*, ed. E. V. Gordon (Oxford, 1953), in *Durham University Journal*, 46 (1953–4) 33–5.
10. Review of *Middle English Dictionary*, Parts E1–3, ed. Hans Kurath and Sherman M. Kuhn (London, 1952–3), in *Durham University Journal*, 46 (1953–4) 129–30.
11. Review of *Poems by John Wilmot, Earl of Rochester*, ed. Vivian de Sola Pinto (London, 1953), in *Durham University Journal*, 46 (1953–4) 130.
12. Review of Thomas Hardy, *Our Exploits at West Poley* (London, 1952), in *Review of English Studies*, n.s. 5 (1954) 107.
13. Review of *New Zealand Poetry Yearbook 1953*, ed. Louis Johnston (Wellington, 1954), in *Landfall*, 8 (1954) 233–5.

14. *Dobsons Drie Bobbes: A Story of Sixteenth Century Durham*, ed. E. A. Horsman (London, New York, Toronto, 1955) pp. xxiv + 110.
15. *The Canadian Journal of Alfred Domett: Being an extract from a Journal of a tour in Canada, the United States and Jamaica 1833–1835*, ed. E. A. Horsman and Lillian Rea Benson (London, Ontario, 1955) pp. xi + 66.
16. Review of Keith Sinclair, *Strangers or Beasts* (Christchurch, 1954), in *Landfall*, 9 (1955) 169–71.
17. *The Pinder of Wakefield*, ed. E. A. Horsman (Liverpool, 1956) pp. xii + 95.
18. *Dickens and the Structure of the Novel* (Dunedin, 1959) pp. 11.
19. Review of James Sutherland, *English Satire: The Clarke Lectures 1956* (Cambridge, 1956), in *AUMLA*, 9 (1958) 88–90.
20. Review of S. C. Roberts, *Doctor Johnson and Others* (Cambridge, 1958) in *AUMLA*, 9 (1958) 90.
21. Review of James K. Baxter, *The Fire and the Anvil: Notes on Modern Poetry* (Wellington, 1957), in *Landfall*, 12 (1958) 186–9.
22. Ben Jonson, *Bartholomew Fair*, ed. E. A. Horsman (London, 1960) pp. xxxiv + 177; second, revised edition, 1965.
23. 'The End of the Golden Weather', *Landfall*, 14 (1960) 191–2.
24. 'Problems and Methods of Teaching Small Classes in English', *New Zealand University Journal*, 9 (1961) 40–4.
25. Review of *The Penguin Book of New Zealand Verse*, ed. Allen Curnow (London, 1960), in *Comment: A New Zealand Quarterly Review*, 2 (1961) 40–2.
26. Review of Diana Athill, Maurice Duggan, Maurice Gee and C. K. Stead, *Short Story One* (London, 1961) in *Landfall*, 16 (1962) 79–82.
27. Review of C. K. Stead, *Whether the Will is Free: Poems 1954–62* (Hamilton, 1963), in *Landfall*, 18 (1964) 273–7.
28. 'The Art of Frank Sargeson', *Landfall*, 19 (1965) 129–34.
29. 'The Design of Wordsworth's *Prelude*', in *Proceedings and Papers of the Tenth Congress, Australasian Universities Language and Literature Association* (Auckland, 1966) 154–62. Reprinted in *Wordsworth's Mind and Art*, ed. A. W. Thomson (Edinburgh, 1969) 95–109.
30. 'The Burns Fellowship', *Landfall*, 22 (1968) 247–8.
31. Citations, Centennial Convocation, *The University of Otago Centenary: Official Record* (Dunedin, 1969) pp. 45–62.

32. Review of Geoffrey Durrant, *William Wordsworth* (Cambridge, 1969), in *AUMLA*, 33 (1970) 122–3.
33. Review of Hardwicke Drummond Rawnsley, *Reminiscences of Wordsworth among the Peasantry of Westmorland* (London, 1969), in *AUMLA*, 33 (1970) 122–3.
34. William Shakespeare, *King Lear*, ed. E. A. Horsman (New York, 1973) pp. xi + 239.
35. Review of A. L. French, *Shakespeare and the Critics* (Cambridge, 1972), in *AUMLA*, 37 (1973) 116–17.
36. Review of Reuben A. Brower, *Hero and Saint: Shakespeare and the Graeco-Roman Heroic Tradition* (Oxford, 1972), in *AUMLA*, 37 (1973) 116–17.
37. Charles Dickens, *Dombey and Son*, ed. E. A. Horsman (Oxford, 1974) pp. lx + 871.
38. Review of Charles Dickens, *Pictures from Italy*, ed. David Paroissien (London, 1973), in *The Dickensian*, 70 (1974) 134–5.
39. *On the Side of the Angels? Disraeli and the Nineteenth-Century Novel* (Dunedin, 1975) pp. 64.
40. Review of Stephen Prickett, *Romanticism and Religion: The Tradition of Wordsworth and Coleridge in the Victorian Church* (Cambridge, 1975), in *AUMLA*, 47 (1977) 67–8.
41. Review of Joan Rees, *Shakespeare and the Story: Aspects of Creation* (London, 1978), in *AUMLA*, 51 (1979) 91–3.
42. 'Charlotte Brontë's Originality in the Construction of *Villette*', in *The Interpretative Power: Essays on Literature in Honour of Margaret Dalziel*, ed. C. A. Gibson (Dunedin, 1980) pp. 69–83.
43. Charles Dickens, *Dombey and Son*, ed. E. A. Horsman (Oxford, 1982) pp. 755.
44. Review of Thom Braun, *Disraeli the Novelist* (London, 1981), in *Review of English Studies*, n.s. 35 (1984) 401–2.
45. *The English Novel 1832–1880, Oxford History of English Literature*, vol. XI, Part I (forthcoming).

Index